THE STALKER OF THE SKY

A CONCISE WWII HISTORY OF
THE ROYAL AIR FORCE'S NO. 266
RHODESIAN FIGHTER SQUADRON

THE WAR YEARS
1939 - 1945

BARRY WOODHOUSE

Typeset in Minion Pro

Design, typesetting and publishing by UK Book Publishing

www.ukbookpublishing.com

Cover Painting: © Robin Smith

ISBN: 978-1-912183-21-0

Dedication

This book is most humbly dedicated to those young pilots of the United Kingdom, the Commonwealth, and other Free Nations, who made the ultimate sacrifice in combat, and gave us the freedom that we enjoy today.

We must never forget their sacrifice.

Preface

It has taken me many years to compile in what I have intended to be a concise wartime history of No. 266 (Rhodesian) (Fighter) Squadron of the Royal Air Force. I first started back in 1964, making notes of anything related to the squadron that I had read in the hundreds of books which I had purchased over the years relating to the Battle of Britain and the air war of World War II. I have also used photographs obtained over many years from now unknown sources. Where I am certain of the original source I have asked permission to publish and have given an appropriate credit. I hope I have not infringed on any persons or organisations copyright, but as the vast majority of photographs used can be discovered on many websites it is impossible to attribute any particular photograph to a particular person or organisation.

Oddly enough it was never my intention to produce a book. As an ex-serving member of the Squadron I had a keen interest in its history, going back to when, one day in 1961, while waiting in the Squadron Headquarters (for some reason which I now forget), I discovered three photograph albums on one of the tables in the outer office. In these albums were photographs of Gloster Meteors, de Havilland Vampires and Venoms along with their pilots, it was this that first aroused my interest in looking into its long and colourful history. These albums have sadly 'vanished', their location now unknown.

My aim is not only to inform the reader about the Squadron's operational record and aircraft, but also to discover as much as I could about the pilots and ground crews who served faithfully during the years of the Second World War. To that end I have produced a list of those pilots that I have been able to trace, plus, where possible, a brief biography of each.

Typing errors in the Squadron's Operations Record Book complicate correct identification of pilots or ground crew. The omission of the letter 'e' for example. Is the pilot's name Whitford or Whiteford? Both are used in these reports. Which is correct? Are they two individual pilots who have different surnames, or one pilot whose name is mis-spelt? Without their initials or service number it is impossible to know. This has undoubtedly caused some errors for which I now apologise. Abbreviations used in the ORBs have been written in full where appropriate to enable the reader to follow the events described more easily.

Ground crew records are practically non-existent unless a mention of a particular ground crew member is noted when referring to a particular event or Operations Record Book entry. This is a great pity, for without these 'un-sung heroes' no Royal Air Force squadron could have operated during the conflict. Again where I have discovered their names I have listed these also.

This book covers the periods from 1919, when the Squadron was first formed, to its disbandment in 1945. Ranging from slow, flimsy bi-plane torpedo carrying floatplanes, through to the Supermarine Spitfire, a solitary Hawker Hurricane and Hawker Typhoons.

An appeal for any ex-members of the Squadron to contact me through the Royal Air Forces Association periodical 'Air Mail' resulted in just four ex-members responding and I thank them for the assistance they have given. I have asked ex RAF colleagues that I know, that should they know of any possible leads that may put me in contact with any ex-members, to forward my details onto them with a view of meeting and talking to them.

Time passes us all by. The Second World War ended over 70 years ago. Sadly not too many of these old warriors still survive today. There must be those, like me that served during the 1950s and 1960s that are still with us but locating them is very similar to the proverbial 'needle in a haystack'.

So this book centers on World War II and the men that served during that period. The prelude to the Battle of Britain saw the squadron patrolling the skies above Dunkirk during the evacuation from the beaches of the British Expeditionary Force and French Forces; the air war in the sky over Southern England; taking the war to the enemy before the Normandy invasion, and through to the Liberation of Europe. During all of these momentous events No. 266 (Rhodesian) (Fighter) Squadron and its personnel were there. No other Squadron has possibly had such a colourful history in operational sorties and aircraft types as this squadron. This is their story,

Barry Woodhouse

No. 266 (Rhodesian) (Fighter) Squadron

An Introduction

Initially part of the Royal Navy Air Service (RNAS), the squadron was first formed towards the end of the Great War of 1914 -18 on 27 September 1918 at Mudros, Greece. It was formed from two existing Flights, Numbers 437 and 438. The newly formed squadron was used briefly on anti-submarine patrols over the Aegean Sea flying Short Admiral Type 184s and 320s as well as Felixstowe F3s. During February 1919 it was transferred to the Caucasus on board HMS Engadine. It also operated from Petrovsk aboard HMS Aladar Youssanoff and HMS Orlionoch before being withdrawn from service on 27 August 1919, finally disbanding on 1 September 1919.

Unfortunately there does not appear to be any surviving Operations Records Books (ORB) from this period or any great records of any description.

With the start of World War Two in September 1939, the Squadron was reformed as No. 266 Squadron at Sutton Bridge, on 30 October 1939 as a medium bomber squadron.

From money donated by Rhodesian citizens, and with the

posting into the Squadron during 1941 of Rhodesian pilots, it
was renamed No. 266 (Rhodesian) (Fighter) Squadron.

The Squadron's motto is 'Hlabezulu' - 'The stabber of the
sky', and it's crest display's the image of a Bataleur Eagle, this
being a common bird in Rhodesia and excellent at aerobatics.

Originally planned to be equipped with Bristol Blenheim's
it was equipped instead with the Fairy Battle light bomber
from December 1939 to May 1940 for training purposes,
until Supermarine Spitfire Mk Is arrived in January 1940 as
its operational type making it the second RAF squadron to be
equipped with Spitfires after 19 Squadron. Also during this
period Spitfire IIs were in operation from September 1940 to
October 1940, and again from March 1941 up until September
1941. Spitfire IIbs also had a brief appearance during September
1941.

The Squadron was equipped with Spitfire Vbs from
September 1941 until June 1942 as well as Hawker Typhoon IA's
from January 1942 to September 1942. These were gradually
replaced with Typhoon Ibs from March 1942.

The Squadron moved from Sutton Bridge to Wittering on
7 April 1940 from where it saw its first combat on 2 June over
the beaches of Dunkirk during the evacuation of the British
Expeditionary Force and French Forces from encircling German
forces, as well as taking part in the Battle of Britain after the fall
of France.

It moved briefly to Tangmere on 9 August 1940 and to
Eastchurch on the 12th, to defend against possible anti-shipping
operations. On the 13th Eastchurch was bombed and severely
damaged which resulted in six of the Squadron's aircraft
being destroyed on the ground. On the 14th it was moved to
Hornchurch for seven days before returning to Wittering as
a 'rested Squadron' after being in action during the Battle of
Britain, where it remained until January 1942.

From Wittering the Squadron moved to Duxford in January 1942 where is was re-equipped with Hawker Typhoons and its role was changed to a fighter-bomber squadron, eventually supporting the invasion of Nazi occupied Europe at Normandy on 6 June 1944 - D-Day - on armed reconnaissance missions, closely following in support of the advancing Allied Forces through France and into Nazi Germany. At the end of the European War the Squadron was disbanded at Hildesheim, Germany, on 31 July 1945.

On 1 September 1946 it was reformed at Boxted when 234 Squadron was re-numbered as 266 (Rhodesian) (Fighter) Squadron. Now an operational jet fighter squadron it was equipped with the Gloster Meteor F3s, twin jet fighter, the Gloster Meteor being the first jet fighter aircraft to enter RAF service replacing outclassed propeller driven aircraft.

Returning to its earlier Battle of Britain base at Tangmere during 1948, it was re-equipped with the Meteor F4. On 11 February 1949, the Squadron was re-numbered as No. 43 Squadron and disbanded.

14 July 1952 and the Squadron was reformed at Wunstorf (in the then West Germany), flying the de Havilland Vampire and later the de Havilland Venom in the ground attack role. On 16 October 1955 it was moved to Fassberg (West Germany) for 12 months before returning to Wunstorf. One year after this move, on 16 November 1957, it was again disbanded.

Moving from the jet age into the missile age, No. 266 (Rhodesian) (Fighter) Squadron was reformed for the final time (at the time of writing) as a surface to air missile Squadron (SAM) operating the Bristol Bloodhound Mk 1 anti-aircraft missile at RAF Rattlesden in Suffolk, (a Second World War USAAF B17 Flying Fortress base,) as a satellite station of nearby RAF Wattisham.

Its main purpose was to defend the Thor Inter Continental

Ballistic missile (ICBM) and RAF Vulcan bomber bases from air attack by the Warsaw Pact (Soviet Union) countries during the period known as 'the Cold War'.

No. 266 (Rhodesian) (Fighter) Squadron was finally disbanded on 30 June 1964. The author was privileged to be a serving airman with this Squadron during its period of operation at Rattlesden.

What follows is a wartime history of this Squadron taken from its Operation Record Books during the Second World War. Mainly reproduced as originally typed more than 70 years ago, but the 'eagle eyed' amongst you will undoubtedly spot some errors in English grammar. These have been deliberately unchanged as it was my intention to attempt to convey to the reader the atmosphere of the period. Spelling mistakes have however been rectified, and I have inserted the occasional word to make these reports more readable. The reader should be aware of this.

From the Operations Record Books

1939

30th October

From the ORB of 30 October 1939 - "No. 266 Squadron formed at Sutton Bridge on the 30th October, 1939 under the command of Squadron Leader J. W. A. Hunnard, posted from RAF Station Hucknall."

This was the announcement of the re-formation of the Squadron and the commencement of air operations during the Second World War by 266 Squadron as part of 41 Group. Also in the same entry is the establishment of the squadron comprising of thirteen Officers - eleven for flying duties, and 204 airmen, including ten NCOs (non commissioned officers) pilots and twenty aircrew.

5th November

Fourteen Pilot Officers and four airmen pilots (Sergeant Pilots) reported for flying duty direct from Services Flying Training Schools on completion of their flying training.

7th November

Flight Lieutenant I. R. Gleed arrived as a Flight Commander, from 46 Squadron, Digby. At this stage of the formation of the squadron, no equipment had been received and "a percentage of the pilots were granted leave until 19 November."

11th November
Another Flight Commander arrived today - Flight Lieutenant J. B. Coward, from 46 Squadron, Duxford. Also on this day three Magister aircraft were collected from No. 10 MU (Maintenance Unit) at Hullavington by squadron pilots.

13th November
These aircraft were put into good use for local flying exercises. Lectures were also arranged and a visit to Wittering to view the Operations Room there. The Squadron apparently had the use of a Link Trainer as well, as it was also put into good use.

The first ground crew accident occurred on this day. At 09.00 hours, 530787 Leading Aircraftman B. Walker was "injured when airscrew (propeller) swung round when engine backfired. The airman was admitted to SSQ (Station Sick Quarters) for treatment."

18th November
The Squadron was informed (Air Ministry postagram dated 17 November) that it would be equipped with the Fairy Battle light bomber instead of the planned Bristol Blenheim's.

20th November
The first Squadron Adjutant arrived - Pilot Officer S. W. Cobb RAFVR. (Royal Air Force Volunteer Reserve.)

25th November
There were several postings to other squadrons on the 25th. Three Pilot Officers going to 222 Squadron at Duxford, and

three Pilot Officers plus two NCO pilots going to 229 Squadron at Digby. This reduced the number of pilots to eleven officers and two NCO pilots

The most obvious reason for these postings was the fact that the Squadron was not yet 'operational' in as much that it still did not have any aircraft! These pilots were possibly needed on squadrons that were 'operational'.

27th November
Pilot Officer J. B. Stevenson was sent on attachment to Northolt to attend an Air Firing Instructors Course, and eleven RAFVR air gunners proceeded to various Air Gunners Courses on the same day.

The Magister had been put to good use as some 109 flying hours are recorded, and Leading Aircraftman B. Walker was discharged from SSQ and sent on sick leave.

The Squadron strength at the end of November consisted of one Squadron Leader, two Flight Lieutenants, nine Pilot Officers (one detached), two NCO pilots, one air observer, nineteen air gunners (eleven detached), one Warrant Officer, three Flight Sergeants, seven Sergeants, 129 Corporals and other airmen (non flying) personnel.

4th December
Squadron Leader J. W. A. Munnard, Flight Lieutenant I. R. Gleed and Flight Lieutenant J. B. Coward collected the first three Fairy Battle aircraft from No. 24 MU, Ternhill, today.

6th December
Training on these three aircraft commenced. Thick fog the following day, and then rain and low cloud on the 8th stopped all flying.

9th December

A further three Fairy Battle aircraft were delivered and flying practice resumed the same day.

One Fairy Battle suffered damage to an engine and underside of the fuselage when the pilot, Flight Lieutenant J. B. Coward landed with the undercarriage retracted. Both the pilot and Pilot Officer J. L. Willis, a passenger on board, were uninjured.

10th December

Five more Fairy Battles were collected from No. 24 MU at Ternhill. Flown by Pilot Officer W. S. Williams, Pilot Officer J. L. Wilkie, Pilot Office N. G. Bowen, Sergeant A. W. Eade and Sergeant W. Jones.

A busy day for the Squadron with more flying practice - formation flying and experience on type - and three more pilots report for duty from No. 6 FTS (Flying Training School), Montrose. They were - Pilot Officer C. A. G. Clark, Pilot Officer P. H. G. Mitchell, and Pilot Officer R. J. B. Roach.

12th December

A Fairy Battle landed heavily causing the tail wheel to collapse up into the undersurface of the fuselage during a practice flight. The pilot, Pilot Officer N. G. Bowan was not injured.

13th - 15th December

Flying practice over these three days, including formation flying, local reconnaissance and cross-country navigation exercises.

16th December

Another Fairy Battle was delivered. Flying Officer N. W. Burnett reported for duty from No. 5 SFTS. (Services Flying Training School.) Pilot Officers D. G. Ashton, D. L. Armitage and E. G. Barwell also reported for duty from No. 2 SFTS. These three pilots having just been commissioned. Sergeant Pilot R. G. V. Barraclough also reported for duty, also from No. 2 SFTS.

19th December

The weather is recorded as being cold, but with good visibility. More flying practice. A further three Fairy Battle aircraft were collected from No. 24 MU at Trenhill by Flight Lieutenant J. B. Coward, Pilot Officer J. B. Stevenson and Pilot Officer H. M. T. Heron.

31st December

The Squadron lost Pilot Officer E. G. Barwell who was posted to 12 Group Pool at Aston Down.

An interesting report in the ORB for the same day states that ground equipment for the Squadron is still outstanding and many aircraft are now due their 30-hour inspections. These aircraft would have been suspended from flying but for the kind co-operation of the Officer Commanding, Upwood, who arranged that these 30-hour inspection could be carried out at Upwood provided the ground crews from 266 Squadron carried out the checks.

To that end these aircraft were flown to Upwood. It was anticipated that all ground equipment "will be forthcoming at an early date."

Summary of 1939

So 1939 came to an end. In the two months since the Squadron was reformed some aircraft had been delivered, albeit the Fairy Battle and not the Bristol Blenheim as was originally planned, and training for the Squadron's personnel was pressing ahead flying the Fairy Battle aircraft.

The Squadron was still short of basic ground equipment however, which resulted in aircraft being unserviceable until the Commanding Officer of Upwood stepped in with an offer of assistance. Things can only improve.

1940

1st - 5th January
With a mixed bag of weather - heavy frosts and thick fog, flying practice was limited, although some cross-country flying to Upwood, formation flying, fighter attack practice and instrument flying did take place.

6th January
No flying today - thick fog. Pilot Officers S. A. C. Sibley and T. A. Vigors reported for flying duties from Cranwell, and Sergeants Kidman and Land also reported for flying duties from No. 12 SFTS.

10th January
This was a Red Letter day for the Squadron. From Fighter Command came the news that the Squadron was to be re-equipped with Supermarine Spitfires Mk Is. The allotment was to be made with immediate effect.

16th January
Snow blizzards forced a Fairy Battle to crash at East Kirby, flown by Pilot Officer J. L. Wilkie; the aircraft was damaged beyond repair. The pilot and passenger, Pilot Officer P. H. G. Mitchell, were un-injured.

17th January

Another flying accident. This time engine failure caused a Fairy
Battle to make a forced landing near Sutton Bridge. The pilot,
Pilot Officer D. L. Armitage (RAFVR) was un-injured. The
damage to the aircraft was to the undercarriage.

Pilot Officers S. A. C. Sibley, T. A. Vigors and Sergeant G.
Land were posted to No. 12 Group Pool at Aston Down.

18th January

Pilot Officers D. G. Ashton and R. M. Trousdale collected two
Fairy Battles from No. 6 MU.

19th January

The first three Supermarine Spitfires were collected from No. 6
MU by Squadron Leader J. W. A. Hunnard, Flight Lieutenants I.
R. Gleed and J. B. Coward.

20th January

The Squadron's fourth Spitfire was collected from No. 6 MU by
Flight Lieutenant I. R. Gleed
The remainder of January was taken up with more flying practice
- bad visibility and heavy snowstorms permitting. Cross-country
flying to Duxford, Abingdon, Wittering and Digby took place
over several days.

1st - 8th February

Poor weather conditions and a waterlogged airfield during early
February meant that very little flying took place.

9th February

Now that the Squadron was being gradually re-equipped with
Spitfires, it was time to return its Fairy Battles. A 245 Squadron
pilot collected the first aircraft.

10th February
At last the pilots started their conversion to fly the Spitfire! 245 Squadron collected another Fairy Battle. Things were looking up at last.

12th February.
Four more Spitfires were collected from No. 8 MU by Squadron Leader Hunnard, Flight Lieutenants Gleed and Coward, and Pilot Officer Williams.

14th February
The Squadron's conversion to Spitfires was going well as the same pilots collected another four from No. 8 MU as on the 12th. It is quite possible that these four pilots were the only pilots that at that time were fully checked on the Spitfire Mk I.

245 Squadron collected another Fairy Battle, and three more delivered to 234 Squadron by Pilot Officers Armitage, Ashton and Heron.

15th February
A very sharp frost over night and in the morning, but this did not prevent the Spitfire conversion from continuing at a pace.

Three more Spitfires were collected from No. 27 MU by Flight Lieutenant Coward and Pilot Officers Trousdale and Williams who had all now been converted to fly Spitfires.

16th February
As more pilots were checked out on Spitfires, so the pace of re-equipping the Squadron picked up as another four were collected by Flight Lieutenant Coward and Pilot Officers Cale, Clark and Williams from No. 27 MU.

18th February

The first Spitfire casualty! Flight Lieutenant I. R. Gleed was forced to bale out of his Spitfire and was slightly injured on landing. The aircraft was wrecked, crashing at Little Ouse, Littleport at 14.40 hours. No reason is given for the cause of the accident. The weather at the time was snow with moderate visibility.

26th February

The Squadron practiced 'Operation Exercise No. 6' - rapid re-fueling and re-arming of aircraft. A warning order was received from HQFC (Head Quarters Fighter Command) for the Squadron to prepare to move from Sutton Bridge to Martlesham Heath on 1 March.

28th February

Flight Lieutenant Bazeley reported from 611 Squadron for duty as a Flight Commander with Flight Lieutenant Gleed as his second in command.

29th February

The Movement Order was received for the Squadron to move to Marlesham Heath. An advance party left with Pilot Officer D. L. Armitage in charge. Now fully equipped the Squadron was on the move and hopefully into the action at last.

1st March

The main party now left Sutton Bridge by road and rail arriving at Martlesham Heath the same day. The party included three officers and 91 airmen. The officer in charge of the rail party was Pilot Officer P. H. G. Mitchell.

All serviceable aircraft left Sutton Bridge at 10.15 hours, arriving at Martlesham Heath 30 minutes later. This party included fifteen officers and twelve airmen. The officer in charge of this party was Flight Lieutenant J. B. Coward.

2nd - 5th March
Most of this period was taken up with practice flying - local area reconnaissance, battle climbs, formation flying, cloud penetration, cross-country flying (navigation) and gunnery practice firing into the sea at Orfordness plus Operational Exercises Nos. 1, 2, 3 & 5 and Fighter Command Attack No. 5. These were 'set piece' exercises, which at the time, the RAF considered to be the 'best method' of attacking enemy aircraft. This outdated ideology was to drastically change at the onset of the coming Battle of Britain after the fall of France.

6th March
More 'set piece' exercises are recorded for this day. The weather was very cold, frosty with showers of snow and sleet.

A Spitfire Mk I was damaged whilst taxying across the aerodrome when the propeller struck the ground. The pilot, Pilot Officer N. G. Bowen was un-injured.

Spitfires were notorious for the tail to 'bounce' up if taxying too fast over rough ground, causing the propeller to strike the ground. The usual 'remedy' was for a member of the ground crew to sit on the tail to add weight!

7th March
Sector formation flying, Operational Exercise No. 6 ('scramble' take off), and a navigation exercise to Sutton Bridge. As well as these practice flights the base was visited by the AOC. (Air Officer Commanding.)

11th March
With an improvement to the weather - reported as 'very mild',

the Squadron was kept busy putting into practice the skills it would need in the very near future.

Two Spitfires were collected from No. 24 MU by Pilot Officer Stevenson and Sergeant Jones.

16th March
Sergeant R. G. V. Barraclough was un-injured when his Spitfire was slightly damaged when taking off in formation.

1st April
Although now re-equipped with Spitfire Mk Is, the Squadron still had several Fairy Battles and one was collected from No. 32 MU and delivered to the squadron, the reason for this is not stated.

Also on this day Pilot Officer C. A. G. Clark damaged another Spitfire when he taxied it onto soft ground, damaging the propeller. He was un-injured.

5th April
Notification from HQ at 12 Group that 'A' and 'B' Flights were to make a temporary move to Wittering to replace 610 Squadron.

7th April
At 09.30 hours 'A' and 'B' Flights left for Wittering. The main party left shortly after by air.
The Fairy Battle, which joined the Squadron on 1 April, was handed over to the Experimental Flight at Martlesham Heath.

9th - 16th April
Most of the entries for this period relate to more practice flights. 'A' Flight was at readiness over a number of days; while 'B' Flight practiced (among other things) filming attack exercises using cine

cameras to record, for later viewing, their results.

Flying Officer H. H. Chalder reported for duty from 66 Squadron at Duxford on the 16th, and 'A' Flight was at readiness at Bircham Newton.

10th April

Flight Lieutenant Coward, Pilot Officer Wilkie and Pilot Officer Clark of 'A' Flight flying Spitfire Mk Is, at readiness at Bircham Newton on convoy patrol, covering the area Outer Dowsing and South to East Dudgeon. No interceptions were reported.

Later Flying Officer Burnett, Pilot Officer Trousdale and Pilot Officer Mitchell flying Spitfire Mk Is at readiness at Bircham Newton also on convoy patrol, covering the area Outer Dowsing and South to East Dudgeon. No interceptions were reported.

17th April

No. 5 Operational Training Unit based at Acton Down collected a Magister aircraft and a Spitfire was damaged at Bircham Newton whilst engaged on night flying practice. The pilot, Pilot Officer F. W. Cale, was un-injured.

Flight Lieutenant Coward, Pilot Officer Cale, and Pilot Officer Clark of 'A' Flight flying Spitfire Mk Is were at readiness at Bircham Newton. Their duty was to investigate an 'X' Raid. They were ordered to intercept an unidentified aircraft, which was found to be a Wellington bomber.

Suspected raids by German aircraft were designated as 'X' Raids in the early months of the war.

20th April

The weather was recorded as "much milder than late". 'B' Flight was at readiness at Bircham Newton having replaced 'A' Flight, which returned to Wittering. (The Squadron is still actually based at Martlesham Heath.)

Another Spitfire damaged its undercarriage when it collapsed during takeoff from its base at Martlesham Heath. The pilot, Squadron Leader J. W. A. Hunnard was un-injured.

21st April

Pilot Officer N. P. W. Hancock un-injured when landing his Spitfire at Bircham Newton after the aircraft ran into soft ground. A new pilot arrives, Flying Officer I. R. Gleed reported for duty.

Flight Lieutenant Bazeley, Pilot Officer Ashton and Pilot Officer Hancock of 'B' Flight at readiness at Bircham Newton. Blue Section ordered to carry out investigation patrol but no enemy aircraft seen.

Pilot Officer Williams, Pilot Officer Roach and Pilot Officer Heron of 'B' Flight at readiness at Bircham Newton. Green Section ordered to carry out investigation patrol, again no enemy aircraft seen. Blue and Green Sections patrolled as 'B' Flight.

22nd April

'A' Flight conducted low flying attacks for anti-aircraft operations, while 'B' Flight were conducting identification patrols and night flying practice. Pilot Officer P. S. Gunning reported for duty.

Flight Lieutenant Bazeley, Pilot Officer Heron and Sergeant Barraclough of 'B' Flight at readiness at Bircham Newton. Blue Section ordered to investigate 'X' Raid at 20,000 feet. No aircraft were sighted.

23rd April

Flight Lieutenant Bazeley, Pilot Officer Ashton and Sergeant Barraclough of 'B' Flight at readiness at Bircham Newton. Blue Section ordered to investigate 'X' Raid at 14,000 feet. No aircraft sighted.

24th April
Flight Lieutenant Bazeley, Pilot Officer Chalder and Squadron Leader Hunnard of 'B' Flight at readiness at Bircham Newton. Blue section ordered to investigate 'X' Raid. No aircraft sighted.

26th April
Pilot Officers Gunning and J. L. Wilkie posted to No. 10 MU for duty.

27th April
Flight Lieutenant Bazeley, Pilot Officer Ashton and Pilot Officer Armitage of 'B' Flight at readiness at Bircham Newton. Blue Section ordered to investigate 'X' Raid at 15,000 feet. No aircraft sighted.

Flight Lieutenant Coward, Pilot Officer Bowan and Pilot Officer Clark of 'A' Flight at Wittering were ordered to patrol the airfield and local area. No aircraft were sighted and so were ordered to land.

30th April
Pilot Officer Stevenson, Sergeant Jones and Pilot Officer Roach of 'B' Flight at readiness at Bircham Newton. Green Section ordered to investigate 'X' Raid patrolling at 10,000 feet, but no aircraft sighted.

1st May
The Squadron was by this time 'split' into two bases. Its Headquarters and the Maintenance Flight was located at Martlesham Heath, while 'A' and 'B' Flights were operational at Wittering, 'B' Flight having returned to Wittering from Bircham Newton today. A Master aircraft was delivered to the Squadron for training purposes.

3rd May

Squadron Leader J. W. A. Hunnard was slightly injured when his Spitfire hit a tree and crashed when landing at night.

4th May

Flight Lieutenant J. B. Coward, Pilot Officer W. S. Williams and Pilot Officer N. G. Bowan on patrol operating from Bircham Newton. Red Section was ordered on patrol but re-called after 25 minutes.

7th May

Another Spitfire was damaged when landing at Martlesham Heath. The aircraft overshot and collided with a Hurricane of 17 Squadron. The pilot, Pilot Officer H. H. Chalder, was un-injured. The last Fairy Battle aircraft that the Squadron still held was delivered to No. 38 MU.

11th May

Pilot Officer N. P. W. Hancock posted to 1 Squadron for flying duties.

13th May

Flight Lieutenant J. B. Coward, Pilot Officer C.A. Clark and Sergeant Eade on convoy patrol duty over Wells - on - Sea. Returned to Cromer on patrol, then returned to base at Bircham Newton.

14th May

Today the squadron was re-united again. Squadron HQ and the Maintenance Flight moved from Martlesham Heath to Wittering. The only exception to this was that 'A' Flight was still operating from Bircham Newton. In all the Squadron had been 'split' since April the 7th. Flying Officer I. R. Gleed posted to 87 Squadron for Flight Commanders duty.

16th May
Pilot Officer Heron and Sergeant Eade collected two Spitfire Mk Is from No. 27 MU.

20th May
Blue Section comprised of Flight Lieutenant Bazeley, Pilot Officer Armitage, Pilot Officer Ashton, Sergeant Barraclough, and Green Section comprised of Pilot Officer Stevenson, Pilot Officer Roach and Pilot Officer Heron scrambled to investigate 'X' Raid. Ordered to patrol Wells at 3,000 feet. When they were in position Green Section ordered to return and land. Blue Section vectored (vectored simply means the pilot is instructed to fly a particular compass bearing) off of Sheringham and orbited until they too were ordered to return and land. All aircraft operating from Bircham Newton. Three aircraft were sighted over Sheringham and identified as Blenheim's.

21st May
A single Spitfire Mk I, flown by Pilot Officer Stevenson, was scrambled and ordered to patrol over Aylsham at 20,000 feet to investigate 'X' Raid. He was given a vector and height (10,000 feet) when he was then ordered to return.

23rd May
Wing Commander Broadhurst from Fighter Command visited the Squadron and discussed German air fighting tactics with all pilots.

26th May
'A' Flight aircraft dispersed to the satellite aerodrome of Collyweston from dusk to dawn.

27th May
Today was 'B' Flights turn to be dispersed at Collyweston from dusk to dawn.

28th May
Nine Spitfires proceeded to Martlesham Heath at 11.45 hours for operational purposes. These were at readiness until 19.15 hours when all aircraft returned to Wittering.

Unfortunately a Spitfire flown by Acting Flight Lieutenant J. B. Coward hit a grass cutter damaging the starboard main plane. The pilot was un-injured.

29th May
Seven Spitfires proceeded to Duxford at 14.20 hours for operational purposes. These were at readiness until dusk.

30th May
The seven Spitfires at Duxford returned to Wittering at 12.45 hours. Pilot Officer Burnett was scrambled at 19.05 hours and ordered to patrol at 3,000 feet to investigate 'X' Raid. After just a few minutes he was ordered to return to Wittering and landed just 15 minutes after taking off.

2nd June
The Squadron is finally in action covering the withdrawal of the BEF (British Expeditionary Force) and French Forces from the beaches of Dunkirk. Sadly not without casualties. Pilot Officer J. W. B. Stevenson and Sergeant R. T. Kidman are both reported as missing.

One Spitfire was damaged on landing back at Wittering, the pilot; Pilot Officer N. G. Bowen was not injured.
From Appendix 1 of the ORB -
"Squadron ordered to patrol Dunkirk between 07.45 hours

and 08.30 hours. Aircraft left Wittering at dawn and proceeded to Martlesham Heath for refueling. Squadron then proceeded to Dunkirk and was in position at 07.45 hours, and patrolled at 22,000 feet until 08.30 hours.

Eight pilots had engagements with the enemy, the definite results of these were very difficult to obtain, owing to the height at which the engagements took place and the large number of aircraft engaged in dogfights. Enemy casualties appear to be one Me 110 (confirmed) and four Me 109s (unconfirmed). Seven aircraft returned to Martlesham - one arrived at Duxford and one at Wittering. Two aircraft piloted by Pilot Officer J. W. B. Stevenson and Sgt. R. T. Kidman failed to return and were reported as missing."

The Squadron on patrol comprised of - Squadron Leader Hunnard, Flight Lieutenant Coward, Flight Lieutenant Bazley, Flying Officer Burnett, Pilot Officer Stevenson, Pilot Officer Roach, Pilot Officer Trousdale, Pilot Officer Cale, Pilot Officer Bowen, Sergeant Jones and Sergeant Kidman.

If the reader refers to the list of pilot's names at the end of the Squadron's history further details as to the outcome for both pilots, and others, can be found.

Also on this day Lord Trenchard, Marshall of the Royal Air Force, paid an unofficial visit to the station.

Twelve Spitfires were sent to Martlesham Heath for refueling and operational instructions. These were kept at readiness from dawn to dusk for several days.

4th June
Air Transport Auxiliary (ATA) ferry pilots delivered three replacement Spitfires from No. 9 MU at Cosford.

6th June
Three Squadron Spitfires were scrambled to investigate a

suspected raid by a single German aircraft. Pilot Officer Armitage, Pilot Officer Williams and Sergeant Barraclough took off at 13.45 hours as Blue Section and were ordered to patrol at 27,000 feet over Upwood and then to Spalding at the same height. Blue 1 had a radio malfunction, so Blue 2 took the lead. Given several vectors at varying altitudes from 20,000 to 27,000 feet over the Skegness area, no enemy aircraft was sighted, so they were ordered to return and land.

In the evening three more Spitfires were scrambled. Pilot Officer Chalder, Pilot Officer Ashton and Sergeant Jones flying as Green Section, again to investigate a suspected raid by German aircraft. Patrolling over Kings Lynn at 7,000 feet, then ordered to patrol Hunstanton at 7,000 feet, They were ordered to return and land, but Green 2 and Green 3 misunderstood the order and were in the air for 25 minutes longer.

7th June

A new Intelligence Officer arrived from the Air Ministry - Pilot Officer A. R. H. Downing.

8th June

A Spitfire slightly damaged when landing. Pilot Officer R. J. B. Roach, the pilot, was uninjured. There were four raid investigations flown. The first - Flight Lieutenant Bazley, Pilot Officer Heron and Pilot Officer Ashton were ordered to patrol over the base at 15,000 feet. Several vectors were given resulting in one aircraft sighted at 16,000 feet, which was identified as a Hampden bomber.

The second - Pilot Officer Armitage, Pilot Officer Roach and Pilot Officer Chalder were dispatched to Peterborough at 10,000 feet. No aircraft sighted so they were ordered to return.

The third - Flight Lieutenant Bazley, Pilot Officer Heron and Pilot Officer Ashton as Blue Section ordered to patrol Market

Harborough at 20,000 feet to look out for unidentified aircraft. They were warned that it might be a new type of twin-engine aircraft on test.

Their height was increased to 25,000 feet and later to 27,000 feet, but no aircraft were sighted so they were given a vector to return home.

And the fourth - Pilot Officer Armitage, Pilot Officer Roach and Pilot Officer Chalder ordered to patrol Grantham at 8,000 feet. After 10 minutes ordered to climb to 20,000 feet and patrol a line from Grantham to Wittering.

Asked to investigate unidentified aircraft, a Hampden bomber was sighted at 5,000 feet shortly after it had taken off.

9th June
Flight Lieutenant Bazley, Pilot Officer Heron and Sergeant Barraclough ordered to investigate a single plot at an uncertain height north east of Upwood.

Almost immediately after take off Blue 2 and 3 were ordered to land. Blue 1 continued and patrolled between 15,000 and 20,000 feet. No aircraft sighted. Blue 1 was then ordered to return.

12th June
Yellow Section of 'A' Flight in tactical exercises with Blenheim bombers of 101 Squadron from West Raynham. Two Sergeant Pilots reported for flying duty from No. 5 OTU - R. H. Gretton and F. B. Hawley.

13th June
Not a very good start for Sergeant F. B. Hawley who was only posted in yesterday. He overshot on landing in his Spitfire, badly damaging the aircraft, but as many pilots were being 'rushed' through their initial flying training to get the squadrons 'up to

strength', this was probably simply lack of experience on his part.

15th June

A captured German aircraft, the much acclaimed Me 109, was to be air tested by Acting Flight Lieutenant S. H. Bazley at Farnborough.

Pilot Officer Clark, Flight Lieutenant Coward and Pilot Officer Bowan flying as Red Section, ordered to investigate a plot and orbited Grantham at 20,000 feet, but owing to cloud they did not fly above 15,000 feet. They orbited Grantham for 10 minutes then returned. No aircraft was sighted.

18th June

The weather so far for June has been recorded as "rather warm", but from this day on it changed completely becoming cool and "rather cold". A single Spitfire was collected from 610 Squadron.

19th June

Flight Lieutenant Bazley, Sergeant Barraclough and Pilot Officer Williams flying as Blue Section, ordered to patrol Sutton Bridge at 12,000 feet, then ordered to patrol from Hunstanton to Wells. They were ordered to return to base, but this order was cancelled almost at once and a southeasterly vector given, but no aircraft was sighted.

21st June

Flight Lieutenant Bazley flying as Blue 1 was scrambled to investigate a plot at 15,000 feet over Boston. After taking off he was ordered to patrol Grantham and when in position at 15,000 feet ordered to proceed to Boston at maximum speed.

From Boston was ordered to orbit Digby and Lincoln, then ordered to Boston again. No aircraft was sighted, so a vector to home base was given.

23rd June
Sergeant D. E. Kingaby reported for flying duties from No. 5 OTU.

24th June
Pilot Officer C. A. G. Clark posted to Fighter Interception Unit for flying duties.

27th June
Pilot Officer J. F. Soden reported for flying duties from No. 5 OTU, and Flight Lieutenant J. B. Coward posted to 19 Squadron at Duxford.

Flying Officer Burnett, Sergeant Eade and Sergeant Gretton scrambled to investigate plot. The aircraft were identified as two Hurricanes at 16,000 feet over Spalding.

Pilot Officer Cale, Pilot Officer Mitchell and Pilot Officer Bowan took off to investigate a plot but were ordered to land when airborne as the plot was identified as a Blenheim bomber over Downham Market.

Squadron Leader Hunnard, Sergeant Eade and Sergeant Gretton ordered to patrol Wittering at 10,000 feet, but no aircraft were seen.

A single Spitfire flown by Flying Officer Burnett was scrambled to investigate a plot. Flying at 20,000 feet between Upwood and Ely, again no aircraft was seen.

29th June
A new CO arrives. Squadron Leader R. L. Wilkinson posted from No. 5 OTU pending taking over command from Squadron Leader J. W. A. Hunnard.

30th June
Twelve Squadron Spitfires and twelve Hurricanes from 229

Squadron practice Wing Formation flying under the leadership of Squadron Leader J. W. A. Hunnard.

lst July
Sub Lieutenant H. C. Greenshields (RNVR) and Sergeant Pilot H. W. Ayres arrived from No. 7 OTU for flying duties. The RAF was desperate for fighter pilots. Posting pilots in from other services, as in the case of Sub Lieutenant Greenshields, was very necessary to keep the RAF flying during the Battle of Britain.

Sergeant Gretton, Flying Officer N. W. Burnett and Pilot Officer P. H. G. Mitchell scrambled to investigate possible raid. Ordered to patrol over Kettering at 15,000 feet above broken cloud and haze, the visibility was about 1 mile. After 30 minutes the Section was ordered to patrol Crowland. This was cancelled while the aircraft were en-route and the Section was ordered to return to base.

2nd July
Flying Officer N. W. Burnett, Pilot Officer P. H. G. Mitchell, Sergeant Gretton, Pilot Officer R. M. Trousdale, Sergeant Hawley and Pilot Officer F. W. Cale patrolled Market Harborough at 20,000 feet searching for two German weather reporting aircraft returning from the centre of England, but no interception was made.

3rd July
Pilot Officer H. H. Chalder, Sergeant Barraclough and Sergeant Jones on patrol over Peterborough at 20,000 feet above cloud. After five minutes ordered to patrol below cloud cover. Approaching Peterborough at about 5,000 feet to investigate a single aircraft, which proved to be an Oxford. After one circuit of Peterborough they returned to base.

4th July

The Squadron took part in a tactical exercise with Hurricanes from 229 Squadron, and Blenheim's from 23 Squadron. Flight Lieutenant D. W. Balden reported from No 5. SFTS for Flight Commander duties.

6th July

Today the Squadron's first CO since its formation on November 1st 1939, Squadron Leader J. W. A Hunnard, was posted to HQ 12 Group pending posting to HQ 14 Group for operational duties (Wing Commander post.) Squadron Leader R. L. Wilkinson assumes command from today.

8th July

Flight Lieutenant S. H. Bazley, Pilot Officer D. L. Armitage and Sub Lieutenant Greenshields patrolling over Sheringham at 20,000 feet given four differing vectors to investigate 'X' Raid which had appeared out at sea but did not approach near enough for the section to search for them.

10th July

This is the official date for the commencement of the Battle of Britain.

11th July

Squadron Leader Wilkinson, Pilot Officer N. G. Bowen and Pilot Officer F. W. Cale were ordered to intercept a Blenheim bomber believed to be hostile. Patrolling to a point about 20 miles seaward of Great Yarmouth, no Blenheim was seen. Ordered to return to base they encountered a Beaufort near Stradishall but it proved friendly. It was not unknown for captured RAF aircraft to be flown by German crews over England.

14th July

Pilot Officer R. M. Trousdale, Sergeant Gretton and Pilot Officer P. H. G. Mitchell ordered to patrol base at Angels 15. At Angels 7 the Section was instructed to land.

Squadron Leader Wilkinson and Sergeant Gretton ordered to patrol their base at Angels 10 and then ordered to orbit north of Sutton Bridge at Angels 20. No aircraft were observed so they were instructed to return to base.

The term 'Angels' indicates 1,000 feet height, thus Angels 10 is equal to 10,000 feet.

15th July

A Spitfire was damaged after landing heavily during night flying practice. The pilot, Flight Lieutenant S. H. Baxley was not injured.

Flying Officer N. W. Burnett, Sergeant Hawley and Pilot Officer P. H. G. Mitchell ordered to patrol at 20,000 feet, were vectored to Warwick where they patrolled for 20 minutes when they were ordered to investigate a single aircraft over Banbury. From there they were ordered to Market Harborough. Nothing was seen and they were ordered to return to base and land.

17th July

Flight Lieutenant D. W. Balden and Sergeant Pilot H. W. Ayre were posted to No. 1 RAF Depot at Uxbridge for temporary duties with 418 Flight.

18th July

Not a very good day today for flying accidents. In the first a Spitfire flown by Pilot Officer D. G. Ashton collided with a tractor while taxying and was badly damaged. The pilot was uninjured.

The second happened to a Spitfire flown by Pilot Officer R.

J. B. Roach when it suffered engine failure and was forced to land in a cornfield. The pilot was uninjured, and the aircraft was slightly damaged.

20th July
Flight Lieutenant S. H. Baxley ordered to patrol the airfield at 20,000 feet. Reaching 11,000 feet the height was altered to 25,000 feet. At 23,000 feet he was ordered to investigate an aircraft at 5,000 feet over Thrapston. After orbiting Bedford (he didn't understand the name Thrapston) was ordered to return and land. The aircraft was later identified as a friendly fighter.

21st July
A replacement Spitfire Mk I, was delivered to the squadron by an ATA ferry pilot.

24th July
Flight Lieutenant S. H. Bazley and Sergeant Kingaby ordered to patrol Melton Mowbray at 3,000 feet and when airborne vectored to 170o to investigate an aircraft flying at 3,000 feet and force it to land. A further vector of 210o given after a short time, but by then the section was almost out of RT (radio transmitter) range. They carried on for a further five minutes then turned back to base. Duxford relayed this radio instruction because they were by then out of radio range with their own base.

Sergeant Jones and Sergeant Kingaby were ordered to take off and patrol base at 5,000 feet. After reaching this height and orbiting for five minutes the section was instructed to land as the suspected enemy aircraft had changed course towards another sector.

25th July
Squadron Leader D. G. H. Spencer reported from Kirton Lindsey on attachment. Flying Officer N. W. Burnett and Pilot Officer J. F. Soden were ordered to patrol Skegness at 10,000 feet. When nearly there they were diverted to cover a convoy 36 miles northeast of Skegness to identify two or more aircraft at 15,000 feet.

Approximately 18 miles northeast of Skegness they were vectored back and patrolled Skegness at 17,000 feet for 10 minutes then instructed to land. The convoy had been bombed and the enemy aircraft had retired.

26th July
Squadron Leader D. G. H. Spencer damaged his Spitfire when landing during heavy rain. He was not injured.

27th July
Pilot Officer H. M. T. Heron attached to St. Athen for Fighter Navigation Instructors course lasting three weeks.

Squadron Leader D. H. Spencer and Pilot Officer R. M. Trousdale ordered to identify aircraft over Bourne. Identifying it as a friendly, they returned to base.

Pilot Officer D. G. Ashton was ordered to patrol base at 12,000 feet to investigate a single aircraft approaching from the east. The aircraft proved to be a Hurricane. He was instructed to return and land.

29th July
Flying Officer N. W. Burnett posted to 46 Squadron for Flight Commander duties.
Squadron Leader R. L. Wilkinson, Squadron Leader D. G. H. Spenser, Sergeant F. Hawley, Pilot Officer N. G. Bowen, Pilot Officer P. H. G. Mitchell and Pilot Officer J. F. Soden

ordered off from Duxford to patrol convoy at 16,000 feet off of Felixstowe arriving at 16.00 hours. After 15 minutes they came down to 2,000 feet. Poor visibility due to clouds. There were also six Hurricanes, two Anson's and one Blenheim patrolling the convoy.

One trawler was believed to have struck a mine, and two other vessels were in a sinking condition about two or three miles behind the convoy. These appeared to have been mined or bombed several hours previously.

Flight Lieutenant S. H. Bazley, Pilot Officer R. J. B. Roach, Sub Lieutenant Greenshields, Sergeant Kingaby, Sergeant W. Jones and Pilot Officer M. H. Chalder were ordered off from Duxford to patrol a convoy approximately 12 miles off of Orfordness. They arrived in position over the convoy at 17.00 hours, proceeding north northeast and patrolled until 18.20 hours. Six Spitfires, six Hurricanes and two Anson's were also patrolling the convoy at various heights.

The patrol began at 4,000 feet and worked its way up to 10,000 feet as the cloud began to break and visibility improved. As nothing suspicious was sighted they were ordered to return to Duxford.

30th July
Pilot Officer N. G. Bowen ordered to patrol base at 7,000 feet. After climbing through 6,000 feet of cloud, instructed to vector 045o for two minutes, then ordered to return and land.

1st August
Flying Officer Burnett was posted to 46 Squadron for Flight Commander duties.
Sergeant Jones and Sergeant Barraclough ordered to patrol the airfield at 15,000 feet. Were then vectored to Kettering to investigate unidentified aircraft at 20,000 feet. No aircraft

sighted so returned to base.

3rd August

Flight Lieutenant D. W. Balden and Sergeant Pilot H. W. Ayre
ceased to be attached to 418 Flight for temporary duty, and were
posted to 261 Flight.

Pilot Officer D. L. Armitage was appointed as Acting Flight
Lieutenant (unpaid) and took over duties as Flight Commander
of 'A' Flight. Flight Lieutenant D. W. Balden assists.

Pilot Officer D. G. Ashton and Sergeant Jones were
both were ordered to patrol their base at 15,000 feet. They
patrolled for 35 minutes when ordered to return and land. No
interceptions.

9th August

Twelve aircraft took off from Wittering at 06.00 hours for
Northolt, but owing to poor visibility the Squadron landed at
Hatfield. One Spitfire was damaged on landing by an obstruction
on the runway. Sergeant Pilot A. W. Eade, the pilot, was
uninjured. At 08.45 the remaining eleven aircraft took off and
landed at Northolt at 09.05 hours.

At 17.00 hours the Squadron was ordered to Tangmere for
operational duties under Coastal Command, arriving at 17.25
hours.

10th August

The Squadron was at readiness at Tangmere. A warning order
was received for the squadron to move to Eastchurch.

11th August

An advance party of one officer and thirty-three airmen left for
Eastchurch.

12th August

All Squadron aircraft flown by - Squadron Leader R. L. Wilkinson, Squadron Leader D. G. H. Spencer, Pilot Officer P. H. G. Mitchell, Flight Lieutenant D. J. Armitage, Pilot Officer R. M. Trousdale, Pilot Officer N. G. Bowen, Flight Lieutenant S. H. Bazley, Sub Lieutenant Greenshields, Sergeant Barraclough, Pilot Officer W. S. Williams, Pilot Officer D. G. Ashton and Sergeant Kingaby - were ordered from Tangmere to intercept enemy aircraft over Portsmouth.

The Squadron arrived after the enemy bombers had dropped their bombs and were making their way home at 250 mph, flying at heights between 7,000 and 12,000 feet. Attacking the enemy aircraft the following casualties were reported. Four enemy aircraft were destroyed, two probably destroyed and nine others damaged.

Sadly Pilot Officer D. G. Ashton did not return and he was presumed shot down over the sea. Pilot Officer W. S. William's aircraft was damaged and on fire, and was forced to land at Bembridge, Isle of Wight. The aircraft was totally destroyed by fire. The pilot escaped any injury.

The main party of personnel and equipment left Wittering for Eastchurch by road at 06.00 hours, arriving at 13.30 hours. The Squadron aircraft arrived at Eastchurch from Tangmere at 17.40 hours.

13th August

The Squadron's first day at Eastchurch, and the station was bombed and machine gunned by enemy aircraft from 07.05 hours until 07.20 hours. Two waves of fifteen Dornier bombers in 'vic' formation from the south and east appeared over the airfield dropping over 100 high explosives and incendiary bombs. The Airman's Quarters suffered sever damage and twelve personnel were killed and several more injured.

Squadron casualties were one killed - AC2 J. B. Brawley, one seriously injured - AC2 E. Crossley (AC2 - Aircraftsman 2nd class) and four slightly injured. Pilot Officer H. H. Chalder received severe cuts on a foot. These casualties were admitted to the County Council Hospital at Minster. Several other airmen received minor cuts and bruises, but after treatment resumed their duties.

All hangers were hit, and the Squadron hanger was set ablaze. Three Spitfires and two Magister aircraft were in the hanger at the time but were hauled out after one Spitfire had been damaged by fire. All of the Squadron's ammunition, spare ammunition tanks and some equipment was destroyed. One bomb fell on the Officer's Quarters, shattering windows and dislodging plaster. Water supplies to fight the fires were seriously effected.

14th August

After the destruction of the previous day the Squadron was moved rapidly to Hornchurch. Transport aircraft were placed at the disposal of the squadron and flight personnel and equipment moved by air, the remaining personnel and equipment was transported by road.

Sadly the airman who was seriously wounded in the raid, AC2 E. Crossley, died in the County Council Hospital from his wounds.

15th August

The Squadron was scrambled at 16.00 hours to intercept enemy aircraft. These were intercepted off of Dover. After the engagement one Spitfire, piloted by Pilot Officer F. W. Cale was reported as 'missing'. His Spitfire was afterwards reported as burnt out at Teston, near Maidstone. Later in the evening the County Police at Maidstone reported finding a parachute with burnt straps but no trace of the pilot. The following day his body was recovered from the river at Teston.

The following was taken from the ORB for that day. But Appendix Four of the ORB details a differing take off time. The Squadron did in fact take part in two combats that day as below. Pilot Officer F. W. Cale took off at 18.20 on the second interception, and not at 16.00 hours as per the ORB.

"Sergeant A. W. Eade, Sergeant W. Jones, Pilot Officer R. J. B. Roach, Pilot Officer J. F. Soden, Flight Lieutenant S. H. Baxley, Sergeant F. B. Hawley, were scrambled at 16.00 hours from the advanced base at Manston to intercept enemy aircraft three miles east of Deal. The enemy aircraft, a He 111 bomber, was sighted approximately twelve miles east of Deal flying at about 300 feet. It was attacked and destroyed, crashing into the sea eight miles southwest of Dunkerque. The Squadron lost one pilot, Sergeant Hawley did not return. He was last seen going into the attack by Green Leader.

At 18.20 hours Squadron Leader R. L. Wilkinson, Sub. Lieutenant Greenshields, Flight Lieutenant D. L. Armitage, Sergeant A. E. Eade, Pilot Officer R. J. B. Roach, Pilot Officer F. W. Cale, Flight Lieutenant S. H. Bazley and Sergeant D. E. Kingaby were ordered to patrol base at 20,000 feet. When they were at 15,000 feet two waves of enemy aircraft, numbering about 200, were sighted south east of Dover travelling at 250 mph. These were attacked and three enemy aircraft were destroyed and one damaged. One of our Spitfires piloted by Pilot Officer F. W. Cale was reported as burnt out at Teston, near Maidstone. On the following day his body was recovered from the river at Teston."

16th August

The Squadron left for operational duties at Manston and were again soon in action. At 12.15 hours they were ordered from

Manston to intercept enemy aircraft. The engagement, which followed, resulted in many casualties for the Squadron.

Squadron Leader R. L. Wilkinson was discovered dead at Eastry, near Deal. His death was due to multiple injuries and burns. Sub Lieutenant H. L. Greenshields (RNVR) is reported as 'missing'. Pilot Officer N. G. Bowen was found dead at Adisham, near Canterbury, death due to multiple injuries and burns.

Flying Officer (Acting Flight Lieutenant) S. H. Bazley escaped by parachute when his Spitfire caught fire and he landed in a cornfield near Canterbury and was taken to hospital suffering from burns and minor injuries. Pilot Officer J. F. Soden was hit by shell fire and force landed north of Faversham. He received slight shrapnel wounds to his legs.

The ORB Appendix Five for that day states - "Squadron Leader R. L. Wilkinson, Flight Lieutenant S. H. Bazley, Pilot Officer Roach, Pilot Officer R. M. Trousdale, Pilot Officer J. F. Soden, Pilot Officer N. G. Bowen, Pilot Officer P. H. G. Mitchell, Sub. Lieutenant Greenshields, Sergeant W. Jones and Sergeant R. H. Gretton were ordered to patrol advanced base (Manston) at 20,000 feet when between twenty and thirty enemy aircraft flying in line astern formation appearing to be going round in large circles.

An engagement followed with one enemy aircraft destroyed and three probably destroyed. Squadron Leader R. L. Wilkinson and Pilot Officer N. G. Bowen were both killed, and Sub Lieutenant H. L. Greenshields failed to return and was reported 'missing'.

Flight Lieutenant S. H. Bazley baled out and was taken to Canterbury Hospital with minor burns and injuries. Pilot Officer J. F. Soden received minor injuries to his leg and crashed on landing north of Faversham."

An ATA ferry pilot delivered a single Spitfire to the Squadron.

17th August

Ten Spitfires were delivered to the Squadron. Nine by ATA ferry pilots, and one from the Air Stores Unit at Hamble. These were to replace those aircraft lost in action and those that were still unserviceable. Experienced fighter pilots were not as easy to replace!

18th August

The Squadron departed Hornchurch for their advanced base at Manston. En-route they were diverted to intercept enemy aircraft in the Dover area. After the engagement they landed at Manston to refuel and re-arm when they were attacked on the ground by German fighters firing 20mm cannon and machine guns. Two Spitfires were destroyed by fire and another five badly damaged which were repairable by a MU. Sergeant Pilot D. E. Kingaby was slightly wounded and Sergeant Pilot W. Jones was treated for shock.

From the ORB Appendix Six. "Taking off at 13.15 Squadron Leader D. G. H. Spenser, Flight Lieutenant D. L. Armitage, Pilot Officer W. S Williams, Pilot officer R. J. B. Roach, Pilot Officer R. M. Trousdale, Sergeant Barraclough and Sergeant D. E. Kingaby were ordered from Manston to patrol Rochford at 10,000 feet from where they were vectored to Dover.

At 20,000 feet over the Channel area about twenty enemy aircraft were spotted in groups of five or six and in line astern. The Squadron attacked, and one enemy aircraft was destroyed, one probably destroyed, and one damaged. None of the Squadron's Spitfires were damaged. Returning to base to refuel and re-arm German fighters strafed the aircraft on the ground resulting in two aircraft destroyed by fire and five badly damaged."

Squadron Leader D. G. H. Spencer was to command the Squadron following the death of Squadron Leader Wilkinson.

Seven more replacement Spitfire Mk Is were delivered. Two from No. 24 MU, and five from No. 6 MU.

19th August
Two Spitfire Mk Is delivered from No. 6 MU.

20th August
Re-placement pilot, Pilot Officer C. Logan, reported from 12 Squadron at Eastchurch, for flying duties.

Flight Lieutenant D. L. Armitage and Sergeant A. W. Eade were ordered to proceed to Manston from Dover at full speed and intercept enemy aircraft approaching Manston, but on the way were ordered to return to home base (Hornchurch) and land.

22nd August
Today the pilots, flight personnel, and main party moved back to Wittering by air, road and rail.

23rd August
The Squadron moved back to Wittering was now complete with the arrival of the rear party.

24th August
More replacement pilots arrive today. Flying Officer E. H. Thomas and Flight Sergeant C. Sydney, both from 19 Squadron.

The AOC of 12 Group visited the Station, talking to pilots about their recent experiences.

26th August
Pilot Officers W. A. Middleton, H. D. Pool, J. G. Pattison, R. H. Thomas and E. P. Well, together with Sergeant Pilots H. Cook and W. Ellis reported for flying duties from No. 7 OTU.

27th August
Pilot Officer J. C. R. Clarke reported from No 7 OTU for flying duties.

28th August
The Squadron was certainly getting back up to strength, for today two more pilots reported for duty. Pilot Officer T. D. Davey DFC, and Pilot Officer G. M. Hayton from 12 Squadron, although the Squadron did lose one pilot as Pilot Officer R. H. Thomson was posted to 66 Squadron.

30th August
Flight Lieutenant D. L. Armitage ordered to investigate a raid going north through the Squadron's section. Immediately after take off he was ordered to land. At readiness was again ordered to investigate suspected enemy aircraft over Nottingham at 15,000 feet, but after five minutes was ordered to return.

31st August
Flight Lieutenant D. L. Armitage, Pilot Officer R. M. Trousdale and Sergeant R. H. Gretton ordered to patrol Duxford and Debden at 25,000 feet but being out of radio range returned towards base till just north of Cambridge where they were instructed to patrol north of Cambridge at 10,000 feet but they were then ordered to land.

Pilot Officer W. S. Williams, Pilot Officer H. M. T. Heron and Sergeant Barraclough ordered to patrol Duxford to Debden at 25,000 feet. When in position over Duxford were ordered to remain in position and orbit. Later they descended to 10,000 feet and were instructed to return to base and land.

1st September

At Wittering, Air Chief Marshall Sir Robert Brooke-Popham visited the Station in connection with Squadron establishment. ('Establishment' is referring to the strength in personnel and equipment of the squadron.)

Pilot Officer R. M. Trousdale, Flight Sergeant Sydney and Sergeant Gretton ordered to patrol at 14.25 hours. They were vectored 220o at Gate. They then climbed to 18,000 feet on course, and were then vectored to 180o and chased enemy aircraft to Watford. They did not engage the enemy and returned to base landing at 15.05.

4th September

The Squadron was to lose its Mk I Spitfires. Information received from Fighter Command states that the Squadron is to be re-equipped with Spitfire Mk IIs immediately. Good news indeed.

5th September

Ferry pilots of the ATA delivered the first five Spitfire Mk IIs.

6th September

ATA pilots delivered another thirteen Mk IIs. The Squadron was now fully equipped with this new Mark. These ATA pilots also flew the squadrons older Mk Is to other squadrons. Five were delivered to 72 Squadron, and four to 66 Squadron.

7th September

Five more of the Squadron's Spitfire Mk Is were delivered to 616 Squadron, again by ATA Ferry pilots.

The delivering of RAF aircraft, which these ATA pilots did,

cannot, in my opinion, be, praised enough. If this organisation were not set up at the onset of hostilities, then the RAF would have had to use its own pilots to carry out this very important role, thus reducing the fighting strength of the RAF. It should also be remember that many were female pilots, and many were killed whilst on ferry duty.

Pilot Officer Williams, Pilot Officer Roach, both flying Spitfire Mk IIs, and Pilot Officer Trousdale flying a Mk I, were ordered from Coltishall to patrol Yarmouth at 25,000 feet and vectored towards enemy aircraft first sighted at 09.00 hours west of Norwich at 30,000 feet.

"Tallyho" was given but due to sun dazzle enemy aircraft were twice lost sight of. When next seen they were at 23,000 feet, approximately twenty miles north-west of Walseheron Island. The chase continued until nearly over the island when the section made a surprise attack. The enemy aircraft took no evasive action, although one of our aircraft experienced apparent cannon fire from the rear of one of the enemy aircraft. After further attacks black smoke was observed from the starboard engine. The aircraft was seen to go into a vertical dive and crash into the centre of Walseheron Island in flames. There were no casualties to squadron pilots or damage to aircraft.

10th September

Six Squadron aircraft proceeded at 06.45 hours to Duxford for operational duties. Squadron Leader D. G. H. Spenser was posted to 257 Squadron at Debden having been CO since 17 August 1940. Flying Officer E. H. Thomas and Pilot Sergeant R. H. Gretton were both posted to 222 Squadron for flying duties.

11th September

Pilot Officer H. M. T. Heron, Pilot Officer J. G. Pattison and Sergeant Pilot H. Cook posted to 92 Squadron for flying duties.

Ordered to patrol London at 25,000 feet, Flight Lieutenant Bazley, Pilot Officer Roach, Pilot Officer Williams, Pilot Officer Heron, Pilot Officer Pattison and Sergeant Barraclough in Spitfire Mk IIs from Duxford as part of the Duxford Wing. Shortly after take off a formation of thirty Do 215s were sighted over Dartford and Gravesend flying northwest at about 240 mph at 22,000 feet. Further behind these was a wave of thirty He 111s with approximately ten Me 109s flying 2,000 to 3,000 feet above.

The Do 215s were being hotly engaged by AA (anti-aircraft) fire. The Squadron aircraft flying in line astern attacked the starboard wing of Do 215s, coming out of the sun from above, ahead and to port. Enemy casualties were three probably destroyed and five damaged. One Spitfire flown by Pilot Officer Roach was hit by cannon fire and crashed near Billericay, Essex. He baled out over the town and spent the night at North Weald before returning to the Squadron the next day.

12th September
Squadron Leader H. W. Mermagen AFC temporarily assumes command of the squadron.

13th September
Pilot Officer W. Jones (recently commissioned from Sergeant Pilot) and Sergeant Pilot A. W. Eade posted to 602 Squadron for flying duties.

14th September
Pilot Officer J. F. Soden posted to 603 Squadron for flying duties.

15th September
Pilot Officer H. H. Chalder was posted to 41 Squadron.

16th September
To replace those pilots recently posted away to other duties, the Squadron received an intake of new pilots. Pilot Officers A. H. Humphry, H. A. R. Prowse, Sergeant Pilots L. O. Allton, R. A. Boswell, R. A. Breeze, J. T. Dunmore and A. N. MacGregor all reported from No. 7 OTU.

17th September
Squadron Leader P. G. Jameson assumes command of the squadron from today.

21st September
Sergeant Pilot W. T. Ellis posted to 92 Squadron for flying duties.

23rd September
Sergeant Pilots K. C. Pattison and J. A. Scott reported for flying duties from an OTU.

24th September
From the Squadron's base at Wittering, there was a regular temporary transfer of aircraft to Duxford. Six were sent today for operational duties. Also today Sergeant Pilot W. Sadler arrived from 92 Squadron for flying duties.

25th September
Sergeant Pilot D. E. Kingaby was posted to 92 Squadron for flying duties.

26th September
Pilot Officer R. J. B. Roach gave Hendon factory 'observers' a demonstration of the Spitfire Mk II today. The ORB doesn't specify who the observers were.

Wing Commander J. Barwell from HQ 12 Group visited the Squadron in respect of training new pilots.

Sergeant Pilots K. C. Pattison, W. Sadler and J. A Scott were all posted to 611 Squadron for flying duties.

These postings of pilots who had only arrived a few days earlier, and the visit by Wing Commander J. Barwell, points to the probable conclusion that the Squadron was training new pilots in aerial combat before they were posted on to other squadrons.

27th September

Flight Lieutenant Bazley, Pilot Officer Roach, Pilot Officer Davy, Pilot Officer Williams, Pilot Officer Middleton, Sergeant Barraclough, Squadron Leader Jameson, Pilot Officer Wells and Pilot Officer Logan ordered to patrol as part of the Duxford Wing and investigate activity at the North Weald and Biggin Hill area as near to the cloud base as possible (17,000 feet). No enemy aircraft or AA fire see. Another Wing of Hurricane and Spitfire aircraft were seen over the Sheppey area. The Duxford Wing was then ordered to return and land at Duxford.

The Duxford Wing, sometimes referred to as 'The Big Wing', was Douglas Bader's idea of getting large formations of fighters into the air, at the right height, and en-mass to take on the large formations of enemy aircraft. Debate still continues to this day as to its success or not.

28th September

Pilot Officer T. D. Davey DFC was posted to 72 Squadron, while Sergeant Pilots R. A. Boswell and A. N. MacGregor went to 19 Squadron for flying duties, and from No. 7 OTU Pilot Officer M. K. Hill arrived for flying duties with the squadron.

The Duxford Wing was scrambled. Squadron Leader Jameson, Pilot Officer Logan, Pilot Officer Pool, Flight

Lieutenant Armitage, Pilot Officer Trousdale, Pilot Officer Thomas, Pilot Officer Williams, Pilot Officer Humphrey, Sergeant Barraclough, Flight Lieutenant Bazley, Pilot Officer Roach and Pilot Officer Prowse were ordered to patrol above the main wing of Hurricane aircraft acting as cover against a surprise attack from enemy aircraft.

The Wing patrolled North and East London, and the Thames Estuary at approximately 20,000 feet, with 266 Squadron flying at 25,000 feet. Several enemy fighters were seen at 30,000 feet over the South Coast flying east, but turned at once to the south at high speed. They were too far away to engage. No further activity was observed and the Wing was ordered to return to Duxford.

29th September
Two more pilots reported for flying duty today. Pilot Officer R. C. Gostling and Sergeant Pilot G. A. Ford, both from No. 7 OTU.

30th September
Sergeant Pilots T. A. Cooper, M. A Beatty and S. A. Godwin reported today for flying duties also from No. 7 OTU. Sergeant Pilot L. C. Allton was posted to 92 Squadron for flying duties.

1st October
Six Squadron Spitfires were 'at readiness' for immediate scramble if called upon. Sergeants R. A. Breeze and J. T. Dunmore were both posted to 222 Squadron for flying duties.

2nd October
Average temperatures, an overcast sky with visibility moderate. Four raid investigations by Squadron aircraft from Wittering.

On a training flight orbiting Wittering Flight Lieutenant

Bazley was ordered to intercept one enemy aircraft four miles north of base at 9,000 feet. There was 10/10th cloud cover from 4,000 to 7,000 feet. He patrolled the position for two minutes and was then given an easterly vector and ordered to descend below cloud and 'Gate'. When over Sutton Bridge he was ordered to return and land. But the enemy aircraft didn't escape. It was intercepted and destroyed by an aircraft from Digby.

'Gate' means that the pilot can get extra speed from his aircraft by pushing the throttle lever through a 'gate' to give the engine more rpm. The 'gate' itself is a metal plate that normally would prevent the throttle lever from travelling too far. Not recommended for long periods as damage to the engine could result.

Pilot Officer E. P. Well posted to No. 41 Squadron for flying duties.

3rd October

A film unit from the Ministry of Information arrived at Wittering to make a film named 'Air Communiqué' under the supervision of Squadron Leader Gillman from Fighter Command.

Pilots and aircraft of the Squadron together with 1 Squadron and their ground crews were to take part in the making of this film. It was decided that the best results would be obtained by shooting the entire sequence on the station.

Two un-planned away landings today! Pilot Officers Trousdale and Mitchell searching for reported enemy aircraft in the Wellingborough area flew into thick cloud. Descending to 1,000 feet from 2,000 feet, they could find no break in the cloud. Descending further to 50 feet, they were forced to land in a field, seven miles south east of Mildenhall.

Pilot Officer P. Pool and Sergeant Terry posted to Biggin Hill for flying duties.

4th October
Filming began today with the Squadron's aircraft taking off and completing circuits of the station, landing as required for camera and sound purposes.

Sergeant S. A. Goodwin piloting a Spitfire Mk II forced landed at Little Bythem with undercarriage retracted during bad weather. He was uninjured but the aircraft was badly damaged.

5th October
The Squadron was by now used to operating from other airfields. At 10.15 hours they flew to Duxford, again to patrol with the Duxford Wing.

6th October
More filming took place today. Owing to bad weather no flying sequences were possible so all inside sequences were filmed in 'B' Flight dispersal hut. 900 feet of film being shot completing the inside shots.

7th October
Exterior shooting for the film with over 1,200 feet being shot. Pilot Officer B. E. Tucker and Sergeants J. W. Allan, E. A. King and S. F. Tomalin reported for flying duties.

8th October
Back to Duxford as part of the Duxford Wing. Twelve of the Squadron's aircraft left at 09.00 hours for Operational Duties, returning at 16.25 hours. They were not sent on any patrols at Duxford, but remained 'at readiness'. The shooting of the Ministry of Information film is now completed.

11th October
Weather was cloudy with visibility average to poor. Twelve

Squadron aircraft sent to Duxford at 15.00 hours, returning at 18.00 hours. Three of these aircraft were scrambled, flown by Pilot Officer Logan, Sergeants Beatty and Cook. They were ordered to patrol over the base at 5,000 feet, and then vectored to Kings Lynn. One aircraft was seen at 3,000 feet and another at 5,000 feet, both identified as Blenheim bombers. They were then instructed to return to Duxford and land. Take off 13.10. Landed 14.00.

As a point of interest, Spitfire P7350, flown here by Pilot Officer Logan, survived the war and escaped being scrapped and is now flown by the Battle of Britain Memorial Flight at RAF Coningsby.

12th October

A misty morning and evening although warm. Visibility good except in mist. The Squadron left for duty at Duxford at 09.45 hours, returning at 17.25 hours.

13th October

Sergeant S. A. Cooper posted to 92 Squadron at Biggin Hill for flying duties.

14th October

Sergeant S. A. Goodwin posted to 66 Squadron at Biggin Hill for flying duties, while Sergeants C. E. Ody, R. J. Thorburn and D. W. Thomas reported from No 7 OTU for flying duties.

15th October

An escaped barrage balloon was shot down by Squadron Leader Jameson today. Squadron Leader Jameson was ordered to search for, and shoot down yet another barrage balloon that had broken away from its moorings. He intercepted it at 24,000 feet northeast of Peterborough and destroyed it.

16th October
A 'backward' step today when instructions received from HQ Fighter Command that the Squadron's Mk II Spitfires were to be exchanged with Mk I Spitfires from 603 Squadron. Fourteen aircraft were delivered to that Squadron at Hornchurch, the remaining four to be delivered when serviceable.

17th October
Thirteen Mk I Spitfires were received from 603 Squadron. One Spitfire piloted by Sergeant C. E. Ody was damaged on landing, the pilot was not injured.

18th October
An official RAF photographer, Mr. Devon, took photographs of the Squadron landing and flying in formation.

20th October
Pilot Officer H. A. R. Prowse posted to 603 Squadron for flying duties.

21st October
Pilot Officer Williams was ordered to intercept a raid attacking Cambridge. He chased the enemy aircraft out in an easterly direction but could not make contact. Landing at Stradishall to refuel, he crashed on take off to return to base and was killed.

22nd October
Sergeant F. W. Morse reported for flying duty from 56 Squadron.

25th October
Eleven aircraft were sent to the Duxford Wing at 11.15 for operational duties returning later that day. Pilot Officer B. E. Tucker posted to 66 Squadron.

26th October

Eleven aircraft sent to Duxford, carrying out one patrol from there. Pilot Officer G. M. Hayton posted to 66 Squadron.

27th October

The Squadron was again sent to Duxford, but did not return to Wittering due to bad weather, although they did carry out two patrols with the Wing. On the first patrol all squadron aircraft were airborne. No interceptions were made, but Pilot Officer Humphrey became detached from the Squadron and landed away at North Weald.

28th October

The Squadron was flying with the Duxford Wing again and were ordered to patrol the base below cloud and then ordered above the cloud to join the rest of the Wing patrolling the Thames Estuary. There were no interceptions and the Squadron was ordered back to Wittering.

One Spitfire Mk I piloted by Pilot Officer Gosling became detached from the Squadron and landed away at Luton. The Squadron returned from Duxford at 18.00 hours.

29th October

Flying with the Duxord Wing the Squadron was ordered to patrol over Duxford at 25,000 feet. Eleven Me 109s were spotted at about 30,000 feet. A short combat followed but no damage was inflicted on the enemy aircraft or to the squadron except for a tyre on one Spitfire being shot up. The enemy aircraft had the advantage of height, breaking off the combat at great speed.

The Squadron was at this stage now broken up when Pilot Officer Trousdales attention was attracted by AA fire. Climbing up into the sun, he identified three Me 109s flying in a wide 'vic' formation towards the south east coast. An engagement followed resulting in one Me 109 being shot down in flames about 10 to 15 miles north of Lympe Airport.

30th October

The weather today was very cold. Visibility was good at first, but quickly deteriorating during the morning. Again the squadron was sent to Duxford.

The Squadron had taken off from Duxford to return to Wittering, when three were detached - Flight Lieutenant Bazley, Pilot Officer Roach and Pilot Officer Humphrey - and detailed to investigate unidentified aircraft over Ely. On reaching Ely the section was ordered to orbit over the city and then proceed to Newmarket. Three Blenheim bombers were intercepted between Ely and Newmarket. The section was then informed that the enemy aircraft had already been engaged and shot down. They were then ordered to return to Wittering.

31st October

Not a great deal of activity today, mainly because of poor weather - rain and poor visibility.
This day is the official date of when the Battle of Britain concluded.

2nd November

Squadron Leader Jameson, Pilot Officer Mitchell, Pilot Officer Logan, Pilot Officer Trousdale, Sergeant Beatty, Flight Lieutenant Bazley, Pilot Officer Middleton, Pilot Officer Hill, Pilot Officer Roach, Pilot Officer Humphrey and Sergeant Barraclough were ordered to patrol Duxford at 20,000 feet to join up with 72 Squadron (Spitfire) over Duxford.

There was considerable haze and the interception was made only after some considerable time had passed, 72 Squadron being sighted below and approaching from the northeast. 266 Squadron was ordered to lead with 72 Squadron following astern. Shortly after this was achieved the Squadron was ordered to land.

4th November
No flying today owing to bad weather - rain and very poor visibility. Pilot Officer C. Logan posted to 222 Squadron for flying duties.

5th November
Two Spitfires flown by Sergeant R. J. Thorburn and Sergeant F. W. Morse, collided. Both aircraft were badly damaged, but both of the pilots uninjured. The ORB doesn't record how they collided, but as both pilots were uninjured it can be assumed that the collision was during taxying.

Six new pilots arrived for flying duties from No. 7 OTU. No details of name or rank are given in the ORB.

8th November
Pilot Officer H. E. Penketh posted to the Squadron from 611 Squadron. The Squadron was again flying as part of the Duxford Wing.

9th November
The six newly arrived pilots were 'put through their paces' today. Formation flying and 'circuits and bumps' was the order of the day for them.

10th November
On this day the Wittering Wing was formed. Comprising of No. 1 Squadron (Hurricane), No. 19 Squadron (Spitfire) and No. 266 Squadron (Spitfire Mk I.)

1 and 266 Squadrons operating from Wittering joining up with 19 Squadron when airborne for the first patrol of the new Wittering Wing took place the same day it was formed.

11th November

Flying as the Wittering Wing, Squadron Leader Jameson, Pilot Officer Thomas, Sergeant Beatty, Pilot Officer Trousdale, Sergeant Cook, Flight Lieutenant Bazley, Pilot Officer Gosling, Pilot Officer Humphrey, Pilot Officer Roach and Pilot Officer Hill patrol Wittering at 25,000 feet. Ordered to Whitstable Bay/Burnham and then onto Maidstone/Canterbury.

Two Me 110s and two or three groups of Me 109s were sighted, but as the Squadron approached to engage the enemy aircraft they at once headed south and out of range appearing to be very reluctant for combat.

14th November

The Magister aircraft used by the Squadron as a training aircraft crashed on landing after such a training flight. The pilot, Sergeant R. F. Lewis and passenger, Sergeant J. Shircore both escaped without injury.

15th November

On patrol with the Wittering Wing one Spitfire over shot the aerodrome on landing and was damaged. The pilot, Sergeant F. W. Morse was not injured.

16th November

Pilot Officer P. H. G. Mitchell was uninjured when his Spitfire crashed on landing in darkness returning from a patrol.

17th November

Another escaped barrage balloon! This time chased by Flight

Lieutenant S. H. Bazley. Breaking from its moorings, it was reported three miles south of Wittering at 9,000 feet. Sighting the balloon he made five attacks without result, expending all of his ammunition. The balloon vanished into cloud at 2,000 feet midway between Wisbech and March. Its final ending is not known, but as it was loosing height it can be assumed that it eventually came down to earth in that area.

21st November
Sergeant R. F. Lewis posted to 57 OTU for further training.

22nd November
Pilot Officer H. E. Penketh was killed during combat. His aircraft was seen to dive into the ground with full engine power, at Holme, near Upwood aerodrome. Both the pilot and aircraft were buried in about thirty feet of earth. The aircraft was identified by pieces of the Merlin engine with the number plate attached found near the crash site. This young pilot had only been with the Squadron for two weeks. His body was recovered on 30 November.

There is an Appendix Fourteen in the ORB for that date, but oddly no mention of the combat, or of his death, is recorded, although there is a clear reference note for that day's report to refer to that particular Appendix.

23rd November
Pilot Officer R. M. Trousdale posted to 255 Squadron for Flight Commander duties.

25th November
Pilot Officer Mitchell was ordered to take off on vector 060o. On climbing to 10,000 feet was immediately ordered down to 5,000 feet and orbit the aerodrome, as an enemy aircraft was

located in the immediate area. Given a new vector in a northerly direction, he was told to orbit again as the enemy aircraft was now six miles to the west. He intercepted the aircraft but it turned out to be a Hampden bomber about seven miles north of Stamford.

26th November

The Squadron, by now, must be getting a reputation for chasing and destroying escaped barrage balloons!

Today Pilot Officer Roach and Flight Lieutenant Baxley were both dispatched to deal with the offending balloon. It was located and duly dispatched! Appendix 18 for the day records that there were three separate take offs in an attempt to destroy this balloon.

First Pilot Officer Roach was scrambled to shoot the escaped balloon down. He carried out the attacking with two guns with 100 rounds per gun, but only fired 70 rounds before there was a stoppage in both guns. He landed to have the guns cleared, took off again and engaged the balloon for a second time due north of Ketton at 4,000 feet. It was observed to have descended to 1,000 feet.

It was now Flight Lieutenant Baxley's turn. Locating the balloon one mile east of Spalding it was now down to 80 feet. He was ordered to stand by, and then ordered to shoot it down. The balloon was now over Fosdyke. He attacked three times and saw it collapse and sink too low for further attacks. At this time it was over the mud flats off of Fosdyke and loosing height.

27th November

Sergeant Pilots Allen and Cooper posted to 64 Squadron at Hornchurch, while Sergeant Pilots King and Tomalin went to 602 Squadron at Tangmere for flying duties.

30th November

Pilot Officer Penkeths body was recovered from the wreckage of his Spitfire at Holme Fen after a week searching for him. (See entry for 22 November.)

2nd December

Average temperatures with fog. Visibility moderate. After today the temperature dropped sharply.

A Spitfire flown by Sergeant J. E. van Schaich was damaged on landing. He is probably one of the six un-named pilots posted to the squadron on 5 November.

4th December

Combat success today. Pilot Officer A. H. Humphrey attacked and destroyed a He 111 over the coast of Holland near Scheldt. Taking the war to the enemy! This is the combat report - "Pilot was flying alone at 15,000 feet on aerobatics practice when five miles south of the Wash at approximately 11.50 he saw an aircraft 3,000 feet below about twelve miles away over the sea. He closed to within 600 yards and identified aircraft as a Ju 88, which was flying eastwards at 220 mph continually into the clouds.

After some 25 minutes the enemy aircraft went through clouds that were 10/10ths at 10,000 feet, pilot followed but did not see enemy aircraft in between two layers at 4,000 feet so proceeded down coming out at 1,000 feet. There was no sign of Ju 88 but less than half a mile away was a He 111 with no special camouflage. Below was an island about five miles long, rather narrow with small red roofed houses - near coast of Holland near the mouth of the Schelde River.

Pilot closed to 400 yards at full throttle then gave enemy aircraft long burst closing at 200 yards. Enemy aircraft made no attempt to avoid until fire commenced when it went into steep spirals towards sea at 250 mph.

The first burst was from directly above and astern and as the enemy aircraft spiraled down, pilot gave two more bursts one of five seconds from port quarter using deflection and firing at the enemy aircraft's pilot.

No return fire was experienced and during last burst enemy aircraft did a steep turn and crashed into the sea approx. ten miles east of the island near some fifteen fishing boats. No damage done to our aircraft."

16th December

Our own aircraft were not safe from attack by friendly fighters as this combat report illustrates.

Flying Officer Thomas was carrying out camera gun practice when he was vectored 140o and ordered to climb to 1,000 feet. Orbiting at this height he was told of an enemy aircraft coming up from the south. He sighted the aircraft and identified it as a Manchester bomber.

He was then vectored to 290o and told that the aircraft intercepted was not the enemy aircraft referred to. He climbed to 17,000 feet and after one or two more vectors intercepted an aircraft leaving a smoke trail which turned out to be a Blenheim bomber L8586 'J' but with no squadron letters.

Forcing it down to 200 feet, and as the aircraft did not fire any recognition signals, he ordered it to land, but just as Pilot Officer Thomas was about to fire warning shots the aircraft gave the correct two star cartridge so identity was established. Film of the interception was taken on the camera gun.

Pilot Officer Hill, Pilot Officer Humphrey and Sergeant Barraclough were also called upon to intercept an enemy aircraft. Flying at 21,000 feet, they were vectored to 240o and then given another vector of 195o when they sighted a Ju 88. After pursuing it for five minutes the Ju 88 escaped into cloud and was not seen again.

20th December
The squadron was visited today be Air Vice Marshall R. E. Saul DFC, Air Officer Commanding 12 Group, who talked to pilots.

22nd December
Two interceptions in one patrol (although six patrols took place today.) Flight Lieutenant Armitage, Sergeant Thorburn and Sergeant Shircore intercepted an aircraft in the vicinity of Grantham which was identified as an Avro Anson. Immediately afterwards they intercepted a Flamingo.

26th December
Sergeant R. G. V. Barraclough claimed as probably destroyed a Do 17 over the mouth of the Thames estuary. Flying his Spitfire, he was vectored onto a Do 17 at 4,000 feet and flying at 200 mph, due east and just south of the London Balloon Barrage. He maneuvered so as to engage the enemy, flying from the sun and gave a quarter attack from above and astern. The Do 17 dived steeply towards the fog layer 2,500 feet below.

A game of hide and seek followed for ten minutes, chasing the Do 17 eastwards. The Do 17 appeared again and Sergeant Barraclough finished all of his ammunition into the fuselage of the enemy aircraft which immediately dropped its starboard wing and disappeared abruptly into the fog in definite distress.

Machine gun fire from the Do 17 top/rear gunner did not appear to cause any damage to the pursuing Spitfire, but on landing it was discovered that there was slight damage to the oil system. From information supplied by Duxford it would appear that combat took place over the sea.

Summary of 1940

The period named as the 'phoney war' at the beginning of 1940. Raids by enemy aircraft - designated as 'X' Raids - were investigated with little success. Dunkirk and the evacuation of the BEF and French Army resulted in the Squadron's first casualties of the war, but there would be more before the year was over.

Protecting the Channel convoys against German bombers and fighter attacks. Losing their Mk 11 Spitfires and being replaced with Mk 1s. There is no explanation as to why the Squadron lost their Mk11s.

The Squadron's first ground crew casualties following an attack by German raiders bombing and strafing the airfield. Two Leading Aircraftman died as a result.

The Battle of Britain in which the Squadron performed very well, albeit not without several casualties. Pilot losses through 1940 were; one killed in a flying accident, three reported as missing in action and sadly seven pilots killed in action.

Enemy aircraft attacked were; one Me 109, one Do 17, one Me 110, five He 111, three Do 215, and five unspecified bombers, all claimed as destroyed. Claimed as damaged were; ten unspecified aircraft, one He 111, five Do 215, and four Me 109s. Probables were three unspecified bombers. Plus of course those three barrage balloons!

1941

1st January

A new identity for the Squadron. Information received from HQ Fighter Command states that "Rhodesian personnel would be gradually drafted to No. 266 (F) Squadron, and when the majority of the personnel are Rhodesian, this Squadron will assume the title of No. 266 (S. Rhodesia) (Fighter) Squadron."

As already described, the Squadron was reformed from donations received by many people living in Rhodesia. It seemed only fitting therefore that Rhodesian pilots should form the backbone of the Squadron. It was in fact known over time as 'Rhodesian' and not as the communiqué stated - 'S. Rhodesia'.

Flying Officer J. S. Howitt arrived today to take up the post of Medical Officer.

The weather, as one would expect, was very cold with snow falling to a depth of three inches, and as such flying was limited.

10th January
Pilot Officer P. H. G. Mitchell made a forced landing at Cranwell with his Spitfires undercarriage retracted, and Sergeant J. Shircore crashed at Swinderby when returning to base from a raid investigation. Both pilots were uninjured.

14th January
Flight Lieutenant Armitage was ordered to locate and shoot down an escaped barrage balloon in the vicinity of Bourne. It was located, and although the outer six .303 machineguns were unloaded; he attacked with just the two inner guns.

Expending all of his ammunition, he left it south of Holbeach at 800 feet, falling at a rate of 50 feet a minute.

15th January
Severe winter weather - very cold and heavy snow six inches deep. Sergeant Ody escaped uninjured when his Spitfire ran into a ground obstruction and was slightly damaged.

24th January
The first sixteen Rhodesian personnel arrived today, but

unfortunately the ORB gives no details as to their names.

3rd February

Flight Lieutenant Armitage and Pilot Officer Thomas were scrambled and ordered to intercept a bandit (enemy aircraft) over Feltwell. Climbing through cloud from 1,500 to 7,000 feet, Flight Lieutenant Armitage could not locate the bandit, but while above clouds white puffs of smoke were observed similar to AA fire. He was ordered to descend through the cloud and join up with Pilot Officer Thomas again but this was not achieved owing to the very poor visibility, the snow clouds now down to 1,000 feet. He patrolled between Feltwell and Newmarket, and when orbiting an aerodrome under construction north of Cambridge saw a stick of bombs dropped on the landing area. He was travelling in the opposite direction to the enemy aircraft and below it, so he turned and climbed but was unable to locate it.

Pilot Officer Thomas was given various vectors below the clouds. As visibility was now very bad owing to severe snowstorms, he was ordered to return to base, landing five minutes after Flight Lieutenant Armitage.

4th February

All twelve aircraft left for Martlesham and after refueling they carried outa Fighter Sweep from Boulogne - Calais - Dunkirk along the French coast together with Hurricane aircraft from 242 Squadron. No enemy aircraft contacts due to 10/10th cloud cover, so returned to Martlesham, refueled and returned to base at Wittering.

8th February

An 'endurance test' was carried out by Squadron Leader Jameson DFC and Pilot Officer Thomas. Unfortunately there are no details in the ORB of what the endurance test comprised and no aircraft details.

10th February

The Squadron was ordered to proceed to Northolt in company with 46 Squadron and refuel. Taking off with 46, 601 and 303 Squadrons to proceed to Manston and rendezvous with six Blenheim bombers to act as bomber escort. An unknown Hurricane squadron joined up from the direction of Biggin Hill or Kenley. The Wing gained height, with the squadrons at between 14,000 to 15,000 feet, and proceeded to Calais, approaching from the north.

There was no enemy aircraft opposition but strong and accurate AA fire from Calais and Cap Gris Nez which followed the Wing out to sea for some distance on the return trip. 266 Squadron broke away from the Wing south of Maidstone and returned direct to Wittering

11th February

Another endurance test today carried out by Flight Lieutenant Bazley and Pilot Officer Gosling. As before there are no more details recorded in the ORB.

A Spitfire was damaged on landing, flown by Pilot Officer Ferris who was uninjured.

16th February

Flight Lieutenant Bazley and Sergeant Whewell were scrambled and given various courses and heights to intercept unidentified aircraft. Locating the aircraft they identified one Avro Anson, one Tiger Moth, two Hurricanes and one Blenheim bomber in various locations. All of these aircraft had been reported as possible bandits.

Flying at full power for most of the time Flight Lieutenant

67

Bazley landed at Sutton Bridge to refuel, while Sergeant Whewell continued with the chase for a short time and then landed at Bircham Newton.

2Ist February

Ten Squadron aircraft together with Spitfires from 616 Squadron took off from Wittering on a Wing practice flight flying east. Shortly after take off they were ordered to fly due south for a possible operational patrol.

The Wing was taken over in the air by Duxford control and then by Hornchurch when they were vectored to southwest London at 30,000 feet and warned that there were bogeys (suspected enemy aircraft) to the east and south. Many smoke trails were observed, but only friendly aircraft were spotted.

The Wing patrolled Manston for a time and were later warned of more enemy aircraft to the east and southeast. The Wing crossed the Channel and carried out a sweep from Calais upwards in the direction of Dunkirk. Slight AA fire was encountered from the direction of Cap Gris Nez. The Squadron's weaver Spitfire reported seeing enemy aircraft but they were too far off, although one pilot from 616 Squadron, detached, fired his guns but with no apparent result.

The Squadron was ordered to return to Wittering and attempted to do so, but bad visibility and shortage of fuel compelled landing at Hornchurch. One Spitfire flown by Flight Lieutenant Armitage, had landed earlier at Manston with engine trouble.

22nd February

The Squadron operated with 616 Squadron as the Wittering Wing formation carrying out a sweep from Calais to Dunkirk. No enemy aircraft were sighted.

24th February

Sergeant Pilots M. A. Beatty and D. A. Edwards were both posted to 118 Squadron at Filton for flying duties.

1st March

Two aircraft flown by Pilot Officer Middleton and Sergeant Whewell were detached from a training flight and vectored to 080o to investigate unidentified aircraft at 14,000 feet.

When near the coast they were vectored after bandits and joined up with Flight Lieutenant Bazley and Sergeant Barraclough who had also been ordered to investigate. They were given further vectors of 280o and 220o at 16,000 feet. "Tallyho" was called and they set off at full speed after a smoke trail at 24,000 feet. Almost at once the bandit went into a steep dive. The smoke trail stopped and the bandit disappeared into the distance.

They were vectored around in a circle and then vectored to 110o and gave the "Tallyho" again for three smoke trails moving at 28,000 feet. These however turned out to be three Hurricanes chasing a fourth smoke trail about six miles ahead. Owing to doing a goodly part of the patrol at full speed they could not pursue owing to petrol shortage. They landed at Coltishall, refueled and returned to base at Wittering.

2nd March

The first Squadron loss for 1941. On a dusk patrol, Flight Lieutenant S. H. Bazley was killed during a raid investigation when he crashed at Gedney Hill. He had been in command of 'B' Flight since 5 March 1940. He was ordered to patrol Wells-next-the-Sea at 10,000 feet and was in radio contact with Wittering at 07.39 hours and this was the last contact with him.

4th March
Sergeant Pilot D. G. Brandreth was posted to Central Flying School (CFS) at Upavon for an instructor's course.

6th March
Pilot Officer H. S. Jaques posted to No. 58 Central Training Unit (CTU) for instructors duties.

7th March
HQ 12 Group informed the squadron that it would be re-equipped with Spitfire Mk IIs. Pilot Officer R. A. Middleton was posted to 485 Squadron for flying duties.

Pilot Officer Mitchell had to force land at Wittering with his undercarriage retracted when the selector lever became jammed.

8th March
Pilot Officer Ferris and Sergeant van Schaice were scrambled to the east. "Tallyho" when a Ju 88 was spotted and pursued as it flew out towards the sea. The Ju 88 was attacked and crashed into the sea, the three crewmembers baled out and were observed swimming towards the shore. There is no record as to which pilot shot the Ju 88 down or whether the German crew were rescued.

Sadly Pilot Officer Ferris was missing after the engagement and is presumed to have crashed into the sea and drowned.

Pilot Officer Gosling and Pilot Officer Humphrey were scrambled and ordered to orbit Wittering at 10,000 feet. Pilot Officer Humphrey called Pilot Officer Gosling, informing him that he had engine trouble and was landing. He subsequently crashed. There is no record in the ORB Appendix as to his fate.

11th March
The first two Spitfire Mk IIs were delivered by ATA ferry pilots.

13th March

Flying with the Wittering Wing, the Squadron was detached to join up with eleven Hurricanes of 257 Squadron to patrol and cover the return of 11 Group Wing. As the two squadrons crossed the coast at 26,000 feet over Hastings, 11 Group Wing was seen returning below.

Patrolling the Calais, Gris Nez and Boulogne areas they spotted about twenty Me 109s at the same height. The Spitfires did not engage as their duty was to protect the Hurricanes, which were running short of fuel. The Wing landed at Hornchurch, refueled and returned to Wittering.

14th March

Enemy aircraft bombed Wittering today. At 23.30 a single German bomber attacked the station resulting in the deaths of two airmen and the serious injury of another. AC1. P. P. Lowe and AC1 T. Gilmore were killed, and AC2. J. P. Kruger was seriously injured.

18th March

Sadly today, AC2. J. P. Kruger died of his injuries.

20th March 1941

The late Pilot Officer W. S. Williams (Killed 21/10/1940), Warrant Officer J. Pickard and Flight Sergeant A. D. Gillespie were mentioned in dispatches in the London Gazette (No. 35107) dated 17 March 1941.

23rd March

ATA ferry pilots delivered another six Spitfire Mk IIs.

25th March

One more Spitfire Mk II delivered by ATA ferry pilots.

26th March

Four more Mk II Spitfires delivered by ATA ferry pilots. Sergeant Pilot Ody posted to No. 58 CTU for instructors duties.

27th March

Six Squadron Spitfires, Mk I and IIs, flown by Squadron Leader Jameson, Flight Lieutenant Armitage, Pilot Officer Gosling and Sergeant Cook departed Wittering at 13.10, landing at Coltishall at 13.35 to re-fuel, taking off at 14.20 flying towards the Hook of Holland at 10,000 feet.

They carried out a sweep down the coast 20 miles out till north of Walcheren. On return to base flew over a friendly convoy of twenty-one ships proceeding south.

31th March

The new Spitfire Mk IIs were continuing to be delivered by ATA ferry pilots. Two more arriving today.

Eleven Squadron Spitfires Mk I and IIs, together with eleven Hurricanes of 257 Squadron left Wittering at 12.45 and crossed the coast at Dungeness, the Spitfires flying at 22,000 feet and the Hurricanes at 21,000 feet.

Several sweeps were made up and down between Manston and Dungeness our side of mid-Channel. No confirmed enemy aircraft were seen but Sergeant Barraclough, weaving for the Squadron, saw five aircraft, presumably enemy, diving towards the Wing from the southwest out of the sun.

The Wing was sweeping in an easterly direction off of Dover and on Sergeant Barrowclough's warning broke up. The enemy aircraft disappeared into the southeast, reluctant to become involved in any combat.

Two ships, probably destroyers, were seen three miles off Cap Gris Nez making considerable wash. Visibility was excellent.

3rd April

With the last Spitfire Mk II being delivered by an ATA ferry pilot, the Squadron is now fully equipped. Four of the squadron Mk Is were taken over by 111 Squadron.

9th April

The Squadron was now flying Fighter-Night patrols on a regular basis. One such patrol was over Coventry when it was being heavily bombed by German bombers. Flying at 22,600 feet and orbiting the city, the silhouette of an enemy aircraft was seen against the fires of burning buildings. The pilot, Pilot Officer Thomas dived after it, but lost it when it flew out of the glow of the fires.

He was not alone flying over the burning City of Coventry that night. Also on patrol were Sergeant Cook and Flight Lieutenant Armitage. Other squadron Spitfires continued patrolling all through the night and day of 9 April, either as a single aircraft or in pairs and one patrol of three aircraft. The first take off for the squadron being 00.20 on the night of the 9th, and last landing time was 00.30 on the following morning, the 10th. 24 hours of Fighter-Night patrols by the squadron.

Squadron Leader Jameson reports - "At 01.45 hours at 18,000 feet, saw one enemy aircraft with one of our fighters formatting on it and trail of smoke from each engine. He turned to chase it and join in when saw a He 111 at about 17,000 feet.

"I made stern attack at 150 yards. There appeared to be four streams of return fire, one of them green, probably from the top turret. Fired two short bursts, but dazzled by bullets when they hit the enemy aircraft and broke away after first attack.

"Then carried out another stern attack and windscreen was obscured by oil from enemy aircraft. Great burning pieces came off enemy aircraft that dived down through the clouds. No evasive action by enemy aircraft." This He 111 was claimed as destroyed.

10th April

From the combat report of Flight Lieutenant Armitage for his Fighter-Night interception over the patrol area (Birmingham).

"...at 16,000 feet heard over radio that fighter at 15,000 feet had descended lower so dropped to 15,000 feet and after turning south saw twinned engine aircraft about 200 feet beneath travelling south west directly over the fires. Was able to identify as a He 111, but attacked too swiftly, partly through fear of loosing it and partly in an endeavour to get it before it dropped its bombs. As a result did not get sights on until 100 yards away with rather high overtaking speed.

"On opening fire was immediately dazzled, probably by effect of de Wilde (incendiary bullets) striking on enemy aircraft fuselage, which was certainly hit. After a burst of 2.5 seconds, had to break away violently. Made a thorough search in direction in which the enemy aircraft had been going but could not find it again."

11th April

111 Squadron took four more of our Spitfire Mk Is.

14th April

As part of Fighter Commands instruction to place Rhodesian personnel on the squadron Pilot Officer E. O. Collcutt assumed the role of Squadron Adjutant, and Pilot Officer S. W. Cobb arrived taking up his position in Station Headquarters.

15th April

Three Squadron Spitfires were lost today in a Wing sweep comprising of thirty-four aircraft. twelve Hurricanes of 402

Squadron, twelve Spitfires of 65 Squadron and ten Spitfire Mk IIs from 266 Squadron.

On a Channel sweep between Dungeness and Boulogne, Wing Commander Coope became separated due to engine trouble but followed to rendezvous at Dungeness. When at 20,000 feet, 33 minutes after leaving Wittering he was turning to the left when he was attacked from the port quarter by an Me 109. He went into a steep dive to evade but was hit by two cannon shells, one of which went through his parachute. The port aileron and petrol tank was also hit. He came out of a second dive and crash landed at Manston, uninjured.

Another nine aircraft of the Squadron had swept to Boulogne at 23,000 feet, the Hurricanes at 20,000 feet and 65 Squadron just above. 266 Squadron were spread out widely in pairs and were at 10,000 feet returning to Hornchurch. When commencing to close in, four Me 109s dived on them from the south out of the sun. Sergeant Barraclough's Spitfire was badly damaged by shellfire and he landed at Hornchurch, he was unhurt.

Another Spitfire flown by Sergeant Whewell was also badly damaged, crashing at Hawkinge, the pilot receiving slight superficial injuries.

Pilot Officer Holland fired a full deflection shot, a two second burst at one Me 109 which suddenly dived beneath on the tail of a Spitfire. Thinking that another Me 109 was on his tail, he broke off with a steep climbing turn and did not see the enemy aircraft again. Whilst this Me 109 is not claimed as damaged, three pilots saw a Me 109 dive past them at 300 mph with its wheels partly down.

Seven Spitfires landed at Hornchurch to refuel and returned to Wittering.

16th April

Replacement aircraft quickly arrived to bring the Squadron up to strength. An ATA pilot delivered one new Spitfire Mk II.

17th April

Yet another Spitfire arrived today. Plus Squadron Leader J. B. de la P. Beresford on posting supernumerary, ex 58 OTU. The first Rhodesian pilot arrived, Sergeant Whitford also from 58 OTU.

21st April

During a practice Wing sweep, two Hurricanes of 46 Squadron collided in mid-air, resulting in the death of one pilot, Pilot Officer Lloyd. The other Hurricane pilot, Pilot Officer Curtiss made a crash landing and was uninjured.

24th April

Sergeant Pilots Cochrane and Cole arrived from 57 OTU for flying duties.

27th April

Two Spitfire Mk IIs took off from Coltishall for a strike over the Dutch coast. Squadron Leader Jameson and Pilot Officer Thomas flew to Gilze aerodrome at 4,000 feet, but owing to poor visibility and good camouflage no aircraft were seen on the ground. The section dived simultaneously, one aiming at goods trucks and the other at light gun posts with no results observed as only one attack carried out. Intense but inaccurate flak seen.

A dummy or new aerodrome under construction seen about four miles southeast of Gilze and attacked. Neither of our aircraft were hit, the enemy being taken by surprise.

After setting course for Coltishall about fifty barges were noticed in the Maas Canal where it joins the Niewe Waterweg.

No ships seen off Dutch coast. One large power driven barge seen coming out of the canal heading north.

Two more Squadron Spitfires were also flying a strike over Holland at the same time. Wing Commander Coope and Pilot Officer Holland's object was Schipol aerodrome. They crossed the sea at 14,000 feet crossing the Dutch Coast in unbroken cloud between 6,000 and 7,000 feet. Breaking out of the cloud one mile north of Ijmuiden after 47 minutes flying time from base at Coltishall.

Wing Commander Coope considered conditions unsuitable for strike, so section returned to Coltishall below cloud.

30th April
A new Intelligence Officer arrives today, Pilot Officer J. L. Browne from 12 Group.

2nd May
Two new Rhodesian pilots reported for flying duties, Pilot Officer Allen White and Pilot Officer Parry, both from 260 Squadron.

3rd May
Having had two pilots posted in from 260 Squadron, one 266 Squadron pilot was posted to them in exchange - Sergeant Pilot Morris, whilst Sergeant Pilots Cochrane and Cole were posted to 145 Squadron.

6th May
Two Squadron pilots, Pilot Officer Gosling and Sergeant Bowman, both flying Spitfire Mk IIas, left Coltishall on a strike over Holland, arriving at Texel.

They sighted a convoy of fifteen vessels which appeared to be stationary. One of about 7,000 tons, the others, 2,000 tons.

Another two small vessels sighted proceeding north of convoy. On returning to the English Coast Pilot Officer Gosling saw and attacked a vessel of between 300 and 500 tons proceeding north and about twenty miles west of Texel. He fired a three second burst that hit the bridge.

7th May
The exchange of pilots continues. A Rhodesian pilot, Sergeant Matthews, was posted from 145 Squadron.

8th May
Five Spitfire Mk IIas flown by Flight Lieutenant Armitage, Squadron Leader Beresford, Squadron Leader Jameson, Sergeant Shircore and Sergeant Lewis were on a Fighter Night patrol over Derby. Squadron Leader Jameson was vectored for Derby where he orbited for ten minutes. He sighted many incendiaries dropping near Nottingham where there appeared to be much activity. Flying there he saw a He 111 below him at about 10,000 feet on the starboard beam, on an opposite course travelling west.

He carried out a steep diving turn to starboard and attacked from astern and slightly below with a two second burst at about 100 yards range. He was blinded by de Wilde striking the enemy aircraft and broke away.

The enemy aircraft climbed steeply, turned almost on its back, stalled and dived vertically out of control, disappearing from view against the dark background. He dived after it but failed to sight enemy aircraft again. He claimed this as a probably destroyed.

9th May
Another Squadron Fighter Night patrol by four Spitfire Mk IIas, again over Derby, the section being, Flight Lieutenant Roach,

Pilot Officer Gosling, Pilot Officer Humphrey and Sergeant van Schaick.

Pilot Officer Humphrey observed a vapour trail at 22,000 feet when he was at 10,000 feet. He pursued this until the trail ended, then shortly after he saw a He 111 above his starboard beam at about 300 yards range, on a course diagonally across his track.

He made a climbing turn to port to bring enemy aircraft to port quarter and fell into position 50 yards astern. Firing a short burst, but blinded by the de Wilde. He fell back to 150 yards when enemy aircraft again became visible. He opened fire with the immediate result that the port engine of the enemy aircraft caught fire. Enemy aircraft swung to port and his top rear gunner was able to open inaccurate MG (machine gun) fire with tracer.

Pilot Officer Humphrey continued firing until the rear gunner was silenced and starboard engine glowing and emitting long stream of smoke. The enemy aircraft dived steeply, obviously out of control. He did not follow it down as he thought another enemy aircraft was sighted. He claimed one He 111 as destroyed.

10th May
Sergeant Pilot Copp posted to 46 Squadron.

11th May
Four Spitfire Mk IIas took off from Wittering to carry out a Fighter Night patrol over Southend - Romford. The pilots, Squadron Leader Jameson, Squadron Leader Beresford, Pilot Officer Cook and Sergeant Thorburn.

Squadron Leader Jameson climbed to his allotted height of 14,000 feet over the Romford area. He sighted a twin-engine aircraft at 4,000 feet below him against the fires of London, flying on course 080o in the opposite direction and dived after the enemy aircraft. After loosing it, he sighted it against the moon and closed to attack from slightly below and astern.

From about 75 yards range he opened fire with a four second burst, having identified the enemy aircraft as a He 111. There followed a lucid flash, sparks from both engines and the enemy aircraft suddenly lost speed and fell into a series of side-to-side glides. He followed it down to 3,000 feet but could not get behind to deliver further attack as enemy aircraft was going too slowly.

At this height the enemy aircraft became invisible against dark ground, eight to 10 miles east north east of Romford, near Brentwood. Intense but ineffective fire met from rear upper gun of enemy aircraft. One He 111 claimed as destroyed.

But the action for this night was not yet over. Another section of squadron Spitfires flown by Wing Commander Coope, Pilot Officer Gosling, Pilot Officer Humphrey and Pilot Officer Barraclough were patrolling the same area as the earlier combat when Pilot Officer Humphrey flying at 18,000 feet and a few miles out to sea off of Southend, sighted a vapour trail at 20,000 feet and followed it on course of 080o for about 15 minutes.

He sighted a He 111 over the sea and nearly opposite the coast climbing below him. The He 111 dived steeply, evidently realising he had been seen. Overtaking at 3,000 feet over an aerodrome near the coast he attacked on port quarter at 100 yards, the enemy aircraft blowing up in mass of flames.

After recovering from the glare he sighted another He 111 taking off from the aerodrome with navigation lights on. Opened fire from dead astern and above at 250 yards closing rapidly. He gave a 15 second burst and the enemy aircraft went into the ground where it was seen to crash and break up. He was then at 50 feet and much light flak opened up without effect. Attacked it from above in steep turn to port with one second burst. de Wilde struck the enemy aircraft but no other results were seen.

Having finished his ammunition he returned to base. Two He 111 claimed as destroyed.

12th May

Rhodesian pilots were still being posted in from other squadrons. Pilot Officer Buchanan arrived from 260 Squadron.

13th May

A visit from the High Commissioner for Southern Rhodesia, Mr. S. Llanigan O'Kemfe CMG, no doubt to see how the transfer of Rhodesian pilots was progressing, and to make their acquaintance.

Yet another Rhodesian pilot arrived today, this time from 235 Squadron, a Flying Officer Green.

17th May

The Squadron made a temporary move from Wittering to a satellite station referred to as K3.

26th May

Sergeant Devenish arrived from 145 Squadron. Another Rhodesian pilot.

31st May

The Squadron loses a pilot to 145 Squadron - Sergeant Smith was on the move. There is a pattern appearing of 266 Squadron pilots going to 145 Squadron, and visa versa.

4th June

Twelve Spitfires from the Squadron joined 19 Squadron over Duxford for a Wing sweep from Dungeness to Portland at 22,000 feet.

Two small boats were spotted about 10 miles south west of

Dover when Wing Commander Coope broke away, throttled down, turned on his back and spun down, and was seen to dive into the sea, no parachute having been observed. No enemy aircraft were seen in the vicinity at the time. Wing Commander W. E. Coope was reported as missing presumed killed.

9th June
Squadron Leader P. G. Jameson DFC posted to Wittering as a Wing Commander, while Squadron Leader T. B. de la P. Beresford was posted to the squadron as CO. Another posting, Flying Officer P. H. O. Mitchell was posted to 57 OTU.

19th June
Pilot Officer Thomas was posted to 129 Squadron as a Flight Commander.

21st June
The Squadron was flying with 19 and 65 Squadrons as part of the Wittering Wing to patrol an area 10 miles from Dunkirk at 12,000 feet to cover bombers returning from an operation. The Wing stayed on patrol for five minutes after the bombers had departed before being ordered to patrol seven miles east of Deal. Although many friendly aircraft were observed, there were no enemy aircraft. A convoy of five enemy ships off of Matique was seen. Pilot Officer Barraclough made a forced landing in a field due to petrol shortage, he was not injured.

23rd June
Another Wing patrol, again as fighter cover for returning bombers leaving France between Le Tourquet and Boulogne at 19,000 and 21,000 feet.

There were numerous attacks on the bombers by Me 109s about six miles inland from Boulogne. Wing Commander

Jameson flying at 20,500 feet, fired a short burst at one Me 109 which he claimed as destroyed.

Pilot Officer Cook flying at 10,000 feet inland from Le Tourquet, fired a three second burst from a slight deflection at an Me 109 and saw it turn on its back and dive. He claimed this as a probable as it was seen by other pilots to overturn and dive.

Returning to the coast Pilot Officer Cook was met by two Me 109s. He turned 180o and fired short bursts from astern but missed and broke off as the second enemy aircraft was closing in on him.

Flight Lieutenant Roach was climbing to engage a Me 109 when another Me 109 got in a short burst which damaged his port wing. He returned safely to Wittering.

Pilot Officer Cunliffe, 12 miles inland from Boulogne, was attacked by several enemy aircraft. He did a stall turn but his Spitfire was hit by one cannon shell which hit the trimming tabs and passed through the fuselage. He was unhurt and returned safely back to base.

27th June

Twelve aircraft took off from West Malling at 16.15 hours, joining 19 and 65 Squadrons for an offensive Wing sweep over Hardelot, St. Omer and Gravelines.

Encountering Me 109s near St. Omer, the Wing attacked and Sergeant Lewis destroyed one Me 109 during the combat, firing three bursts using 660 .303 rounds.

Flight Lieutenant Green noticed glycol leaking from Pilot Officer Cook's aircraft after an engagement with the two Me 109s. Pilot Officer Cook turned and headed back to Wittering with Flight Lieutenant Green following. At about 10 miles out from the French coast at 6,000 feet Pilot Officer Cook disappeared and is reported as missing.

Sergeant Bowman's Spitfire was struck by several machine

gun bullets during the engagement and suffered damage to an undercarriage oil pipe, managing to land at Manston on one wheel, slightly damaging a wing tip. Pilot Officer Holland was not seen taking part in the engagement, but he is reported missing.

On a second patrol the same day to protect bombers returning to England, nine squadron aircraft took off from West Malling at 20.45 over the same area. Pilot Officer Gosling and Sergeant Whitford both fired on Me 109s but did not make any claims. Sergeant Whitford's oxygen mask had worked loose, coming off, and this affected his aim.

Heavy flak was experienced over Boulogne at 16,000 feet. Pilot Officer Gosling saw an Me 109 dive down behind him, he turned, got onto the Me 109s tail and fired a one second burst. No hits were seen.

1st July
Sergeant Pilot Sergeant was posted to 129 Squadron.

3rd July
Flying as a Wing with 257 and 401 Squadrons to patrol over Hazeborough district about 50 enemy aircraft were encountered.

Dogfights resulted in which the Squadron claimed to have destroyed two enemy aircraft, one probable and four damaged. Sergeant Thorburn is missing, believed killed, and Sergeant Matthews is also missing, believed killed. Pilot Officer Allan-White's Spitfire and Pilot Officer Parry's Spitfire were both damaged, but returned to West Malling, both pilots were unhurt.

7th July
Two pilots, Squadron Leader Beresford and Pilot Officer Dawson were dispatched to search for dinghies. Taking off at 13.00

hours, they were vectored to 105o for 27 minutes. Having reached the search area they could see no sign of any dinghies. The search was called off, and they returned to base crossing the coast at Manby.

Also taking part in the search, having taken off at an earlier time (12.00 hours) were two more squadron pilots, Pilot Officer Barraclough and Pilot Officer Parry. They were given a vector of 125o and searched the area for 21 minutes flying at 190 mph, looking for rescue launches, but did not see them. Given another vector of 065 o which they flew for 9 minutes as instructed and saw aircraft wreckage. They searched and spotted one dinghy with four or five men on board. They both circled until 13.30 and then set course of 290 o and after flying for 25 minutes at 180mph, would have reached Wells after another five minutes. As they were short of petrol they flew straight to Coltishall, but saw no rescue boats. There is no report of whether the men in the dinghy were rescued or not.

11th July

Returning from an Offensive Fighter Sweep to Northern France, Sergeant Barlow's Spitfire's engine stopped after he had run out of fuel and he made a forced landing in a field with the undercarriage up. He was uninjured.

21st July

Two pilots, Sergeant Leggo and Sergeant Lees were instructed to escort two damaged ships into harbour which were being towed by destroyers 15 miles north of Sheringham.

That evening the Squadron took off from West Malling together with 19 and 65 Squadrons, crossing the English Channel at 18,000 feet, the other two squadrons were stepped up to 24,000 feet, but due to cloud visual contact with the other two squadrons was lost. Instructed to orbit seven miles off of

Boulogne where there was very heavy flak. The Squadron was then ordered to proceed to St. Omer where fifty enemy aircraft were reported, but only a few were seen, either in pairs or singly. There was no combat. Re-crossing the French coast south of Boulogne at 18,000 feet, very accurate flak was experienced. Pilot Officer Parry's Spitfire was slightly damaged in the fin and tail.

23rd July

Taking off at 19.55 hours, the Squadron joined up with 401 and 601 Squadrons for an Offensive Fighter Sweep over Northern France. Crossing the coast at Rye, flying at 12,000 feet the Wing proceeded to Le Touquet where they experienced very heavy flak north of the city.

Patrolling inland to Fruges the squadron saw several small formations of Me 109s too far off to attack. Yellow Section led by Flight Lieutenant Green with Sergeant Leggo saw two Me 109s making a diving attack onto White Section. They engaged the two enemy aircraft at long range without result and later engaged them again at shorter range, but no claims are made, and no return fire was experienced.

Pilot Officer Johnston became separated from the Squadron as was attacked by four Me 109s, but was not hit and in turn he attacked and fired at three of them but without any result. He landed at Manston, Yellow Section landed at Detling, and the rest of the Squadron landed at West Malling. No casualties were reported.

25th July

Sergeants Devenish and Plagis were scrambled to search for a dinghy in the Wash with two pilots in it. They located a large oil patch in the water about 200 yards off shore near Hunsanton. A small boat appeared to be picking up someone from out of the water. They reported this and were ordered back to base.

26th July
Another dinghy search, this time by Wing Commander Jameson and Squadron Leader Beresford. Vectored on to a line between Spalding and Hunstanton, they were over the Wash searching for the dinghy but saw nothing. They then heard that the downed crew had waded ashore at an Air Firing Range near Sutton Bridge.

1st August
Sergeants Spense, Ross, Carine, Smithyman and Hardy, all Rhodesians, reported for flying duties at Wittering.

5th August
Another Rhodesian pilot, Sergeant Browne, reported for flying duties at Wittering.

10th August
Sergeant Browne, who was only posted to the Squadron five days ago, was killed at Hawarden. No further details as yet.

11th August
Pilot Officers Wright and Allen, both Rhodesians, were posted to the Squadron at Wittering.

12th August
The Squadron took off from Ipswich together with 65 and 19 Squadrons to patrol a line between Schouwen Walcheren in Holland to cover the withdrawal of sixty-two Blenheim bombers which had attacked Cologne power station. They were patrolling from 1,500 feet down to sea level, when the first Blenheim's (about twenty-five) were spotted flying at sea level.

Wing Commander Jameson damaged a Me 109 which he chased round Schouwen Island. Flight Lieutenant Green fired at three Me 109s as they dived after another Me 109 in the rear of the Blenheim's, (the second enemy aircraft succeeded in shooting one of the Blenheim's down into the sea,) but preventing the first and third enemy aircraft getting into line with the Blenheim's. No claim was made by Flight Lieutenant Green.

Sergeant Whiteford fired at three Me 109s without visible results and his own aircraft was hit by two bullets in the wing from a fourth Me 109 which was engaged by Sergeant Munro. No claims were made by either pilot.

The Squadron remained in formation of loose fours throughout and returned to Ipswich by 13.25 hours. Pilot Officer Parry's aircraft had a bullet (or flak hole) in the airscrew.

A dinghy was seen in the sea 10 miles off of the Dutch coast near a balloon also in the water. Shortly after landing seven pilots involved in the bomber escort took off at 14.45 from Ipswich in search of the dinghy which had been spotted. They managed to locate the balloon in the water, but could see no sign of the dinghy. No enemy aircraft or surface ships were seen. They landed back at Martlesham at 16.20 hours.

14th August

Sergeants Sherwood and Plagis were carrying out an inner sweep of the inner channel (the ORB is not specific to where, but possibly the Wash Estuary) searching for a Do 17 flying on a southwesterly course. Squadron Leader Beresford, Pilot Officers Allen-White and Dawson patrolling the outer channel at 2,000 feet saw a Do 17 flying at right angles to them, out to sea at 2,000 feet.

The section turned and Squadron Leader Beresford (leading) fired in a quarter attack at 200 yards range and experienced return fire, he then made a second attack with a two second burst and lost sight of the enemy aircraft.

Pilot Officer Dawson saw these attacks but could not catch up. Finally using emergency boost he got to within 400 yards and opened fire. He experienced return fire at first but not later when he again opened fire. He finally lost sight of the enemy, but no claim made.

19th August
Blue and Black Sections were patrolling Outer Dousing, Smiths Knoll independently, when about 20 miles east of Winterton, Blue Section saw an He 111 flying at sea level.

Blue Section - Flight Lieutenant McMullen and Sergeant Munro turned and attacked from the port quarter at 150 yards range. Thereafter twelve attacks were made almost alternately by one aircraft from all directions, 5,000 rounds being fired. There was considerable return fire, when suddenly the enemy aircraft dropped its nose and disappeared into the sea, leaving no survivors or wreckage.

21st August
The Squadron now had a full compliment of Rhodesian pilots. From this day on the Squadron was officially known as No. 266 (Rhodesian) (Fighter) Squadron.

Four aircraft were ordered to patrol Outer Dousing-Smith Knoll area to carry out an outer channel sweep. The two sections comprised of Flight Lieutenant McMullen, Sergeant Barlow, Sergeant Thompson and Squadron Leader Beresford. Visibility was very bad so it was decided to return to base when AA fire from a convoy was observed. Investigating, a He 111 was spotted flying at 200 feet over them.

Flight Lieutenant McMullen (Blue 1) had already become separated from his Number 2. He chased the enemy aircraft and fired a burst of one second and saw strikes on the enemy aircraft that dived. He then gave it two more very short bursts and then lost sight of it against the dark sea background. No claim is made as Blue 2 and Black Section did not see anything.

27th August
Sergeant Whiteford (Rhodesian) and Pilot Officer Buchanan were both posted to 41 Squadron, while Sergeant Spence-Ross (Rhodesian) was posted to 129 Squadron.

26th August
Squadron Leader Cheatle was posted supernumerary to the squadron.

30th August
Sergeant Elcombe, a Rhodesian, was posted to 19 Squadron.

1st September
Sergeant Pilot Gain, a Rhodesian, reported from 57 OTU to Wittering.

2nd September
Sergeant Pilot Deall, a Rhodesian, reported from 65 Squadron to Wittering

3rd September
The Squadron received the first Spitfire Mk IIb. 20mm cannons were now installed, far more effective than .303 ammunition.

8th September
Sergeant Pilot Welby, a Rhodesian, was posted from Leconfield to Wittering.

10th September

Four aircraft were ordered on a strike to the Dutch coast. Flight Lieutenant McMullen, Pilot Officer Johnston, Wing Commander Jameson and Pilot Officer Parry attacked a wireless boat and other small craft with machine gun fire. No flak was returned.

Crossing the Dutch coast at Wlacherren Island to north of Beveland Schouwen and north of Overflake, they attacked a 1,000 ton ship south-west of Zierinzef killing two gunners. Haamstede aerodrome was passed, but no aircraft seen on the ground. No flak, and 10/10th cloud at 5,000 feet.

12th September

News was received today that the Squadron was to be re-equipped shortly with the four cannon armed Spitfire Mk Vb.

Four Spitfires flying in two sections were dispatched on a strike to Gravelines. Several small escorted convoys were seen and one 4,000 ton ship was attacked by one section with machine gun fire. Light flak was encountered from the other ships. The second section attacked a sailing boat and became separated from the other section.

Flying Officer Parry was attacked by six Me 109s, but avoided them by flying into clouds. On emerging he saw two Me 109s in front of him, he fired and sent one into the sea. Claimed as destroyed. The two sections took off at 13.55 and landed 15.50.

A busy day for the Squadron. Taking off at 19.00 hours, six squadron aircraft - Flight Lieutenant McMullen, Sergeant Bartlow, Pilot Officer Parry, Sergeant Hagger, Squadron Leader Beresford and Pilot Officer Dawson were north of Smiths Knoll when Flight Lieutenant McMullen saw a He 111 at 2,000 feet on an opposite course. He turned and got onto its tail, firing a six second burst and saw its port engine well on fire. He claimed this as a probable.

He then saw AA fire from a convoy that had reported on the

radio that they were being attacked. He saw and fired at another He 111, but without any visible results.

Sergeant Barlow also saw an aircraft that he chased nearly to Hull when a searchlight illuminated him instead of the other aircraft, and he lost sight of it.

15th September

Four more Rhodesian pilots were posted to the Squadron at Wittering. Pilot Officer C. R. M. Bell and Sergeant Pilots Miller, Howard and MacNamara, all coming from 58 OTU.

Two aircraft piloted by Wing Commander Jameson and Sergeant Sherwood, were sent on a strike to Holland from Coltishall. When 40 miles from the Dutch coast Sergeant Sherwood saw four Me 110s astern of them. Both aircraft turned, meeting the enemy aircraft head on and fired at both, but observed no results. Wing Commander Jameson then got onto the tail of one Me 110 and with a two second burst sent it into the sea. Claimed as destroyed. Sergeant Sherwood made a second attack on another and saw a large flash in cockpit of the enemy aircraft. This he claimed as damaged.

19th September

The Squadron was now fully equipped with twelve Spitfire Mk IIbs. The Mk Vb 20mm cannon equipped Spitfires were expected shortly.

24th September

Sergeant Pilot Hardy, a Rhodesian, was posted to 129 Squadron.

26th September

Six Squadron Spitfires, a mixture of Mk IIa, IIb and Vbs, went on dusk patrol over the inner and outer channels of the Wash. Sergeants Munro and Thompson spotted a Do 17 when they were 30 miles southeast of Outer Dowsing.

They attacked this seven and four times respectively and saw its port engine well on fire after the penultimate attack. During the last attack the enemy aircraft disappeared in cloud. They claimed it as a probable. All of the Mk Vbs .303 machine guns and 20mm cannon jammed at sometime during the attack.

27th September

In a sweep over France, the Squadron, together with 411 and 412 Squadrons, were patrolling a line south of Montreuil, the squadron flying at 15,000 feet with 411 and 412 staggered above them.

The Wing was on patrol for 30 minutes when fifteen Me 109s were spotted and chased. Some engagements followed, but 266 did take part in any of these.

Nine aircraft landed at Manston, one at Detling and one at Biggin Hill. No Spitfire Mk IIAs took part in this patrol.

28th September

Twelve aircraft plus fourteen pilots, in all fifty-five personnel, left by air and road for Martlesham Heath to take part in manoeuvres with the Army titled Bumper. The exercise lasted from September 29th up to October 3rd. The Squadron's Spitfires were duly installed at Martlesham Heath by 14.30 hours today.

30th September

As part of Operation Bumper, the squadron was ordered to carry out low level attacks on the 'enemy' at Standborough, Sandridge and Redburn. The 'enemy' were spotted and the attacks were successfully carried out. The Squadron is now equipped with the new Spitfire Mk Vb.

1st October
Operation Bumper was still continuing. Flying from Martlesham Heath, the squadron was to 'attack' motor transport along the Coldham to Brownheath road. The target was located and successfully 'attacked'. Later they 'attacked' motor transport on roads leading to Bishop Stortford, and a third target in the Chiswirl Barkway district.

2nd October
More targets in the Bumper Exercise were located and 'attacked' along the roads between Redbourn, Harpenden and Wheathampstead, a second from East Turvey and Barham, and a third at the western entrance roads to Bedford. The Bedford road 'attacks' had to be abandoned because of low cloud and mist. Could these practice attacks on motor transport be a rehearsal for the Squadron to be equipped with Typhoon aircraft?

3rd October
The Squadron departed Martlesham Heath now that the Army co-operation Exercise Bumper had concluded. All aircraft returned to Wittering at 13.00 hours, with other personnel returning by road, arriving at 18.00 hours.

4th October
Flying Officer Scott arrived to take up the post of Medical Officer from the Princess Mary (RAF) Hospital at Halton Camp, near Aylesbury. Buckinghamshire, taking over from Flying Officer Howitt.

6th October
Flying Officer Howitt posted to Wittering. The ORB does not state in what role.

8th October
Two more Rhodesian pilots are posted to the Squadron from 58 OTU - Pilot Officer Small and Sergeant Wilson.

9th October
Sergeant Lees, a Rhodesian, posted from Wittering from non-effective to flying duty.

13th October
Twelve Spitfire Mk Vbs took off from West Malling at 12.55 together with 411 and 412 Squadrons on a sweep patrolling Boulogne - Hardelot. 266 leading at 20,000 feet in loose fours.

Flight Lieutenant MacMullen saw two Me 109s flying 1,000 feet above him. He gave one a short burst and saw streams of glycol issuing from it. He was not able to continue the attack as he was unsure where the second enemy aircraft was. He claimed this as damaged.

He later saw several enemy aircraft diving, and selecting the nearest, followed it down and fired his cannon at only 250 yards. Black smoke issued from the enemy aircraft that crashed on the beach at Le Touquet. Claimed as destroyed.

Flight Lieutenant Green saw two Me 109s separate from a group of six or eight and dive onto four Spitfires in front of him. Both enemy aircraft flew directly through his gun sight at 150/200 yards range and he gave each a burst but stalled his aircraft and was not able to continue to follow them. He claimed one as damaged. Sergeant Hagger fired a burst at long range at two Me 109s without seeing any results. In all about forty enemy aircraft were seen.

18th October
Squadron Leader Beresford posted to Wittering. The ORB does not state in what role. Flight Lieutenant Green promoted to

Squadron Leader, and Pilot Officer Allen-White promoted to Flight Lieutenant as a Flight Commander.

23rd October
Sergeant Chaplin, a Rhodesian pilot, posted from 58 OTU to the squadron at Wittering.

25th October
Four pilots, Flight Lieutenant McMullen, Pilot Officer Allen, Pilot Officer Johnstone and Pilot Officer Hill flying Spitfire Mk Vbs were sent on a 'rhubarb' operation from Martlesham Heath to Oostvoorne (Holland). After 20 minutes Pilot Officer Allen was forced to return with radio failure.

Flight Lieutenant McMullen, after about 30 minutes into the Rhubarb and 40 miles off of Oostvoorne, saw five Me 110s. He attacked the rearmost from 350 yards, closing to 100 yards and saw both engines emitting smoke, oil and glycol, with pieces falling off the wings and fuselage. As the other four Me 110s had started turning towards him he broke off the combat. He claimed the enemy aircraft as destroyed.

The other squadron section flew to Haamstede, and when about eight miles off of the Dutch coast saw two enemy aircraft who saw them and at once took cover in a rainstorm. The section turned south, flying at cloud base and were two miles from the Dutch coast where they saw six Me 109s which quickly disappeared into clouds.

They patrolled for another 10 minutes off of the coast, but because of insufficient cloud cover over the coast they returned to base.

27th October
Two Spitfire Mk Vbs on dusk patrol, Squadron Leader Green and Sergeant Sherwood were searching for a convoy near

Haisborough Light when Squadron Leader Green saw an aircraft about 1,000 yards away, on closing he identified it as a Do 17 flying at 500 feet.

He opened fire at 100 yards and saw strikes. The starboard engine ceased working and the Do 17 dived to sea level. He followed it down and gave it another burst when the enemy aircraft was seen to cartwheel into the sea. There were no survivors. Claimed as destroyed.

28th October
Squadron Leader Cheatle posted to 92 Squadron.

29th October
A fatal flying accident when Sergeant Gain flying from Nottingham back to Wittering, crashed during a snowstorm near Grantham. No further details are available.

1st November
Warrant Officer Pickard appointed to commissioned rank for engineering duties.

2nd November
Sergeant Pilot Elcombe, a Rhodesian pilot, reported from 19 Squadron.

3rd November
Flight Lieutenant McMullen DFC and Bar, posted to 257 Squadron, while Pilot Officer Parry assumes command of 'B' Flight and is promoted to Flight Lieutenant.

4th November
Pilot Officer Menelaws and Sergeant Lucas (Rhodesian) reported arrival at Wittering from 19 Squadron.

5th November

From Martlesham on a Rhubarb operation, four Mk Vb Spitfires piloted by Pilot Officer Johnston, Sergeant Deall, Sergeant Lees and Sergeant Sherwood were flying about 10 miles off of the Dutch coast in 2/10ths cloud cover.

Proceeding north at the edge of the cloud for five minutes, it was decided that as there was no enemy activity and the cloud was increasingly thickening that the patrol would end. Two aircraft returned to Wittering and two landed at Marham.

I5th November

Taking off from Docking, four Spitfire Mk Vbs piloted by Pilot Officer Dawson, Sergeant Chaplin, Pilot Officer Wright and Flight Lieutenant Allen-White were patrolling a channel which had been swept for mines 15 miles south-east of Outer Dousing, saw a floating mine and two more about a mile away. Some wreckage and another mine were also observed. They reported an accurate position of the mines and wreckage when landing back at Docking.

24th November

Flight Lieutenant Allen-White, Pilot Officer Bell, Squadron Leader Green and Sergeant Plagis flying Mk Vb Spitfires, took off from Docking on a dusk patrol.

When about to return Yellow Section (Flight Lieutenant Allen-White and Pilot Officer Bell) saw five small ships which were not part of a convoy, and the saw a He 111 about 2,000 yards away approaching the ships at 500 feet. Yellow Section at once pursued it using full boost. The He 111 turned eastwards, jettisoned its bombs and dived to sea level.

The section continued the pursuit but only gained slowly on the Heinkel and realising that petrol was running short they opened fire at 500 yards range but saw no strikes. They saw considerable yellow and orange coloured tracer fire by the enemy but it was very wide. On landing at Docking the Spitfires had less than seven gallons of petrol left. No claims were made.

25th November
Promotion for three Sergeant Pilots. All Rhodesians, Sergeant Pilots Munro, Leggo and Sherwood were all commissioned as Pilot Officers.

1st December
One flight from Wittering stationed at Docking to cover the Coltishall Sector. Three sections of the Squadron flight at Docking were dispatched to locate and maintain cover for a shot down bomber crew in a dinghy. The first section, Pilot Officer Johnstone and Sergeant Miller took off at 12.00 hours, and were successful in locating the dinghy which was being orbited by a Wellington bomber until their arrival.

The second section, taking off at 13.00 hours, consisted of Sergeant Hagger and Sergeant Wilson, took over from the first section, patrolling over the dinghy until a Lysander and then a Hudson took over the cover.

The third section, Pilot Officer Allen and Pilot Officer Menelaws, taking off at 14.00 hours observed two launches in the vicinity of the dinghy. They were recalled and presume the downed bomber crew were rescued.

3rd December
The Squadron badge was presented to the CO of No. 266 (Rhodesian) (Fighter) Squadron by the High Commissioner for Southern Rhodesia in the presence of Air Vice Marshall R. E. Saul CB DFC. The squadron was duly inspected and conducted a march past.

4th December

Taking off at 16.00 hours on a sea patrol, Flight Lieutenant Allen-White and Pilot Officer Wright flew over Docking and were then vectored onto 055o for 12 minutes. Flying just above thick haze and they saw some balloons flying just above the haze. When 300 yards from the balloons considerable AA fire was experienced and some ships could just be discerned through the haze.

The section was then recalled on account of the weather. No British convoy was advised as being in that sector.

6th December

Exercise Scorch. Personnel took part in an exercise to defend the aerodrome from attackers. The attackers were members of the Army, but the ORB does specify which branch.

7th December

Exercise Scorch continues. The attackers take the aerodrome, but lose 75% of their force. A counter attack using six tanks is successful and the aerodrome is taken back.

This day also marks the attack on Pearl Harbor by Japanese forces and the declaration of war on Japan by the United States of America.

9th December

Pilot Officer James, a Rhodesian, is posted to the Squadron at Wittering from 57 OTU.

10th December

A very temporary move to Honiley Aerodrome. A road party left Wittering at 07.00 hours, followed by fourteen Mk Vb Spitfires, remaining there for one day until the 11th.

15th December
Sergeant Reid, a Rhodesian pilot, arrived at Wittering from 275 Air/Sea Rescue Squadron.

22nd December
Sergeant Reid is posted to 19 Squadron, having been posted in only a week earlier.

25th December
Christmas Day, and to celebrate it a special lunch is organised for NCOs and airmen who were unable to get away on leave.

26th December
Boxing Day, and an informal visit to the Squadron by the Rhodesian Air Minister, Colonel Guest, and Air Vice Marshall Meredith.

Summary of 1941

The Squadron was re-equipped with Mk11 Spitfires that would be upgraded to Mk11bs fitted with 20mm cannons. In September these were exchanged for Spitfire MkVbs that had 2 x 20mm cannons.

August and the Squadron was officially known as No. 266 (Rhodesian) (Fighter) Squadron and had a full complement of Rhodesian pilots. A new Squadron badge was produced during December.

Squadron action included attacks on enemy shipping over Holland and fighter sweeps to France and Holland. Army co-operation manoeuvres in dummy attacks on motor transport convoys as well as working with Air/Sea Rescue to locate downed aircrew in the Wash and English Channel.

The Squadron lost three Spitfires in one day, fortunately without any loss of pilots. But the Squadron didn't get off scot-free. Casualties among pilots during 1941 were - six killed in action, two missing in action and two fatalities through flying accidents. Sadly three ground crew were also killed - two Aircraftmen Second Class and one Aircraftman First Class.

Enemy aircraft tally is - one Ju 88, seven He 111s, one Do 17, one Me 110, five Me 109s, and two unspecified aircraft destroyed. Plus of course, one barrage balloon!

1942

2nd January

In the first operation of the New Year, four aircraft, piloted by Squadron Leader Green, Pilot Officer Lees, Pilot Officer Munro and Sergeant Deall took off from Martlesham at 11.25 to carry out a Rhubarb patrol.

Flying at 'zero' feet to the Dutch coast, their target was a barge concentration at Verne, north of Walcheren, but landfall was actually made south of Walcheren. ('Zero feet' means they were flying at very low level.)

The cloud cover was very poor so they flew inland of the coast to near Gravenhage. Three 500-ton boats were seen near Oostvoorne which fired light AA fire at the Spitfires. Seven smaller boats west of Hook also fired AA rounds at them and two 1,000 ton ships fired both heavy and light AA. No attacks were made and no aircraft were hit. The section landed back at Martlesham at 13.20 hours.

6th January

The ORB for today states that "One Typhoon aircraft arrived." No other comment is made, but this must be the commencement of equipping the squadron with Typhoons.

11th January

Three aircraft, all Spitfire Mk Vbs, flown by Flight Lieutenant Allen-White, Sergeant Lucas and Pilot Officer Small took off from Docking having been scrambled to intercept a possible bandit approaching the base.

Visibility was good although there were large cloud patches. The section flew over a convoy but could not locate the enemy aircraft. They then heard on the radio that the bogey was 20 miles east of Cromer Knoll. The enemy aircraft was spotted five miles away at Angels 5. The section chased the enemy aircraft for eight minutes in line abreast, with Pilot Officer Small to port and highest, Flight Lieutenant Allen-White in the centre and Sergeant Lucas to starboard.

When they were at 600 yards the enemy aircraft, a Ju 88, opened fire, closing to 200 yards. Pilot Officer Small opened fire but with machine-guns only, in a slightly diving quarter attack. The Ju 88 turned steeply to starboard into a cloud. Pilot Officer Small followed, firing. In the cloud the Ju 88 did a climbing turn and rolled onto its back, with Pilot Officer Small copying the manoeuver, but he overshot and emerged from the cloud base in a vertical dive.

Sergeant Lucas now saw the Ju 88 turn to starboard, i.e. directly towards him. He fired his guns as the Ju 88 passed across his gun sights at 150 yards range. He turned and followed the Ju 88 into cloud, then rejoined Pilot Officer Small to search for the Ju 88, trying to make radio contact with Flight Lieutenant Allen-White, but without success.

Asking for a heading for home they were vectored onto 220 o making landfall at Skegness. They could hear Control calling Flight Lieutenant Allen-White without any success. He was reported as 'missing in action'.

28th January
A second reference regarding the Typhoons arriving on the squadron, simply "Typhoon flown to Duxford."

11th February
Ten Squadron Spitfires flew to Duxford and it would appear from the ORB that these ten pilots then undertook conversion to the new Typhoon, although this is not specifically noted.

One incident occurred when a Typhoon was landing and actually touched down with only one wheel lowered. The pilot immediately took off again, managed to get the other wheel down, and landed safely.

12th February
The two German 'pocket battleships', the Scharnhaus and Gneisnau were attacked today, with nine Squadron Spitfires involved in the operation, covering the withdrawal of the bombers 40 miles from the Dutch coast. Taking off from Coltishall the nine aircraft flew to a position 40 miles off of the Dutch coast to cover the safe withdrawal of the bombers carrying out the attack. The bombers were located and escorted back to their base. No enemy aircraft were seen.

By this date the Squadron was flying both Spitfire Mk Vbs and Typhoon Mk Is. As the days progressed, more and more of the Squadron's patrols and training involved flying the Typhoon.

13th February
Six Spitfires took part in the search for survivors from yesterdays attack on the two German 'pocket battleships'. None were found.

19th February
Two pilots, Flight Lieutenant Johnstone and Pilot Officer

Small flying Spitfire Mk Vbs were sent on a Jim Crow sortie to Ijmuiden in Holland.

Bad weather forced them to fly to the Hook of Holland where they sighted a fishing fleet and two naval auxiliaries going north of the Hague, and another three ships, possibly mine-layers, eight miles out to sea off of Katwyk-Aan-Bee. Owing to bad weather they flew to within 200 yards of the breakwater at Tmuden where there was a large number of fishing vessels and two flak ships near to the end of the breakwater. These opened up fairly accurate bursts of AA fire, but with just a few guns.

24th February

Two sections of four Spitfires on a dusk patrol, flown by Pilot Officer Barlow, Sergeant Lucas, Pilot Officer Dawson and Sergeant MacNamara sighted their convoy for patrolling and orbited for about an hour, when AA fire from the convoy was observed. At the same time bombs were seen to explode on each side of the convoy.

Yellow Section experienced friendly fire from the convoy, but failed to locate the enemy bombers before being recalled by Control.

White Section became separated as by then it was very dark, but Pilot Officer Dawson saw four or five Do 111s pass across his front. He chased the nearest aircraft and after his third burst saw a big explosion in front engine. The Do 111 caught fire, climbed to 1,000 feet, heeled over to port and dived in flames into the sea. He himself received a six-inch hole in his rudder from the convoy's flak. Pilot Officer Barlow was hit, but no more details of this are in the ORB.

25th February

A strike to Holland consisting of four Spitfire Mk Vbs piloted by Flight Lieutenant Johnstone, Pilot Officer Devenish, Pilot Officer

Small and Sergeant Lucas.

Their primary target was an alcohol distilling plant at Bergen on Zoom. Making landfall at Zeebrugge, they turned left, flying along the coast looking for shipping at the entrance to Flushing. Sighting none they returned to Zeebrugge where they attacked a dredger and a coaster of 1,000 tons inside the Mole, seeing cannon and machine gun strikes on both ships, breaking away out to sea over the Mole from which moderately accurate, light and heavy flak was fired.

8th March

Flying out of Duxford, Pilot Officer Lees was killed while carrying out local flying in a Typhoon. He was seen to spin in with the aircraft's engine stopped from 5,000 feet, crashing a quarter of a mile from Duxford village. The Typhoon did not catch fire.

10th March

Two Spitfire Mk Vbs, piloted by Pilot Officer Munro and Sergeant Chaplin were on a Jim Crow operation. Taking off from Coltishall at 11.45, they made landfall south of Hook in bad visibility, flying then northwards to Ijmuiden where they observed six ships outside of the harbour, steaming west. The ships were of about 2,000 to 3,000 tons. Heavy and accurate AA fire was experienced resulting in Pilot Officer's propeller being damaged and his reflector gun-sight being totally smashed. They returned to base, landing at 13.35 hours.

11th March

Another Jim Crow operation today. This time for Pilot Officer Lucas and Sergeant Lucas, both flying Spitfire Mk Vbs. Taking off from Coltishall at 12.30 and flying at zero feet, they made landfall at Ijmuiden and saw five motor vessels, two of which were 2,500 tons and escorted by two destroyers, steaming south about five miles off of the Dutch coast, and escorted by four Me 109s.

The section flew across the bows of the convoy, the leading Me 109 attempting to get onto the tail of Red 1. The section flew along the port side of the convoy and broke up. Red 1 flew over the convoy and delivered a beam attack on another of the Me 109s at 150 feet, a short burst with no results seen. Red One then made for home. The Me 109 did not follow. Red 2 tried to attack the first Me 109, but could not get into a firing position.

Light flak was also experienced at the same time from the convoy. Visibility was about one mile. Both Red 1 and 2 returned independently to Coltishall, landing at 14.10. No damage to either aircraft, and no claims made.

12th March
The Squadron was, at times, flying out of both Coltishall and Duxford. Squadron Leader Green's engine failed, but he managed to land safely at Waterbeach. The ORB doesn't indicate whether he was flying a Spitfire Mk Vb or a Typhoon Mk I. During this period the squadron was operating both types.

15th March
Sergeant Howard was flying a Typhoon when he got into a spin while doing a rate one turn at 2,000 feet, but fortunately managed to recover from the spin with just 150 feet to spare!

Also today Flight Lieutenant Parry, flying in another Typhoon, had a lucky escape when the throttle control broke and he had no control over the engine revolutions, but he managed to land the aircraft successfully. The first dusk flight in a Typhoon also took place, flown by Squadron Leader Green.

18th March
Sergeant Lucas was making a circuit of Duxford in low cloud, lost sight of the aerodrome on three occasions, and finally overshot the runway on landing, severely damaging the aircraft, luckily he was unhurt. The ORB doesn't state what type of aircraft he was flying however.

Sport is taking place within the Squadron! Two rugger teams, two soccer teams and a hockey team are all noted as having games. Unfortunately there is no mention of how the teams are made up or of any names.

23rd March
Now that the Squadron was flying Typhoons, a visit by pilots was arranged to Hawker's production plant at Langley. Here they saw Typhoons on the production line, and also had the opportunity to speak to Hawker's test pilots.

27th March
Another problem with the throttle control on a Typhoon. This time it was Sergeant Lucas who could not control the engine speed when the control broke. He was coming into land at the time. Realising that there was a problem when the aircraft's engine did not respond he retracted the undercarriage and switched off, landing in a field near to Duxford. He was unhurt.

4th April
Possibly following the squadron's pilot's visit to the Hawker works during March, and their conversations with their test pilots regarding any concerns about the new Typhoons, eight modified aircraft arrived. After flying these Typhoons the pilots were 'more favourable' towards the modified aircraft.

As April passed there was an increasing number of Typhoon

operational sorties and training as opposed to the number of Spitfire sorties flown. One Spitfire was flown to Sutton Bridge.

14th April
The first overseas postings. Pilot Officer Hagger and Sergeant Howard were both attached to Abbots Inch from Duxford pending overseas posting.

19th April
Pilot Officer Menelaws crashed on landing after dropping a wing when he misjudged his height. The unspecified aircraft was badly damaged, but luckily the pilot was unhurt.

20th April
The first mention in the ORB of the Squadron pilot's relaxing, spending an afternoon on the River Camm while ground crews inspected all aircraft ailerons. The ORB doe not record why this was taking place but as there were technical issues with the early Typhoons it could probably have been an inspection for possible faults.

21st April
Flight Sergeant Smithyman was commissioned to the rank of Pilot Officer.

22nd April
A new Rhodesian pilot, Sergeant Cooper, arrived at Duxford from No. 58 OTU at Grangemouth.

23rd April
More relaxation by the Squadron's pilots. No flying today so a soccer match was organised between our pilots and 609 Squadron pilots. The result of the friendly match is not recorded.

During the afternoon the pilots went boating on the River Camm.

24th April

During a Squadron interception practice with 609 Squadron, Pilot Officer N. N. Allen flew at very high speed into the ground at Great Casterton near Wittering. The cause of the crash was, at the time of the ORB entry, unknown.

25th April

A Rhodesian pilot was posted from Duxford, and Sergeant Cooper was off to 616 Squadron.

27th April

There are now just three Spitfire Mk Vbs remaining on the Squadron. Unfortunately apart from one being recorded as going to Wittering, the eventual fate of the other two is not recorded, but both, for the time being, remain with the Squadron.

29th April

Two pilots, Squadron leader Green and Flight Lieutenant Johnstone, both flying Spitfire Mk Vbs, were on a Fighter Night patrol north of Norwich at 11,800 feet and 11,500 feet respectively.

Squadron Leader Green saw an aircraft approaching Norwich and dived down after it to 3,000 feet before loosing sight of it in the smoke of the fires from Norwich. Flying towards Yarmouth he was attracted by AA fire and spotted two exhaust glows. He followed this aircraft first in the direction of Lowestoft and then back towards Norwich. He did not open fire and could not definitely identify the aircraft as hostile.

Flight Lieutenant Johnstone at 11,500 feet saw AA fire below him and turning in the direction of the AA bursts intercepted a Ju 88. Turning after it he fired a short burst of machine gun and cannon fire from 300 to 400 yards range. The Ju 88 started weaving and was partially illuminated by a single searchlight intermittently. He fired a longish burst from astern at 200 yards and saw strikes but lost sight of the Ju 88 when six or seven searchlights illuminated him. He claimed one Ju 88 damaged.

Following this engagement Flight Lieutenant Johnstone suggested that AA guns and searchlights should be placed in certain definite belts so that they can continue their good work of indicating targets yet allow our pilots to operate undisturbed when he passes out of their zone in pursuit of the enemy.

30th April
Pilot Officers E. S. Sherwood and L. G. Barlow, both Rhodesians, posted supernumeral to Duxford Station and attached to Abbots Inch pending overseas postings.

9th May
The Typhoons underwent a change of power plant, all being changed to a newly modified type of engine.

10th May
This is undoubtedly a quiet time for the Squadron as the ORB records pilots sunbathing on the banks of the River Cam, and today twelve pilots were sent on leave for four days while the Typhoons underwent the engine change.

25th May
Another football match was arranged. Playing for the Duxford Football Cup, they beat the opposing (unknown) team 3 - 2.

27th May
This report of non-operational training flights illustrates the

amount of inter-squadron practice that was regularly taking place when no aggressive operations were planned. The ORBs contain entries for practically every day when flying was possible and not restricted by adverse weather conditions. It is not really practicable to include all of these entries into this book.

"Two Typhoon sorties including practice Wing with 609 Squadron, nine of our aircraft taking part and led by Wing Commander Gillam successfully jumped a squadron of Spitfires. Tactics being to dive on enemy, have one burst of fire, continue diving and rely on greater speed to get away out of range. No attempts at dog fighting. Tactics seem successful. Low flying, tail-chasing, Air/Sea firing. Co-operation with a Stirling bomber."

28th May
This is the first occasion when the ORB specifies a Typhoon Mk Ia flying on an interception of a suspected enemy aircraft. Pilot Officer Elcombe was scrambled from Duxford and vectored towards the coast. The bogey was plotted at 18,000 feet at which height he could not see it. It was later discovered as being a Spitfire flying at 2,000 feet.

1st June
Six Typhoons were at readiness all day from Duxford to carry out ground attack strafing of targets in an Army co-operation Exercise Blitz. Two sorties were flown, in all cases the targets were located and low level attacks were made.

3rd June
As a brand new type, many RAF squadron pilots had not seen the Typhoon. To help other pilots in the recognition of Typhoons, and prevent them being mistakenly attacked by friendly aircraft, the Squadron flew three Typhoons to Biggin

Hill, Debden, North Weald, Heston, Kenley and Tangmere.

4th June
Today found the Squadron pilots bathing at Royston Baths, but it was not all leisure as the main purpose of the visit was to give dinghy drill in case of ditching into the sea.

5th June
More leisure time for the pilots! A Squadron dance held at Sawston School. As in other leisure activities noted in the ORBs, there is no mention of any of the ground crews being involved.

8th June
Squadron Leader Green flew to West Malling to 'show off' the Typhoon to other pilots.

13th June
Sadly today a Rhodesian pilot, Sergeant Welby, was killed when he crashed into the ground near March while taking part in a training exercise involving flying in cloud.

20th June
Offensive Wing Circus No. 193. Typhoons 1a and 1bs flown by Squadron Leader C. L. Green, Flight Lieutenant R. H. L. Dawson, Pilot Officer C. R. M. Bell, Pilot Officer W. R. Smithyman, Pilot Officer J. D. Wright, Sergeant N. J. Lucas, Pilot Officer G. Elcombe, Pilot Officer J. R. D. Menelaws, Pilot Officer J. Small, Pilot Officer J. D. Miller and Wing Commander D. E. Gillam took off from Duxford at 15.15.

This was the first Typhoon operation involving the whole Squadron as part of the Wing. They were to be at Mardych at 15.38 hours at 20,000 feet to sweep along the French coast to

Cap Gris Nez in the hopes of meeting the enemy coming out after our Spitfires.

The two squadrons making up the Wing, 266 and 56, led by Wing Commander Gillam, together with Duxford's CO, Group Captain Grandy flying as Black 2, took off from Duxford at 15.15, crossed the French coast at Gravelines at 15.38 hours, and swept over Calais to just south of Boulogne where they turned for home. Some aircraft were seen in the distance south of Boulogne but not identified. No flak was seen. One pilot had left his radio switched on, making communication difficult. All Squadron aircraft landed at Duxford by 16.25 hours. Sergeant Lucas landing almost at once with hydraulic trouble.

23rd June

Another offensive operation, this time a Wing Rodeo (No. 78) to Dunkirk. The Wing, consisting of 266 and 56 Squadrons, departed Duxford at 11.35. The 266 Squadron pilots were - Squadron Leader C. L. Green, Sergeant N. J. Lucas, Flight Lieutenant R. H. L. Dawson, Sergeant A. R. Chaplin, Pilot Officer I. M. Munro, Pilot Officer J. J. R. MacNamara, Pilot Officer J. D. Wright, Wing Commander D. E. Gillam, Pilot Officer J. D. Miller, Pilot Officer G. Elcombe, Pilot Officer J. R. D. Menelaws, Pilot Officer J. Deall and Pilot Officer H. Small.

They flew over Martlesham, arriving just east of Dunkirk at the correct ETA (estimated time of arrival) of 12.04 hours. 266 Squadron at 19,500 feet and 56 at 21,000 feet.

No shipping was seen in Dunkirk harbour, although some flak was seen but not directed at the Wing. Turning south west to Guines and Cap Gris Nez, loosing height to 14,000 feet, the Wing turned for home and when halfway to Dover, eight Me 109s were seen at 20,000 feet, (some 8,000 feet above 266 Squadron), flying in two sections of four in line astern and a little to the south.

The Me 109s dived towards 56 Squadron who dived under and across the front of 266 Squadron to draw the Me 109s, but the Me 109s did not follow. The Wing returned to Duxford, landing between 12.35 and 12.40 hours.

Pilot Officer Small did not take part in the operation as, on taking off, his propeller struck the ground, forcing him to return to base immediately. Pilot Officer Wright who had taken off as 'stand-by' took his place instead.

29th June

The weather today was very hot, with good visibility. The Squadron took part in Offensive Wing Circus No. 195 as part of a Typhoon Wing with 56 Squadron, led by Wing Commander Gillam DSC DFC and Bar, AFC, to fly to Mardyck, to arrive at 16.40 to cover Boston bombers returning from a raid.

Arriving at Mardyck at the correct time, the Wing came in behind and above the Boston beehive and their escort as they were crossing the French coast. Many Spitfires were seen but no definite identification of enemy aircraft although the Wing saw three Me 109s at 23,000 feet near Calais but out of range to engage. One unidentified aircraft was seen to crash into the sea four miles off of Dunkirk after several unidentified aircraft were observed milling round five miles inland where flak was seen. Following the bombers out of the English Channel until they were safely back at their base, all Squadron aircraft landed back at Duxford.

6th July

A temporary move to Digby for one day. Sixteen pilots and 65 other personnel went to Digby to take over that sector in the absence of 411 Squadron. The Squadron was at readiness by 20.00 hours.

7th July

Local flying from Digby during the late afternoon. The Squadron returned to Duxford immediately after No. 411 Squadron had returned.

10th July

All Squadron pilots went to the Napier Works at Acton to see the production of the Sabre engine. From here they travelled to London, meeting up at the 'Final' where their 'tanks' were re-filled, and then the pilots went on sorties in loose formation, some weaving more than others! All pilots managed to get back to base safely, although somewhat after the ETA.

This is a nice 'tongue in cheek' item. The 'Final' was probably a code word for a local hostelry, referring to the final approach an aircraft is on before landing, and the 'tanks being re-filled' is a nice reference to the pilots no doubt having a few drinks there. The reader can work out the rest of the report I'm sure!

13th July

A flying visit to 10 Group when two Squadron Typhoons flew to Exeter to tour three aerodromes within the Group to show other pilots what the aircraft looked like and to give flying demonstrations.

15th July

Army Exercise Limpet. The squadron was at readiness to take part in this Army exercise. One flight was scrambled to attack motor transports on the Walton to Thetford road, while two sections were sent south to recko (reconnaissance) south of Dorking.

16th July

The Squadron was again at readiness for the Limpet exercise.

Three targets were given and attacked by a section each and the last target by two sections. The targets were located but no amount of motor transports or troops to beat up.

Two Typhoons, piloted by Pilot Officer Small and Sergeant G. G. Osbourne were scrambled to intercept two Do 217s that came in from the Wash, crossing our Sector, and went on to bomb Lemington. They were ordered to orbit base and then were recalled when it became obvious the enemy aircraft were passing west of the Sector, and on account of the very bad weather. The returning Typhoons had great difficulty in locating their base even while orbiting. The two Do 217s were later reported as both being destroyed by another squadron.

18th July
A not too popular visit to the Stirling bomber repair factory by pilots during the afternoon. The ORB doesn't state why the visit was not a popular outing.

19th July
Friendly fire incidents are nothing new in warfare. The Squadron was part of a Wing Rodeo together with No 56 and 609 Squadrons. Flying along the French coast many Spitfires but no enemy aircraft were seen. One of the Spitfires attacked, and fired upon a 56 Squadron kite (aircraft), luckily without hitting it.

The recent visits by the Squadron to other Sectors and stations to show other non-Typhoon pilots what the aircraft looked like, both on the ground and in flight, was probably an attempt to give these pilots a better awareness of the aircraft if ever encountered by them to prevent just such attacks on friendly aircraft.

28th July
The Squadron departed Duxford at 14.55 hours to carry out a

Fighter Roadstead alongside 56 and 609 Squadrons. Squadron Leader C. L. Green, Sergeant A. R. Chaplin, Flight Lieutenant R. H. L. Dawson, Pilot Officer J. D. Wright, Pilot Officer W. R. Smithyman, Pilot Officer C. R. M. Bell, Flight Lieutenant A. C. Johnston, Pilot Officer J. R. D. Menelaws, Pilot Officer J. C. Thompson, Sergeant W. J. A. Wilson, Pilot Officer G. Elcombe and Sergeant B. McGibbon.

They arrived over Gravelines at 15.15 hours in order to cover North Weald Spitfires in shipping attacks. Control reported nine plus enemy aircraft over Ostend and 50 plus over Mardyck. The Wing turned left at Gravelines and flew along the coast to Ostend and about five miles out to sea. No enemy aircraft, flak or shipping seen, so the Squadron returned to base, landing at 16.00 hours.

30th July

One Typhoon pilot of 56 Squadron had a very lucky escape today, while flying with the Wing.

Taking off from West Malling with 56 and 609 Squadrons on a Circus operation, the Wing flew to 20 miles east of Foreland, climbing to between 18,000 to 20,000 feet, turning to cross the French coast at Gravelines at 12.40 hours. From there they flew to Audruicq when informed by Control that fifty plus enemy aircraft were at St. Omer and another twelve at Gris Nez. The Wing lost height to 15,000 feet and saw twelve aircraft in the middle of the Channel, but too far off to identify.

It was on the trip back over the English Channel that the 56 Squadron pilot was attacked by a single Spitfire and shot down into the sea. Luckily the pilot managed to bale out into the sea and was picked up later by a Rescue Launch. The problem with Spitfire pilots not being able to correctly identify Typhoons was now very apparent!

1st August

Some unusual training for Squadron pilots. During the afternoon they were introduced to decompression chambers, and some more dinghy drill at local baths.

2nd August

The Squadron was on the move. Leaving Duxford for Matlask. It wasn't a very good experience for Pilot Officer Wright however. As the ORB puts it. "Exceedingly bad visibility. Pilot Officer Wright overshooting, but just managed to pull up in time."

Fifteen Typhoons, one Hurricane and the Squadron's Magister left, but unfortunately the Magister pranged (crashed) on take off and broke a wing.

On arrival over Matlask several bogeys were reported in the vicinity and although just one section was sent to investigate the whole Squadron decided to follow! They found one Beaufighter, which apparently "was very frightened." Finally it emerged that Sergeant Howarth reported over the radio that he was the bogey!

So it was a fairly exciting arrival to Matlask, but at least all members of the Squadron were "very pleased with the messes."

3rd August

A new station means new local hostelries! There was "a small reconnaissance of the district, including several pubs embracing in the evening at Sheringham."

9th August

Two pilots, Pilot Officer I. M. Munro and Pilot Officer N. J. Lucas took off from Matlask on a sea patrol at 19.25 hours. Flying north, with Red 1 at 800 feet and Red 2 at 500 feet, they saw an aircraft about one mile away, approaching them from 2 o'clock at zero feet. This enemy aircraft passed under the section and was identified as a Ju 88.

Pilot Officer Munro turned to port and Pilot Officer Lucas to starboard and gave chase. Pilot Officer Munro was dead astern and Pilot Officer Lucas slightly to port. The Ju 88 opened inaccurate green tracer fire at 800/1,000 yards and then started to weave to port, but as this brought him dead ahead of Pilot Officer Lucas he turned to his original course and flew straight using full boost.

The section was overtaking very fast and at 400/600 yards Pilot Officer Munro gave very short bursts of cannon fire, seeing strikes low on the water. Throttling back to +2 boost the range was rapidly closed to 200 yards, and a three second burst given.

Pilot Officer Lucas also opened fire with machine guns, from the port quarter, a very short burst at 600 yards, again at 400 yards and a longer burst at 200 yards. Immediately after opening fire (both pilots firing) flames appeared inboard of both engine nacelles. A hood came off and one of the crew started to climb out but slumped back as fire was continued.

The enemy aircraft bounced on the sea, dropped a wing and went straight in. There were no survivors. Both pilots claimed the Ju 88 destroyed, and were awarded 'half' a claim each.

10th August

An escort for a number of HSLs (High Speed Launches) for pilots Flight Lieutenant R. H. L. Dawson and Pilot Officer C. R. M. Bell.

The HSL crew were searching for a downed Mosquito crew. Although wreckage was found there was no trace of the crew.

11th August

The Squadron had a week to sort out some suitable public houses, and then it was back to Duxford.

The whole Squadron of sixteen Typhoons and the single Hurricane left Matlask during the day, while the road party left later, arriving back at Duxford in the evening. The Squadron's serviceability has remained very good, though Matlask was not very well equipped in this respect.

13th August

An evening sea patrol by four Squadron pilots. Flight Lieutenant A. C. Johnston, Sergeant G. G. Osbourne, Pilot Officer J. D. Miller and Pilot Officer W. J. A. Wilson.

Taking off from Duxford to a point 30 miles east of Southwold, they then flew north for 50 miles, the section flying in line abreast at zero feet. Just east of Cromer Flight Lieutenant Johnston saw an aircraft ahead going westward at zero feet. He at once turned to port and opened up (accelerated), the rest following. The enemy aircraft turned onto 130o with the section following.

The enemy aircraft opened fire at 1,200 yards, and Flight Lieutenant Johnston fearing that he might not get within range before enemy aircraft reached a rain cloud, gave a short burst at 1,000 yards and 600 yards, both falling short. Closing rapidly now, another short burst at 400 yards saw a strike on the starboard engine. The enemy aircraft all the time continued to fly straight and level.

Closing now from 300 yards to 200 yards, Flight Lieutenant Johnston fired a succession of bursts and saw the port engine smoking and the starboard engine and underside of the fuselage well on fire. As he broke away Sergeant Osbourne and Pilot Officer Wilson at 300/200 yards gave a short burst each, but the enemy aircraft was already well on fire.

It climbed to 600 feet, one man baled out and the aircraft dropped a wing and went into the sea and sank. Flight Lieutenant Johnston orbited the spot at 1,500 feet and got a fix on the enemy aircraft, but was informed later that although a Walrus rescue aircraft was dispatched to locate the airman, he was not found. Flight Lieutenant Johnston claimed one Ju 88 destroyed.

15th August

Pilot Officer F. B. Biddulph and Sergeant S. J. Blackwell posted to the Squadron from 56 and 609 Squadrons respectively. These two squadrons were part of the Typhoon Wing at Duxford.

17th August

Duxford must have had a very active sports organisation! An entry for today states that "Station sports held and although we went on a sweep half way through it yet managed with the available men to win the Shield very comfortably (34 points to 14). An excellent show". Unfortunately again, there is no mention of who was in each team or teams, and what the Shield was played for.

19th August

The disastrous Dieppe raid by British and Canadian forces. A Wing Sweep to Le Treport and Dieppe. Twelve Typhoons flow by Squadron Leader C. L. Green, Pilot Officer N. J. Lucas, Flight Lieutenant R. H. L. Dawson, Pilot Officer W. S. Smithyman, Pilot Officer I. M. Munro, Pilot Officer J. D. Wright, Wing Commander D. E. Gillam, Flight Lieutenant A. C. Johnston, Pilot Officer J. D. Miller, Pilot Officer J. C. Thompson, Pilot Officer W. J. A. Wilson and Pilot Officer G. Elcombe took off from West Malling at 14.00 hours. Pilot Officer Wright's Typhoon developed a mechanical malfunction and did not take off.

With 609 Squadron leading, 266 and 56 Squadrons flew top cover. Flying to Le Treport they were warned by Control of approaching enemy bombers. Some of our Squadron at 16,000 feet saw three Dorniers inland of Le Treport with several Me 109s in the vicinity.

Yellow Section (Flight Lieutenant Dawson, Pilot Officer Smithyman), and White 1 (Pilot Officer Munro), were ordered by Flight Lieutenant Dawson to attack the Dorniers. From what other pilots heard on the radio it appears that Pilot Officer Smithyman saw one Dornier crashing, and that Flight Lieutenant Dawson said that it was his.

Pilot Officer Munro, diving fast, fired one burst (100 x 20mm cannon rounds) from 300 yards, closing to 50 yards and saw smoke issuing from the Dornier between the port engine and the fuselage as the bomber dived steeply down. He claimed this Do 217 as probably destroyed. He had to break away and noticed tracer going past his wings. He went down to zero feet, and on coming out over the coast saw a Typhoon and found that it was Flight Lieutenant Dawson.

Flight Lieutenant Johnston as Blue 1, with his Number 2 and Green 1, were at 15,000 feet just north of Le Treport saw ten Me 109s below at 2 o'clock. Flight Lieutenant Johnston dived after them, eight breaking away to port and two diving straight ahead. Following one of these two, he used full throttle, caught up and fired a short burst at 600 yards range, and a series of short bursts as the range closed to 400 yards. The Me 109 steepened his dive to nearly vertical and Flight Lieutenant Johnston and Blue 2 (Pilot Officer Miller) saw thick white smoke issuing from the Me 109. Flight Lieutenant Johnston had to pull out of on account of his speed (480 mph) and low ground haze. He claims one Me 109 probably destroyed.

Flight Lieutenant Dawson and Pilot Officer Munro flew in line abreast over the Channel and got to near Blue and Green Sections. About half way over the Channel a squadron of Spitfires came in on the starboard quarter. All of our squadron aircraft at once used full boost to get away, some weaved but one

Spitfire opened fire on Flight Lieutenant Dawson's aircraft. Pilot Officer Munro saw pieces flying off and Dawson's aircraft half rolled up to 100 feet and then went into the sea. There was no sign of wreckage or the pilot.

Red and Green Sections came home at 14,000 feet, and they too complained that Spitfires attacked them although they themselves did not actually open fire.

Pilot Officer Smithyman is missing. No one saw him after they started to attack three Do 217 bombers. The rest of the squadron landed at West Malling.

26th August

A Wing Rodeo to the French coast. Taking off from Wittering at 08.20, Squadron Leader C. L. Green, Sergeant S. J. Blackwell, Flight Lieutenant I. M. Munro, Pilot Officer C. R. M. Bell, Pilot Officer J. Small, Sergeant A. R. Chaplin, Pilot Officer N. J. Lucas, Wing Commander D. E. Gillam, Flight Lieutenant A. C. Johnstone, Pilot Officer J. D. Miller (reserve pilot), Pilot Officer O. G. Elcombe, Pilot Officer F. B. Biddulph, Pilot Officer J. H. Deall and Sergeant G. G. Osbourne, as the leading Squadron along with 609 and 56 Squadrons, flew at zero feet across the Channel, crossing the French coast at Mardyck at 4,000 feet.

266 Squadron covered the other two squadrons who went on to near St. Omer, turning west coming out at Hardelot at 10,000 feet. 266 flying west just inside of the French coast until Guines where they turned south also coming out at Hardelot at 8,000 feet. It was at this point that five Me 109s attacked the Squadron almost head on. Four of 266 Squadron pilots managed quick bursts, but as they turned the Me 109s also turned, heading rapidly for home. There were no casualties, and no claims made by Squadron pilots.

27th August
Apparently there was dinghy drill in the afternoon, and in the evening a visit to the Bull public house at Sawston.

11th September
A Squadron interception exercise on Spitfires. This developed into individual dogfights, with the honours going to the Spitfires.

The Squadron went down to Exeter with 609 and 56 Squadrons to take part in a sweep that was eventually cancelled. All squadrons returned to Duxford, flying in what was recorded as beautiful weather, very hot and sunny.

15th September
Sergeant J. L. Spence was reported as missing after baling out of his Typhoon over the English Channel. Flying on a Circus patrol with the squadron from Exeter over the Cherbourg Peninsular, he must have had a major malfunction of some kind, baling out over water. He could have baled out over France, but to make certain his Typhoon did not fall into enemy hands opted to attempt to nurse his aircraft back to base. He was forced to parachute into the Channel about 20 miles out to sea.

He was seen in his dinghy and a fix was taken for Air/Sea rescue services to pick him up. A Walrus aircraft was dispatched, but the sea was too rough to land. One flight continued to orbit the dinghy but had to return to base when fuel ran dangerously low. The prevailing wind would have driven him towards the enemy coast. Nothing further was heard of him.

18th September
News came through today that the Squadron was moving to Warmwell. Apparently "all pilots very pleased and hope we see more action."

19th September

Practice attacks on road convoys. The convoy was very well equally spaced apart, but when it became 'clumped up' it offered an easier target.

As for sport, the Station team played Hunsden at soccer, rugby and hockey, most of the Station team being squadron members. The Station team is recorded as winning all of the games. Celebrations must have followed, as there was an accident to one of the RAF transport vans on the way back home. No casualties reported.

Later in the evening there was "a terrific farewell party in the evening, first in the mess and then the Bull, and then back to the mess. More names on the ceiling and buk buk." Despite researching this particular phrase there is no clear or obvious meaning to it. Lost with the passage of time.

20th September

After the previous nights revelries, today was packing up day, with the Squadron preparing for the move to Warmwell.

21st September

The rail party, led by Flying Officer Pickard, marched to the railway station with the Station band playing, and was seen off by the Station Adjutant etc. Various motorcars left in the morning, although the Squadron's aircraft were delayed by poor weather with 10/10th cloud, finally leaving at 16.25 when thirteen aircraft took off without mishap and landed at Warmwell. The rail party and the cars arrived during the evening.

22nd September

Despite the cold and rain all Squadron personnel were very pleased with their new station. The Officers Mess is fine, and sleeping quarters attractively situated on a millstream. A bit overcrowded as yet and rather sparsely furnished. The men's quarters were poor, but the food is good. "We shall soon get things organised."

23rd September
A celebration in the evening for the CO Squadron Leader T. B. de la P. Bereford's birthday. Apparently it was "quiet but pleasant ending up in the Kings Arms."

25th September
Two Typhoons piloted by Pilot Officer J. H. Deall and Sergeant J. Howarth were on an anti-Rhubarb patrol 10 - 15 miles south of Portland and St. Catherines Point at zero feet and later at 3,000 feet when two sections of Spitfires approached to "check them out." On this occasion the Spitfire pilot's aircraft recognition skills proved to have improved after earlier unhappier meetings!

27th September
Radio communication was proving troublesome. Four Typhoons flown by Flight Lieutenant I. M. Munro, Pilot Officer N. J. Lucas, Sergeant S. J. B. Blackwell and Sergeant A. R. Chaplin were on Dusk Patrol over St. Catherines Point and Portland Bill until 19.35 hours.

On returning to Warmwell it took over 20 minutes to 'pancake' due to faulty aerodrome control. "Radio difficult to contact Factor (controller) for 30 minutes before dusk." This was not the first time that there had been problems with the radios.

28th September
An excursion led to the discovery of "a very pleasant country pub, with an exceptionally pretty daughter. Will have to be visited again."

29th September

 A return visit to the unnamed pub. "Paid second visit to pub, all very impressed by the daughter."

30th September

Sergeant R. K. Thompson posted to the Squadron from Llandow, and Flight Lieutenant A. S. McIntyre arrived from Annan.

6th October

The Squadron pilots certainly appeared to be enjoying their new station and the surrounding area - "Pilots went to Home Guard dance in Weymouth in evening, much amusement."

7th October

In an attempt to overcome radio problems twelve pilots went to Middle Wallop and talked to the Controller and Signals Officer reference Ops (Operations) Room procedure, radio procedure etc. The outcome is not recorded, although it is recorded that the pilots stopped at Blandford on the way home and had sandwiches and beer!

9th October

Four new pilots arrived today, but the ORB does not record rank or names unfortunately.

10th October

Another comment in the ORB - "Radio transmission with forward relay station still not satisfactory." The four new pilots were flying the Squadron's sole Hawker Hurricane carrying out Sector reconnaissance patrols.

12th October

A very lucky escape for Pilot Officer J. D. Miller during local flying and dusk bumps. Failing to see the direction of landing strip flare path, he ran 'crooked' and crashed into a quarry. The Typhoon overturned and was severely damaged, but the pilot was not hurt. A comment in the ORB states - "a very lucky escape, due to the strong construction of Typhoon."

14th October
Searching for enemy survivors of a naval action, two Typhoons flown by Flight Lieutenant I. M. Munro and Pilot Officer A. Chaplin took off from Warmwell and flew at zero feet up to 15/20 miles from the Cape de la Hague. About five miles from the French coast Yellow 2 saw an Fw 190 turning onto Yellow 1, about 2,000 yards behind. Doing 320 mph, he closed to within 500 yards of the Fw 190, turning sharply as he tried to engage the Fw 190, but the enemy pilot immediately turned and went into cloud. No survivors of the naval action were seen, and no wreckage on the sea.

17th October
Pilot Officer N. J. Lucas and Pilot Officer J. J. R. MacNamara took off at 09.00 from Warmwell to search the English Channel for survivors from a downed bomber. Although orbiting the position given, nothing was found. They were recalled to base landing at 10.10.

At 11.25 another section flown by Squadron Leader C. L. Green and Sergeant S. J. P. Blackwell were dispatched to continue the sea search. Again, orbiting the area they saw no sign of any dinghy or aircraft wreckage and were recalled.

A Ju 88 shot down by Flight Lieutenant A.C. Johnston on 13 August 1942, was in fact a Me 210, the first to be destroyed. The information was given by a German survivor after some two months interrogation.

21st October

A patrol returning from a weather reconnaissance over the French coast and mainland spotted what they thought were several small fires burning in the grass as they crossed the English coast. They were in fact from an Fw 190, which had just crashed the cause was unknown.

24th October

Squadron Leader Green and Flying Officer C. R. M. Bell were on a weather reconnaissance to Cherbourg at zero feet. When returning they saw three Fw 190s north of Barflour, also flying at zero feet in line abreast, flying straight towards the two Typhoon pilots. Due to the high closing speed it was impossible to get sights on the enemy and they passed through the section.

The Fw 190s turned, chasing the Typhoons but were unable to catch up, and abandoned the chase after a minute. The pilots later commented - "It is pleasant to know that we are faster than the Fw 190s on the deck."

Non-operational flying today sadly cost Sergeant D. D. Audley his life. His Typhoon was seen to break up at 18,000 feet. Pieces of his aircraft were scattered over a five-mile radius. The cause of the failure was not known.

27th October

Sergeant D. D. Audley's funeral took place this afternoon, attended by members of the squadron.

Sergeant Borland overshot the aerodrome and crashed into a bank at the side of the parameter track. As the ORB records - "...the aircraft was rather badly damaged." The pilot was not injured.

4th November

With 10/10th cloud and rain, visibility was very poor. A low lying mist also enveloped Warmwell, so Squadron Leader Green and Pilot Officer MacNamara requested flares to be fired so that they could safely locate the aerodrome after they had been scrambled.

Also today it was learned that one Flight of the Squadron was to make a temporary move to Predannack tomorrow.

6th November
The move to Predannack took place a day later than expected. First reports of the new base stated "...is very cold, and first reports are not very optimistic."

Six Typhoons of 'A' Flight together with the CO flew there. The CO returned later to Warmwell during the day.

8th November
Sergeant D. C. Borland's engine on his Typhoon started to cut out while on a tail-chasing exercise, so he returned to base (which base is not made clear). Coming in to land he discovered that he had no hydraulic power and was forced to make a wheels up landing, damaging the aircraft, although he was uninjured.

A number of short flights in the Magister and Tiger Moth of the Station Flight were given to members of the Air Training Corp.

13th November
'B' Flight attempted to change over with 'A' Flight at Predannack, but all efforts were abandoned due to very bad weather.

Sergeant Thompson, who was bringing Flying Officer D. R. Tidmarsh from Predannack in the Tiger Moth, ran out of petrol and had to make a forced landing in a field.

18th November

Taking off from Predannack, Flight Lieutenant A. C. Johnston and Sergeant G. G. Osbourne patrolled from Lizard to Star Point. On the second leg Blue 1 saw an aircraft ahead which took evasive action and went into clouds. It emerged from the clouds and Blue 1 increased speed and gave it a very short burst at 600 yards as it began to head back into cloud cover again. No results of the firing was seen, Blue 1 then realised that the aircraft was possibly a Typhoon and made a remark to that effect over the radio. Both aircraft returned to base and pancaked. Blue 1 taxied into a steamroller. Damage to the aircraft or the pilot is not recorded.

20th November

Flight Lieutenant A. C. Johnston is promoted to Squadron Leader and is posted to 56 Squadron. Later in the evening there was a farewell party in his honour.

22nd November

A new 'B' Flight commander is appointed. Pilot Officer J. C. Thompson is promoted to Flight Lieutenant.

27th November

Very rarely is there any mention of the ground crews in the ORB, except in the cases of airmen being killed or wounded during German bombing raids or other actions. But today, although unfortunately there are no names recorded - "All pilots and six ground crew in a scratch rugby game in the afternoon, and out to Weymouth in the evening."

28th November

Sergeant G. G. Osbourne crashed near Ibsley today and was killed. He was flying in a Squadron formation that entered cloud.

The cause of his crash is not recorded.

During the same exercise, Flying Officer C. R. M. Bell, also flying in cloud, discovered that he had no instruments. Trying to bale out of his Typhoon, he operated the jettisonable hood lever which failed to operate, so he was forced to fly on and came out of the cloud. The rest of the Squadron, and himself, landed safely back at Warmwell.

30th November

A number of Sergeant Pilots were commissioned. 777721 Sergeant S. J. P. Blackwell, 778630 Flight Sergeant J. Howarth, 778597 Flight Sergeant W. V. Mollet, Flight Sergeant 778635 D. McGibbon and 777692 Sergeant G. G. Osbourne. With effect from 12 October 1942.

The following Sergeant Pilots were posted into the squadron. 778823 Sergeant C. Bailey, 778711 Sergeant G. Eastwood, 77846 Sergeant D. Erusmus, 778745 Sergeant D. S. Eadie and 778813 Sergeant E. V. Horne. With effect from 17 November 1942.

The service numbers of Officers and NCOs are rarely noted in the ORBs. It always helps with correct identification when a service number is recorded.

1st December

The newly arrived pilots carried out a reconnaissance of the sector in the Station Flight's Tiger Moth.

4th December

A mid-day patrol by Flying Officer J. D. Wright and Sergeant R. K. Thompson were ordered to patrol from Portland to the Needles, when 12 miles out on their second leg they spotted two bogeys 5 miles away to port. Both pilots chased after them, asking operations if they knew if the aircraft were hostile or not, but ops did not know.

On closing to 500 yards they were recognised as Spitfires at which point operations said they were friendly. Continuing the patrol the same two Spitfires approached, we waggled our wings but they came to within 150 yards. The pilots radioed ops to tell the Spitfires to stop chasing them which they apparently did as the Spitfires eventually departed.

6th December
Non-operational flying today included sixteen Squadron pilots carrying out camera gun training and circuits and bumps in the Station Flight's Hurricane.

14th December
A night out to London! All Squadron pilots and about thirty of all other ranks went to London 'and dined', after a preliminary session at the 'Final'. Guests included staff from Rhodesia House and the Squadron's former Squadron Commander, Wing Commander Beresford DFC.

15th December
Most of the party met up again at the 'Final' and returned to Warmwell in the evening, and so to bed after two very enjoyable and hectic days.

20th December
A morning anti-Rhubarb patrol on which Sergeant H. V. Borland, after telling his Number 1, Flying Officer L. M. Munro that there was an aircraft behind him suddenly saw strikes on the water just ahead of his own aircraft, he then saw a Typhoon behind his. Luckily no hits were sustained.

Christmas Day. 25th December

An old Armed Force's custom. After some local flying today all Officers served at the Airman's Mess where lunch "was terrific." The Officers lunch was "rather a fiasco as we were all late, but lunch was a cracking success, entertainment continued for rest of day."

Boxing Day. 26th December

The celebrations continue. The officers entertained the sergeants of both 263 and 266 Squadron in the Squadron's Officer's Mess, where the Squadron Sergeants were "ignominiously defeated in beer drinking relay and officers also lost but by a narrow margin." The afternoon was apparently spent resting and recovering. During the evening most officers went into Weymouth to the cinema.

Pilot Officer G. Elcombe was posted to 66 Squadron as a Flight Lieutenant.

27th December

No flying today due to low cloud and poor visibility. In the evening the expected party on account of Flying Officer J. D. Wright's posting as a Flight Lieutenant, was cancelled.

31st December

Squadron Leader C. L. Green and Flying Officer F. B. Biddulph were on a Rhubarb patrol in the Ariel (France) area when they spotted eight locomotives standing motionless. Squadron Leader Green attacked one from broadside at 80 yards range, and saw strikes and a "large volume of steam." The driver of the locomotive jumped clear just before the attack started. Immediately after the attack an anti-aircraft gun opened fire on the two Typhoons from a position north of the harbour north of Isigny.

A large caliber coastal gun was spotted at Grand Camp les Bains, 800 yards west of the harbour. Take off 08.30. Landed 09.30.

Another raid followed at 11.45 when two more Typhoons flown by Flight Lieutenant I. M. Munro and Pilot Officer W. V. Mollett attacked two goods trains standing in Ariel Station and one unconnected locomotive.

Pilot Office Mollet made three attacks; Flight Lieutenant Munro made six attacks. Strikes were seen and steam was seen escaping from the damaged locomotives. The only opposition was reported as being light flak with no damage to either aircraft.

Summary of 1942

The Squadron converted to Typhoon Mk 1s during January, with pilot training commencing in February at Duxford. This was not without problems though. The Typhoons became notorious for, amongst other things, broken throttle controls. After modifications and a new engine for the Typhoons it became a very rugged and able aircraft.

Training flights were organised flying against Supermarine Spitfires to determine the best tactics to use in combat. The first interception by Typhoons during May, and Army co-operation exercises with dummy attacks on motor transports. Providing air cover for the disastrous Dieppe raid by Canadian forces.

The introduction of the Typhoon was not without risk of friendly fire. Instances of the Typhoons being attacked by Spitfires were recorded several times, one attack resulting in the death of the pilot. Part of the answer was to fly to various Spitfire squadrons to show the pilots what a Typhoon looked like!

Offensive patrols to Holland to attack shipping and other

targets of opportunity, and being involved in the attacks on the German pocket battleships.

But everything was not work, work and more work. 1942 has the first record of pilots being granted leave. Sport is also mentioned. Rugby, hockey and football matches were played, and pilots even managed trips to the River Camm boating. And as is the service custom, officers serving other ranks their Christmas Dinner.

Enemy aircraft claims were - one Do 111, one Ju 88, one Me 210, two Do 217s and one Me 109 - all claimed as destroyed. One Ju 88 is claimed as damaged.

As for Squadron pilot casualties - five pilots killed in flying accidents, one killed by friendly fire, and two pilots missing in action. Six good pilots lost unnecessarily!

1943

1st January

Unwelcome news today. The Squadron was informed that they were to move to Exeter. The reasons for the reluctant move were that it took them further away from enemy occupied Europe, and the fact that it was now settled at Warmwell.

Their maintenance section was to be left behind - "which has done us very good service and is partly Rhodesian. The idea of having the Squadron split half at Exeter and half at Bolt Head does not sound convenient."

No date for the move is given but it can be assumed that is was within a matter of a few days as the ORB for the 8th records the Squadron as operating from Exeter.

10th January

Flying Officer J. Small and Pilot Officer S. J. P. Blackwell were carrying out an anti-Rhubarb patrol just off of Teignmouth at 300 feet when they saw eight Fw 190s flying northwest towards Teignmouth at zero feet.

They both turned to starboard and gave chase using full boost. The Fw 190s dropped bombs on the waterfront and Flying Officer Small selected one of two Fw 190s without bombs and gave a short burst at 250 yards. Closing rapidly he gave it a longish burst with little deflection at 100 yards range. He observed a flash in the enemy aircraft that nosed down and hit the sea 500 yards off shore just north of Teignmouth.

His Typhoon flew through the cascading water caused by the Fw 190 crashing suffering a damaged radiator cowling. He looked for further targets, but could not see any.

Pilot Officer Blackwell opened fire on another Fw 190 at about the same time that Flying Officer Small gave his first burst, but at 500 yards range, chasing the Fw 190 for 20 miles until his ammunition was exhausted, seeing strikes on the mainplane and fuselage but was unable to close the range to much less than 500 yards, claiming it as damaged. The eight Fw 190s made no attempt to turn and fight the two Typhoons.

11th January

Four Typhoons flown by Squadron Leader C. L. Green, Flying Officer J. H. Deall, Flight Lieutenant J. C. Thompson and Flying Officer J. R. D. Menelaws crossed the French coast at Point Plouha at zero feet and flew about 10 miles south-west when Green 2 saw his Number 1 (Flight Lieutenant Thompson) aircraft smoking. Flight Lieutenant Thompson said on the radio that he was in trouble and intended to make a forced landing.

His aircraft rapidly slowed down, the other three Typhoons drawing ahead. Squadron Leader Green was about to turn around to see how he had managed his forced landing when AA fire started so instead he ordered the Rhubarb patrol to Target Number 6 to be abandoned.

The three Typhoons flew eastwards meeting considerable flak from the La Plaine/St. Driec aerodrome, crossing out at Point de Pordic.

The position of Flight Lieutenant Thompson's forced landing was approximately mid-way between Etables and Guingamp.

26th January

A number of scrambles took place today. The reports in the ORB for each scramble ended with the comments - "...it was obvious that we were chasing ourselves," and "...think we were chasing ourselves."

On one scramble however, things were very different. Pilot Officer C. R. M. Bell and Sergeant N. V. Borland took off to investigate enemy aircraft over Dartmouth. Sergeant Borland had trouble starting his Typhoon and was "left somewhat behind."

Flying Officer Bell, flying alone, spotted a number of Spitfires, and was instructed to go to Start Point when he saw a lone Fw 190 at 2 o'clock going south at zero feet, 1000 yards ahead. (Imagine a clock face lying flat on the ground. Looking towards 2 o'clock, with you at the centre, that is where the Fw 190 was.) Flying Officer Bell turned slightly on to its tail and overtook at approximately 20 mph, gave a short burst at 600 yards, then at 300 yards and again at 250 yards. In this last burst he saw strikes and pieces flying off of the Fw 190.

The Fw 190 climbed steeply and then plunged smoking into the sea. Flying Officer Bell turned to look for any other enemy aircraft, but saw none. He claimed one Fw 190 as destroyed.

27th January

As recorded in the ORB - "Squadron Leader C. L. Green has been awarded the Distinguished Flying Cross. Announced over the Tannoy to the greatest pleasure of everybody, especially the Squadron, who all realise so much he has done to build up and maintain the Squadron, not to mention the very large number of offensive sorties he has made."

29th January

No less than eight Squadron pilots, in two sorties, took part in searching for the crew of a crashed Boston bomber who might have taken to a dinghy in the English Channel.

The first search section was flown by Flight Lieutenant J. D. Wright, Pilot Officer V. Mollett, Pilot Officer N. J. Lucas and Sergeant N. V. Borland taking off at 15.15 and landing at 16.35.

Five minutes before they landed, the second search section comprising of Squadron Leader C. L. Green, Pilot Officer S. J. P. Blackwell, Flight Lieutenant I. R. Munro and Pilot Officer J. D. Miller took off, again searching an area with co-ordinates of North 4923, West 0342.

Both sections made a thorough search of the area but nothing was seen. Other pilots who had witnessed the crashing Boston did not see any survivors, but a search had to be made in case any of the crew did manage to escape the stricken bomber before it sank into the sea.

2nd February

A fatal flying accident while the Squadron was carrying out a practice flight in clouds. Sergeant Horne could not be contacted on the radio. He was later found crashed near Hampton and would have been killed instantly, his Typhoon completely destroyed. There was no apparent reason for the crash.

3rd February

Another loss for the Squadron today. Flying Officer C. R. M. Bell's engine failed on his Typhoon when flying at just 500 feet, 10 miles out to sea from Torquay. He jettisoned the hood and doors, ditching his Typhoon very successfully, but did not evacuate the aircraft although it floated for five seconds. (The time of ditching is recorded as 14.20 hours.) Apparently he must have been knocked unconscious in the ditching. When the aircraft sank there was nothing left on the water except an oil patch.

The position was orbited by Sergeant G. M. R. Eastwood, who was later relieved by Yellow Section - Flight Lieutenant J. D. Wright and Pilot Officer W. V. Mollett. Yellow Section was joined 20 minutes later by Flight Lieutenant I. M. Munro who continued orbiting until 15.00 hours.

A Walrus and Defiant arrived on the scene, together with a motor launch, but Monty Bell was not found and is presumed drowned.

6th February

Three Typhoon's 'beat up' Exeter in connection with a recruiting drive for the ATC.

7th February

Another engine failure on a Typhoon just four days after Flying Officer C. R. M. Bell's ditching due to engine failure. This time it was Squadron Leader Green's engine causing the problem. His engine failed at 25,000 feet when he was 15 miles south of Bolt Head. He reported that he would try to glide and land, but if he went below 4,000 feet before reaching land he would bale out. Fortunately his engine continued to 'tick over' enabling him to reach land, where he landed - wheels up - at Bolt Head Aerodrome.

By coincidence his Number 2 was Sergeant Eastwood who was also Number Two to Flying Officer Bell. This was also Sergeant Eastwood's second operational mission.

13th February

Lucky 13th for Pilot Officer Haworth when the throttle control broke and he had to force land in a field near to the Squadron's sports field. He had to go under some high-tension cables, hitting a tree with his starboard plane, before coming to rest. Fortunately he was un-hurt, but the Typhoon was almost a complete write off.

15th February

Two Typhoons flown by Sergeant G. M. R.Eastwood and Pilot Officer W. V. Mollett were scrambled to intercept a raid at 30.000 feet, 10 to 15 miles south of Start Point. Sergeant Eastwood (as Number 2) first spotted the enemy aircraft some distance off and gave "Tally - ho!" Number 1, Pilot Officer Mollett followed but became separated from his Number 2 who followed the enemy aircraft which he could just see.

The enemy aircraft flew north to Plymouth with Sergeant Eastwood following 'flat out' and climbing to 31,500 feet over Plymouth. As the enemy aircraft turned south, Sergeant Eastwood 'cut the corner', catching up and closing rapidly, opening fire at 150 to 75 yards range with a two second burst. He saw many strikes and pieces flying off of the enemy aircraft, which appeared to glide slowly down.

Sergeant Eastwood was unable to follow it down as his guns had all jammed and the enemy aircraft had turned to attack. At this point he "Observed a large object hanging underneath it." He returned home, claiming one Fw 190 damaged.

It was not uncommon for fighter aircraft - both German and British - to carry 250lb or 500lb bombs. German aircraft carrying bombs were identified as 'rats'.

16th February

Four Typhoons were acting as rear cover to a large force of

bombers that were raiding Brest, but it developed into an abortive dinghy search.

Two more aircraft escorted a Walrus 60 miles out to sea. In the words of the ORB - "This was a useless operation as by the time the Walrus had reached its position and begun its search, the Typhoons were short of petrol and had to come home leaving the Walrus to look after itself."

17th February
Serviceability of the Squadron's Typhoons appeared to be improving after the unfortunate earlier problems. Twelve Squadron aircraft took off to carry out formation flying with some of the new pilots. Eleven aircraft completed the course, with the formation flying being "quite good." There is no record of who these new pilots were, or how many. Hopefully their names will appear in later ORBs.

20th February
Four aircraft on an anti-Rhubarb patrol spotted an aircraft going very fast at zero feet, flying out to sea. Pilot Officer Small was sure it was a 'Hun' by the way it was behaving and "Tally-hoed", but when near saw it was a Liberator.

This section of two aircraft had been going fast, and Pilot Officer Furber's engine suddenly cut out about 15 miles south east of Torquay. He radioed he was bailing out and undid his straps, but had insufficient height and had to ditch with his straps undone. He made a tail down ditching, but the aircraft either turned over or sank very quickly as Pilot Office Furber was well under water. Somehow or other he "got away with it" and managed to evacuate his sinking Typhoon and into his dinghy.

Flying Officer Small, who had started to fly back to Exeter, did not hear the radio transmission of Pilot Officer Furber but heard Control calling Red 2 (Pilot Officer Furber) without success. Both he and Yellow Section - Pilot Officer Mollet and Pilot Officer Blackwell - turned around and went back, locating the dinghy and eventually managed to contact a trawler/ minesweeper from a nearby convoy to pick him up where he was later transferred to an Air/Sea Rescue launch and taken to Dartmouth, slightly bruised but nothing more. A very lucky pilot to have evacuated a sinking aircraft.

Aircraft serviceability was recorded as "again terribly low, so no operational flying". To make the situation worse seagulls were inflicting damage to the aircraft! A seagull hit Flight Lieutenant Munroe's Typhoon making the aircraft u/s (unserviceable), and Sergeant Eastwood's aircraft was u/s from the same cause the previous day.

Could these and other failures be the result of leaving the squadron's maintenance crews back at Warmwell, or was the Mk Ib Typhoon prone to these types of problems and maintenance was proving difficult with the number of engine failures?

24th February

An interesting comment in the ORB for today. Four aircraft were flown to Henlow and exchanged for modified ones. No further details as to what the modifications were.

26th February

Squadron Leader Greeen and Sergeant R. K. 'Bunder' Thompson flying on an anti-Rhubarb patrol heard (over the radio) 'rats' bombing Exmouth and chased after them.

They first spotted a Spitfire and then saw nine Fw 190s. They rapidly overtook the Spitfire and closed in on the Fw 190s, firing as they got nearer. Squadron Leader Green damaged one and then attacked a second, shooting it down into the sea.

'Bunder' Thompson closed right into the Fw 190 that the CO had damaged, finishing it off, disintegration wreckage severely damaging the Typhoon's spinner. They claimed two Fw 190s destroyed, but not before the enemy aircraft had dropped their bombs on Exmouth causing considerable damage.

'Bunder' is the second nickname recorded in the ORBs. Up to this point the reports have been very formal. A new hand behind the keyboard typing up the reports? See this pilot's story of how he obtained his nickname in the Roll of Honour section.

28th February

Yet more problems with engine failures. Sergeant Bailies's engine cut out and he was forced to land with the under carriage up (no hydraulics) in a field about six miles from the drome. It has since been established that his throttle had broken in the same way as Squadron Leader Greens had on the 7 February, and Pilot Officer Haworth had on the 13th. A comment here was - "It would seem that this rod needs strengthening."

Recorded today is the Official Citation of Squadron Leader Green DFC.

"Squadron Leader Green has an impressive record of operational flights against the enemy. Since May 1941, when he joined his present unit, he has participated in many operational sorties, acting as leader of his squadron on numerous occasions. In addition, he has completed several other flights and defensive patrols and has destroyed one enemy aircraft. Squadron Leader Green has always displayed outstanding leadership and an intense desire to engage the enemy. By his example and keenness he has raised the efficiency of his squadron to a very high standard."

1st March

The Squadron is grounded today! "In consequence of yesterdays forced landing which was caused by a broken throttle control, this being the third example of this failure, the Squadron was grounded pending the fitting of a strengthened unit".

2nd March
Modifications started in earnest today, and some Typhoon flying with the strengthened throttle controls quickly commenced.

3rd March
If the pilots thought that they were going to get few days of rest though they were greatly mistaken.

"Eight pilots dressed in Sidcot suits, flying boots and no hats taken four miles out in an enclosed van then had to find their way back to the 'drome without speaking English and enter the 'drome unseen. All succeeded and one couple captured a RDF Station (Radio Direction Finder - radar) on the way."

4th March
Another eight pilots repeated yesterday's escape exercise. To quote the ORB - "This certainly proves that English farmers take no notice whatever of strangely dressed airmen walking across fields and their suspicions are not even aroused when addressed in a foreign language."

13th March
Flying Officer J. H. Deall and Sergeant D. S. Eadie were on patrol and heard over the radio that bandits were over Salcombe. The section was fortunately flying south, very near to Salcombe, when they saw four Fw 190s coming out from Start Point travelling eastwards and then turning south after the Fw 190s spotted the Typhoon section. The two Typhoons were only 2,000 yards away and closed on the Fw 190s rapidly.

Flying Officer Deall opened fire on one Fw 190 and saw strikes. The undercarriage dropped on the enemy aircraft just as the Typhoon pilot overshot. Sergeant Eadie opened fire on a second Fw 190, seeing many strikes and a flash before he overshot. But he meanwhile had flown up beside a third Fw 190 and overtaken it as the Fw 190 was turning to get his sights on Sergeant Eadie. Flying Officer Deall saw this and shouted a warning to break away which Sergeant Eadie did. He then went and finished off the Fw 190 that Flying Officer Deall had damaged.

In the meantime Flying Officer Deall had turned towards the Fw 190 that had fired at Sergeant Eadie, closed, and gave it a burst. The enemy aircraft climbed steeply and the pilot baled out. The pilot's claimed two Fw 190s destroyed and one damaged.

18th March
Six pilots were taken on a trip aboard an Air/Sea Rescue launch at Exmouth. They then sailed one of the new sailing type of dinghy.

21st March
During aerobatics, Sergeant Baillie found himself lost in bad visibility and found his radio unserviceable. He flew around trying to pinpoint his position without success, and finally, only having 15 gallons of fuel left, he forced landed in a field near Bovey Tracey. The Typhoon was 'smashed' but he was un-hurt.

23rd March
Air Marshall Leigh Mallory, Commander in Chief, Fighter Command, visited Exeter and spoke to pilots from the squadron at dispersal.

Flying Officer H. A. Cooper was posted to the squadron as a pilot.

25th March

No flying today, so instead the pilots were shown Film Numbers 4, 5, and 6. No indication as what these training - presumably - films were about. There was also a lecture from 'Doc' on oxygen etc. A new Engineering Officer arrives, Flying Officer Cockburn.

26th March

During an Air/Sea firing exercise Squadron Leader Green's Typhoon developed engine trouble, and he had to return to Exeter without too much trouble. Also today the Squadron challenged the Station to a game of hockey and beat them 3 - 2.

28th March

On a normal patrol off of Torquay, Sergeant C. W. Baillie and Squadron Leader Green were ordered up to 18,000 feet to look for two bandits. They were then ordered down to sea level. It was at this point that supercharger problems on Squadron Leader Green's Typhoon forced both pilots to return to Exeter. They were on their way back when they saw two enemy aircraft dive down to zero feet. They immediately dived after them but Squadron Leader Green could not engage his supercharger and could do no more than 320 mph, so could not close the gap to less than 1,000 yards.

The enemy aircraft, possibly Me 109s, could not be caught to enable the two Typhoon pilots the opportunity to attack, and the chase was abandoned.

4th April

A party was held in the Officers Mess to celebrate the engagement of Flying Officer 'Bob' Menelaws to Kim which was announced on 1 April.

For the next few days' pilots from 193 Squadron (Typhoons)

from Harrowbeer were flying some patrols with the Squadron to get them accustomed to patrolling.

5th April

The runway at Exeter was blocked after a Mosquito crashed on the intersection of the runways, preventing Flight Lieutenant Munro and Sergeant Borland from landing, forcing them both to land at Harrowbeer.

On returning to Exeter after the runway had been cleared, Sergeant Borland swung on the runway due to cross wind, collapsing the undercarriage of his aircraft. Unfortunately Flight Lieutenant Munro, who was following him down, ran into him. Both pilots were not injured, but their aircraft were very badly damaged.

10th April

'Wings for Victory Week'. Three Typhoons flew over Chudleigh where Squadron Leader Green was speaking to raise funds for the worthy cause.

11th April

Getting engaged was becoming popular! At a dance in the Officers Mess, news was 'leaked' out the CO, Squadron Leader Green, is engaged.

This announcement led to "...a very concentrated celebration in which all the Squadron's Officers took part, and some too much. The pilots celibacy will now go quickly to bits'."

14th April

Three Typhoons in low formation flew over the church just after the wedding of Flying Officer 'Bob' Menelaws and Section Officer Kim Henoco.

The wedding was held at the 14th Century church at

Poltimore, the officiating Padre having been in Rhodesia for many years. The reception was held in the Officers Mess. The couple going away in a taxi driven by a South African.

In wartime many service engagements and weddings took place very quickly. This was no exception. The author hopes that the newly wed couple had a very long and happy life together.

A farewell party for 307 (Polish) Squadron. First in the Officers Mess and then moving to the Sergeants Mess.

15th April

While flying at zero feet, four miles south of Prawl Point, Flight Lieutenant Munro witnessed Sergeant D. S. Peters Typhoon crash into the sea. He immediately returned to the area and saw an open parachute and the pilot on the water. An Air/Sea Rescue launch arrived and recovered Sergeant Peters from the water, but sadly he was dead. He had made no radio transmission so it is not clear what happened, but it is probable that he flew into the sea accidently.

17th April

On the first patrol of the day, just after dawn, Sergeant Eastwood was attacked by one of five Spitfires of 65 Squadron just off of Bolt Head. The Spitfires "had been escorting a MTB (Motor Torpedo Boat) and why on earth the Spitfire should break away from its formation and carry out a long drawn out attack on a Typhoon at short range is difficult to understand."

Sergeant Eastwood managed to fly his aircraft over land and bale out successfully despite his foot becoming stuck in the cockpit, but fortunately his boot came off. He did not attempt to land as his aircraft's ailerons were shot away. His aircraft crashed two fields away.

During the evening, Squadron Leader Green and Flying

Officer Deall had been scrambled after two enemy aircraft flying at 18,000 feet over Plymouth.

They first saw two Fw 190s about 40 miles from the French Coast and had great difficulty in overtaking them. The overtaking speed was very low, so they fired at 1,000/800 yards range to make the Fw 190s weave.

Squadron Leader Green observed strikes, and claimed one Fw 190 damaged. He decided to attack the leading, and faster, Fw 190 so as to stand the best chance of getting both, but in catching this Fw 190 he overshot, and the other Fw 190 promptly attacked him

A 'dogfight' ensued in which the 'Gerry' pilots showed themselves to be very experienced, and a very hectic five minutes was spent by our pilots who were very severely handicapped as only one cannon of Flying Officer Deall's Typhoon was firing. The Fw 190s both vanished into heavy haze. Each pilot claimed one Fw 190 damaged.

19th April
The funeral of Sergeant Peters took place at Exeter cemetery, and was attended by Officers and Sergeants.

22nd April
Information was received today that on a sweep to Airel, France, on 31 December 1942, by Squadron Leader Green, Flying Officer Biddulph, and later the same day by Flight Lieutenant Munro and Flying Officer Mollett, eight locomotives were destroyed by their combined attacks. At the time the Squadron only claimed four as damaged.

26th April
Some testing of firing cannons at high altitude. One Typhoon flown by Sergeant Eastwood was flown to 31,000 feet to discover

whether icing problems at that altitude would prevent the cannons from firing. No icing was experienced, although the Typhoon dropped about 100 feet at each burst.

27th April

A new experience for Flying Officer Mennelaws and Pilot Officer McGibbon. They were sent to intercept two bandits flying north at zero feet, about 25 miles northwest of Torquay. This was the first time that Control had sent any squadron pilots so far out to sea when the enemy aircraft have been flying so low. The two pilots saw the enemy aircraft about 2,000 yards away, turned towards them, but the two enemy aircraft turned almost immediately away and were both lost in the haze.

30th April

During a practice Air/Sea firing and formation flight, Sergeant Henderson's engine failed two or three minutes after take off when he was at 2,000 feet. He radioed he was attempting a forced landing. Squadron Leader Green watched him go down, but he hit a tree and cartwheeled into a field. The Typhoon broke up into pieces and Sergeant Henderson was thrown out. He was taken to hospital badly injured.

1st May

Two Thunderbolts 'took on' two Typhoons in a dogfight. Piloted by Squadron Leader Green and Flight Lieutenant Munro the two Typhoons "definitely won, but the Thunderbolts put up a very good show."

3rd May

The young pilot who took part in the dogfight with the two Thunderbolts was tragically killed today. "Flight Lieutenant Munro took an aircraft up on test, and during a fast dive his wings appeared to break off, then the tail and the aircraft spiralling fast crashed to the ground." He had no chance to bale out and was instantly killed.

4th May
Flying Officer J. H. Deall is promoted today to the rank of Flight Lieutenant.

7th May
Flight Lieutenant Munro's funeral took place at Exeter Cemetery attended by all pilots and 'Ticky' Baggot as a representative of Rhodesia House. The service was conducted by the Reverend Green who is padre at Poltimore Church and has lived for some years in Rhodesia.

10th May
A strict limit was imposed today on the number of hours each Typhoon was permitted to fly during May. Only 300 hours per aircraft was allowed while a new type of 'sleeve' was fitted.

No further details are available, but the new type of sleeve may be a modification to the engine cylinders.

14th May
To support another 'Wings for Victory' week, two pilots 'beat up' Salcombe in aid of their appeal.

15th May
'A' Flight commanders check on pilot's flying capability. Flight Sergeant Meyer was carrying out a new maneuver spin from 10,000 feet to 2,000 feet, apparently, "…shook the Flight Commander more than the Flight Sergeant."

16th May

Time for some relaxation. In the afternoon most pilots went to Ladram Bay bathing and "throwing stones at 'gulls in flight. This giving good practice in deflection (shooting) and showing good examples of evasive action."

Another fly past by two Typhoons, this time to support Torquay's 'Wings for Victory' campaign. In this case the pilots are identified as Flying Officer J. D. Miller and Sergeant D. Erasmus.

21st May

All of the pilots went to West Lulworth by 'bus and saw various types of tanks, and then rode in Churchill tanks over rough countryside. They later went to Weymouth and "had a good party there."

23rd May

The forth-coming marriage of the CO, Squadron Leader Green, was celebrated with a small bachelor's party in the Officers Mess.

26th May

The 'big day' has arrived. The Squadron was released from duty in the afternoon for the wedding of Squadron Leader Green to Miss Betty Bowden.

A quiet wedding at the Registry Office followed by the reception in the Officers Mess "...which was anything but quiet." Mr. O'Keefe was present representing Rhodesia House, and all the Officers and Sergeants of No. 266 (Rhodesia) Squadron.

There were in fact two weddings today. Flying Officer 'Johny' Small was also married today to Mrs. Kay at Weymouth, and he and his wife arrived at Exeter in time for the Squadron dance.

30th May

The Squadron was scrambled to intercept enemy aircraft over Sidmouth. They were then vectored to south of Exmouth, but no enemy aircraft were seen.

Smoke was seen over Torquay, so some squadron Typhoons broke away and headed in that direction where they saw an aircraft burning on the water 12 miles south of Exmouth. Flight Lieutenant J. D. Wright saw an oil patch and a dinghy and gave a fix. The downed pilot, a German, was later picked up by an Air/Sea Rescue launch.

5th June

Improved patrol tactics were implemented today. The two patrolling aircraft will both fly at least 10 miles off shore and at 1,000 feet instead of one flying at sea level and one at 500 feet.

'Wings for Victory' campaign support again. This time Flying Officer J. Small and Flight Sergeant C. W. Baillie were instructed, whilst on a normal patrol, to over fly Teignmouth and Darmouth to boost their campaigns.

10th June

More technical problems for the Typhoons! On inspection part of the tail unit of several aircraft were found to be cracked. All flying suspended until all of the squadron's Typhoons have been examined and the faulty aircraft repaired.

11th June

After examination there were just seven Typhoons serviceable for operational flying.

17th June

Two aircraft were scrambled to intercept a suspect bogey. The two pilots, Flight Lieutenant Wright and Flying Officer Cooper, were given several vectors to fly. Flying Officer Cooper was flying at 300 feet and Flight Lieutenant Wright at zero feet, about 26 miles south of Bolt Head. Flying Officer Cooper said over the radio that he had engine failure and intended to bale out after attempting to gain altitude. He did this but he became caught up in his aircraft's wireless ariel and did not get free until he had dropped to 500 feet. He then pulled the ripcord and the 'chute opened at 300 feet.

He was badly entangled in shroud lines etc. and took many minutes to get free. He had to undo his dog lead, thus loosing his dinghy although his Mae West life jacket kept him afloat. Flight Lieutenant Wright orbited him giving fixes. He managed to cut his own dinghy away from his parachute, partly unfurled it and tried to throw it down to Flying Officer Cooper, but it fouled his tailplane and stuck there, making his aircraft difficult to control. He continued orbiting until relieved by the next section which had been scrambled to assist, Flying Officer N. J. Lucas and Flight Sergeant K. R. Thompson.

A Spitfire dropped a large dinghy near to Flying Officer Cooper but he did not see it. Flying Officer Cooper was picked up after 60 minutes by a Walrus, which was unable to take off, again due to four-foot waves, so it taxied until an Air/Sea Rescue launch took the pilot off to Bolt Head where he was declared fit and un-injured.

18th June

A postscript to yesterday's event. "Flight Lieutenant Wright and Flying Officer Furber (the ditching expert), went down by car to collect Flying Officer Cooper at Bolt Head, and on arrival there found 'Haig' with twenty-five other 'Haigs' lined up and Haig Cooper in very good form". Haig in this instance refers to the whisky!

19th June

Returning from a patrol, Pilot Officer R. K. Thompson's engine cut out when he was in the circuit. He managed to force land, wheels up, on the airfield with a dead propeller, making a very good landing.

21st June

Another engine failure, this time over open water. Pilot Officer N. V. Borland, flying at 1,500 feet had engine failure when 12 miles east of Berry Head. He baled out and made "a very comfortable descent" boarding his dinghy very easily. Flying Officer J. Small observed this.

A Walrus was carrying out practice landings on the sea in Ton Bay and arrived to pick up the pilot, after he had been in his dinghy for 15 minutes, taking him back directly to Exeter.

This rescue by the Walrus was not so straight forward as it might seem, as the rescue aircraft had landed in an area of sea where mines where located. At the beginning of their patrol, the two pilots had witnessed a mine blowing up.

The ORB goes on - "A very successful bale out, but two bale outs and one forced landing all caused by engine failure in five days is most discouraging." The Typhoon Mk Ib was getting a not too good reputation, at least by this Squadron!

22nd June

Squadron Leader Green in London to receive his DFC from Her Majesty the Queen.

Flight Lieutenant J. D. Wright, acting as CO, asked for another squadron to take over the sector from the Squadron "in view of the appalling state of our aircraft serviceability." 183 Squadron sent four aircraft to help the Squadron do their patrols and stand-bys.

23rd June

As many aircraft as possible were required to escort four Bomphoons (Typhoons carrying bombs) of 183 Squadron to attack Maupertus aerodrome. But the Squadron could only send seven to Warmwell, the starting point, with one of these acting as a 'spare'.

Six aircraft took off - Squadron Leader Green, Flight Lieutenant J. D. Wright, Flying Officer J. Small, Flight Lieutenant J. H. Deall, Flying Officer F. B. Biddulph and Pilot Officer J. D. Miller, but one had to force land at take off. The other five flew with aircraft from 257 Squadron to escort the Bomphoons.

The Bomphoons dived from 12,000 to 5,000 feet, releasing their bombs at 7,000 feet. Bombs appeared to fall on the target although no enemy aircraft were seen on the aerodrome. The only enemy aircraft seen was a Me 109 which was seen to be diving below the formation but did not attempt to intercept. Throughout the operation the Squadron gave top cover from enemy aircraft at 13,000 feet. Operation uneventful, with all aircraft returning safely.

25th June

News was received today that Squadron Leader Green was leaving the Squadron and going to Hinkleigh as Wing Commander, Station Commander.

Flight Lieutenant MaCintyre was to take over command of the squadron. As stated in the ORB - "He (Squadron Leader Green) certainly deserves it after 600 hours of operational flying, but he will be sadly missed by the Squadron. Flight Lieutenant MaCintyre will obviously make a very popular and efficient CO."

26th June

Six Typhoons flown by Flight Lieutenant A. S. MaCintyre,

Flight Lieutenant J. D. Wright, Flying Officer N. J. Lucas, Flight Lieutenant J. H. Deall, Pilot Officer J. R. D. Menelaws and Flying Officer J. D. Miller were given the task of escorting three Bomphoons of 183 Squadron on an armed shipping reconnaissance to Guernsey hoping to find some German 'E' Boats.

No shipping or enemy aircraft were seen but when flying over Guernsey they were met by intense light and heavy flak, Flying Officer Lucas's aircraft was hit by a LMG (light machine gun) bullet through his wing which penetrated his nose tank. All aircraft landed safely just before dark.

28th June

Six Typhoons - Flight Lieutenant J. H. Deall, Flying Officer J. R. D. Memelaws, Flight Lieutenant A. S. MaCintyre, Pilot Officer K. R. Thompson, Flying Officer S. J. P. Blackwell and Flight Lieutenant J. D. Wright - took off from Harrowbeer escorting four Bomphoons of 183 Squadron.

Flying at zero feet to Maupertus where they were to meet up with ten Spitfires of 610 Squadron. The Spitfires were seen before reaching the rendezvous point some way out at sea.

Making a rapid climb to 2,000 feet before crossing the coast, the Bomphoons did a diving bombing attack over the aerodrome from west to east. They encountered moderate flak, and while in the dive Flight Lieutenants Wright's port oleo leg came down. His Number 2 escorted him home where he managed to land wheels down, but the port oleo leg collapsed near the end of his ground run, damaging the main plane and propeller.

1st July

It was announced today that the Squadron will be released every other 24 hours, for flying training and offensive operations, this it was hoped, will help considerably: firstly it will reduce by half the very great number of hours on stand-by and also help the

Squadron serviceability which was still very bad with usually only six or eight Typhoons available at any one time.

Flying Officer McGibbon suffered an engine failure on his Typhoon. As one of three aircraft being air tested, his engine cutting out sporadically, luckily he was flying near the landing strip at the time. He thought he could make a normal landing, lowered his undercarriage, but then realised he would not be able to round to use the correct runway, so he had to land downwind onto the shortest runway. Touching down very fast half way along the runway (no flaps to slow him down), it was obvious that he was going to overshoot hopelessly, so he managed to partially raise his undercarriage, became airborne again before crashing in a field. He was unhurt, but the Typhoon was severely damaged. The cause of the engine cutting out was not established.

3rd July
Could today herald a new phase in the Squadron's combat role? Two brand new Typhoons arrived. These are fitted with long range, jettisonable fuel tanks, and bomb racks. The hope among the pilots was that all Typhoons would be equipped like this in the future.

5th July
Three pilots had a game of golf, and Sergeant Henderson who crashed on April the 30th returned to the Squadron but is still not permitted to fly for another two months.

7th July
Squadron Leader Green is now officially posted away from the Squadron but not before "a small party developed in the mess." Flight Lieutenant A. S. MaCintyre is now promoted to Squadron Leader and assumes command.

9th July

A short night's sleep, just four hours, before six aircraft took off at first light to fly with Bomphoons of 183 Squadron. Flying at zero feet to within 10 miles of the French coast before turning west where they spotted five ships to the south near St. Brieuc Bay about 10 miles away from the formations position.

Turning south and increasing speed, they attacked, each of the squadron's pilots selecting one ship. The ships were armed minesweepers.

The Bomphoon's bombs were seen to be fairly near misses and probably not doing too much damage to the ships. The flak was moderate, but Pilot Officer 'Mike' Furber's Typhoon was evidently hit in the engine and he had to ditch. He made a very good ditching about 200 yards from the shore, but his aircraft turned over and he was not actually seen to get out. Pilot Officer Lucas thought he saw something that might have been the pilot come up to the surface. Pilot Officer Lucas had "got away with it" on a previous occasion in similar circumstances, so he thought there is a good chance for the ditched pilot. All other Typhoons returned safely.

13th July

The previous day nine aircraft had flown to Harrowbeer in preparation for today's operation. Making rendezvous over the base with eight Typhoon bombers, the formation flew to Bolt Head and saw aircraft of 193 Squadron over Start Point, but although they should have joined up with Harrowbeer formation they did not. The formation crossed the French coast east of Batz and found the target, Morlaix aerodrome, covered in 10/10 clouds, so could not bomb it. Squadrons of Spitfires were also in support.

20th July

A company of publicity 'merchants' visited the Squadron, taking a number of photographs and collected a lot of 'gen' about the Squadron and its history.

21st July

Station sports day has arrived. Apparently the "squadron did extremely well largely owing to the keenness of Aircraftsman Cowan who collected personnel for training and got them to compete."

The final scores were - 266 Squadron with 60 points; the Regiment 16 points; 131 Squadron 14 points; 125 Squadron 10 points.

Aircraftman Cowan, Green and Stott and Leading Aircraftman Elliot won a number of track events. Squadron Leader MaCintyre was placed in the discus and shot putting.

The Regiment probably refers to the RAF Regiment, established to defend airfields against enemy ground attack.

22nd July

All pilots attended a lecture today by Lieutenant Commander Clarke on ship recognition. It went down very well with the pilots, all agreeing it was needed.

A film was shown later, about the squadron. Compiled by Corporal Marshall of the squadron's Photographic Section. As commented in the ORB - "If this can be released it would be a popular number in Rhodesia."

26th July

Following on from their success at the Stations Sport Day, a cricket match was played between the Squadron and the GRU which the Squadron won by 132 runs to the GRUs 52. Apparently Flight Lieutenant Wright was hit in the eye by a cricket ball "but is still smiling."

30th July

During an aborted raid to bomb Gulpavas aerodrome, Flying Officer Menelaws spun when the squadron flew into cloud, recovering at 2,000 feet, he flew straight back to base at Exeter very fast and alone.

Meanwhile when the rest of the Squadron was coming out over the French coast, Pilot Officer Cooper's engine cut out completely, he jettisoned his hood and doors preparing to bale out, when his engine picked up again. The Squadron climbed and escorted him home. "He looked very naked sitting in his open cockpit. On making a normal approach to land he nearly spun in (due to no hood and doors apparently) so made a faster approach down wind on the longest runway which were under repair and broke his port wing when he groundlooped on overshooting.

'Stand by' and for the first time in a long time the squadron actually had twelve Typhoons serviceable. Taken off 'stand by', 165 Squadron, who had only arrived two days previous were placed on 'stand by', scrambled and shot down two Fw 190s. The comment in the ORB report says it all - "Good show, but rather disappointing to 266 after their hours of 'stand by'."

31st July

More sports today, this time swimming at Exeter baths. Flight Sergeants Baillie, Eadie, Erasmus and Bean, with Aircraftman MacMaster winning the diving. Flight Sergeant Erasmus was second in the 2 x lengths, and the team came 3rd in the relay.

3rd August

Ten Typhoons giving close support to eight Whirlibombers (Whirlwind bombers) on a bombing operation to (the target name is unreadable here) Squadron Leader MacIntyre and Pilot Officer Thompson became involved in a dogfight with eight Fw 190s. Pilot Officer R. K. Thompson was last seen spinning down from 4,000 feet. He was listed as 'missing' believed killed.

A footnote from the ORB - "Whilst training in Southern Rhodesia he had made a forced landing and was lost far away in the Rhodesian bush of Bund hence his nickname of Bund. He saw no human being until meeting a native some 12 days later, his only food having been four pheasants eggs, his only companions were baboons. The Tiger Moth he was flying has yet to be discovered."

The reader should refer to the Roll of Honour for further information on this and all pilots and ground crew.

11th August

A move to Gravesend. The Squadron was to move the following Saturday. The news was greeted as a very good move, as the Squadron now came within the control of 10 Group, which they eagerly wanted to join. Apparently the only down side was that the Intelligence Officer had to be re-called from leave!

13th August

Dismay in the Squadron as the welcome move to Gravesend was cancelled. No 193 Squadron were moving instead.

"The whole Squadron busy packing all morning and had just completed the job by 15.00 hours when it was announced that the move had been cancelled and that 193 Squadron are going instead. We proceeded to unpack."

15th August

Circus Operation Number 51. Whirlwinds of 263 Squadron with escorts from various other squadrons, including 266 and 193, were to bomb Guipavas airfield.

266 and 193 Squadrons were flying as 'free lance'. The bombers and their covering escorts were recalled before reaching the target as it was obscured by cloud, but 266 and 193 Squadrons were unaware of this and continued with the operation.

Between four and seven enemy aircraft were seen in good time. The six Typhoons of 266 Squadron turned to engage them believing that the six aircraft of 193 were nearby to assist, but these six aircraft never saw the enemy aircraft and were in fact well on their way home before they realised that 266 had met and were engaging the enemy.

To quote the ORB. "This engagement somehow or other went most unfortunately. Squadron Leader MacIntyre was apparently shot down early on by a Fw 190 from about 50 yards range, his Number 2, Flight Sergeant Erasmus, immediately engaged this Fw 190 and shot it down in flames, but Flying Officer Small's aircraft was evidently also hit for he was seen to bale out at the same time. Flight Sergeant Erasmus attacked a number of enemy aircraft and was himself attacked several times, and claims one FW 190 damaged also and possibly another."

With two pilots lost Flight Sergeant Erasmus returned alone although three other pilots joined up, flying low out from the French coast.

But that was not the end of casualties sustained on this operation. Midway across the English Channel two aircraft approached from astern, but the Typhoon pilots were not sure if they were hostile or not. Our aircraft broke hard and in doing so Flying Officer Biddulph stalled his aircraft and spun into the sea. Two other pilots, 'Barney' Wright and 'Tusky' Haworth had individual dogfights before they became separated. Eventually 'Barney' Wright, after damaging one enemy aircraft, found himself alone.

'Tusky' Haworth meanwhile (with two starboard cannons out

of action) was being repeatedly attacked by two enemy aircraft and could not get a good sight of them to return fire, was having great difficulty in breaking off the action to streak for home after being hit in the tail by an HE (high explosive) cannon shell.

The Squadron claimed one Fw 190 destroyed and one damaged by Flight Sergeant D. Erasmus. Two damaged by Flight Lieutenant J. D. Wright. Again to quote from the ORB. "..but this is a poor set off against losing the CO, (S/Ldr MacIntyre), Flying Officer J. Small and Flying Officer F. B. Biddulph".

Later that day Pilot Officer Borland flew the IO (Intelligence Officer) down to Port (the name is unreadable here.) This routine flight was not uneventful as they could only communicate with each other and no body else. Apparently on the return trip they sang a duet - "Praise the Lord and Pass the Ammunition."

16th August

A new Commanding Officer arrives - Squadron Leader P. W. Le Fevre, as well as a new pilot, Sergeant Pilot I. Hulley, posted from 56 OTU.

19th August

'A' Flight and about thirty ground crew were sent to its old 'hunting ground' at Warmwell to be a 'standby' flight until further notice.

Some of the ORBs are extremely faint at this point, and reading them is very difficult, if not impossible at times.

22nd August

A captured Fw 190 which is flying to various Stations took part in a practice dogfight with the new CO. Other pilots took the opportunity to see it flying and "watching its amazing quick rolls."

23rd August

Splitting the Squadron into two sections at different bases was taking its toll on pilots and ground crew. From the ORB. "It is hard work keeping a section at 'standby' all day at both Exeter and Warmwell. Pilots having to do 2 hour shifts and at least twice a day."

26th August

Sergeant Pilot R. McElroy arrived from No. 56 OTU.

29th August

Another replacement pilot arrives. Sergeant Pilot K.W. Rogers from No. 59 OTU.

2nd September

Seven Squadron aircraft flown by Squadron Leader P. W. Le Fevre, Pilot Officer N. V. Borland, Flight Lieutenant J. D. Wright, Flying Officer J. J. R. MacNamara, Flying Officer W. V. Mollet, Pilot Officer H. A. Cooper and Flying Officer S. J. P. Blackwell escorted Air/Sea Rescue Boston aircraft to pick up a Mustang pilot who had been in his dinghy since Tuesday. They flew to Bolt Head meeting the Boston and escorted it to the target area where a Walrus aircraft was already on the sea collecting the pilot.

3rd September

Flight Sergeant Erasmus and Flying Officer Blackwell were scrambled from Exeter. When 30 miles off Guernsey saw enemy aircraft 8 miles ahead. Both dived and the ASI (air speed indicator) got up to 350 mph on the clock but they could not close on the enemy aircraft, so fired from 600 yards range and saw what looked like strikes on the enemy aircraft. The pilots were not very pleased with this lack of overtaking speed which is usually blamed on the four bladed props and bomb racks. Flight Sergeant Erasmus claimed one Fw 190 damaged.

5th September

Instructions received that the Squadron is to move to Gravesend for attachment with forty ground crew only. This is terrific news especially after the disappointing cancelation last month. The IO was recalled from a course, this is noted here because this is the third occasion he has been recalled out of the last three times he has been away from the Squadron.

6th September

Weather today noted as fine with good visibility. Twelve aircraft fully serviceable and on top line. The Squadron Adjutant, Medical Officer and Intelligence Officer arrived at Gravesend with 40 ground crew.

7th September

Seventeen Typhoons took off from Exeter and flew to Gravesend, but Sergeant I. Holley had to force-land, wheels up, in a field near Hasselmere, his aircraft badly damaged. He was slightly hurt and is in hospital. The cause was given as short of fuel but there must have been plenty in the tanks.

The other sixteen aircraft and pilots arrived at Gravesend and all flew a sector recce in the afternoon. The officers billeted in the huge Cobham Hall which is a most interesting mansion. Everybody expecting the balloon to go up very shortly. Possibly a reference to the Second Front and the invasion of Nazi occupied Europe.

8th September

In the evening all pilots were briefed for tomorrow's job, a large convoy of invasion craft will be leaving Dungeness and heading for a point 9 miles off Bologne. Eight aircraft of 266, with eight of 193 and eight of 257 Squadrons will patrol this convoy, and two other Wings of Spitfires will continue this patrolling when we leave off, then we re-fuel fast and repeat the performance probably thus making three or four patrols. This is only a feint landing, the object being to make the Hun attack in force and fight him on level terms over the Channel. All aircraft taking part in this operation have their wings painted in black and white stripes. All pilots went to bed early. Black and white stripes were actually used before the D-Day landings at Normandy on June 6th of the following year.

9th September

Weather fine, viability unlimited, but 'drome covered in ground mist for an hour after dawn. Because of the weather at base our operation was postponed and finally cancelled, although the weather cleared.

We then patrolled Bolounge with the other two squadrons at 16,000 feet. Saw the convoy and masses of friendly aircraft and smoke from bomb bursts on the French coast, but no enemy aircraft, not a single one. This is all we do except for a stooge convoy patrol by twelve aircraft without incident.

10 September

Fine after heavy rain in the night. All pilots in the sixteen aircraft flew back from Gravesend to Exeter. Aircraft serviceability is doing fine. The ground crew left in rather a scramble to catch the train but managed it and arrived at Exeter in the evening.

12th September

Eleven aircraft took part in a low-level practice attack on Dunkeswell aerodrome. Squadron flew straight there and carried out attacks without orbiting, thus taking defences by surprise.

We were complimented on our effort.

13th September
Nine pilots took part in the first bombing practice on this aerodrome. The target is in the centre of the airfield and there were low-level practices and all personnel can watch the accuracy, results were quite good. Flight Sergeant McElroy and Flight Sergeant Forresester did their first Typhoon flights.

17th September
Twelve aircraft took off from Exeter with two photographic Bostons, crossed the French coast at point Ponteval, turned west and flew over the river estuary of Aber-Vrach which the Bostons photographed and returned to Exeter, no enemy aircraft or flak.

Eleven aircraft did a practice landing at Bolt Head to familiarise pilots with that 'drome. Four aircraft did a practice bombing exercise at Exeter. We have just heard that the Squadron and echelon is to move to Harrowbeer, the move to take place on Tuesday, September 21st.

21st September
The road and rail parties left for Harrowbeer, but fourteen aircraft had to fly to Preddanack instead as they had to take part in an operation from there.

Fourteen aircraft took off for Preddanack, but operation was cancelled so they flew to Harrowbeer. Squadron started settling down at Harrowbeer. The weather seems a bit colder here and the billets will not be as warm as Exeter's.

22nd September
Eight aircraft with eight of 193 Squadron took part in a large operation. Twelve Mitchells bombed Guipavas aerodrome and our two squadrons acted as 'fighter sweep' over the target, five

minutes after the bombers, and their escort, to shoot down any Huns seen. We were at 15,000 feet but saw no enemy aircraft although we were warned of fifteen by Control. Slight/heavy flak and Flying Officer McGibbon found his tail-plane had been slightly dented on landing.

Fourteen aircraft flew to Preddanack but only eight were required so the rest returned to Harrowbeer. We continued to unpack and settle in.

23rd September

The Squadron took part in Ramrod 84 & 85 operating from Preddanack on both occasions. Eight aircraft with eight aircraft of 193 Squadron and eight Bombphoons of 183 Squadron.

Crossed the French coast at 12,000 feet at Canaret after skirting Ushant. Bombphoons bombed the target Poulmic successfully, probably destroying four twin-engine enemy aircraft on ground. No enemy aircraft airborne. Moderate flak.

Flying Officer Lucas noticed his engine running rough on leaving French coast possibly due to flak and had to bale out when 33 miles off Lizard. Everything worked perfectly, he judged his height from the water when coming down in 'chute by dropping a boot. He was picked up by a Walrus and landed at Portsmouth.

Later eight aircraft of 266 with eight Bombphoons of 193 Squadron repeated the performance, this time smashing a hanger completely. Five twin-engine enemy aircraft seen taking off. No engagements. Considerable flak. A third operation was started against Guipavas but this was abandoned after 20 minutes from take off. Flying Officer Lucas arrived after tea none the worse for his wetting.

1st October

A trip to Plymouth by bus. A terrific high time was had, some visiting the pictures, others to the docks. Several hotels visited.

8th October

Nine aircraft took off from Preddannack with eight aircraft from 193 Squadron to act as target support in a large operation in which eighteen Boston's escorted by several squadrons of fighters were to bomb Poulmic aerodrome. We arrived as arranged over target area before the 'Beehive', saw the bombs fall among buildings near airfield but did not see any enemy aircraft. Otherwise uneventful.

9th October

Seven aircraft took part in a sweep with 193 Squadron to Guipavis. No enemy aircraft seen but heavy flak. The weather over the target was 10/10 and on returning the squadron became separated. Flight Lieutenant Wright, Pilot Officer Eastwood, Flying Officer Lucas found themselves above 10/10 clouds with practically no petrol left.

They came down through a hole in the clouds and saw St. Merryn aerodrome and had to land immediately. This 'drome is under repair and partially obstructed. They landed on any runway and just managed to pull up in time without hitting anything. A very shaky do!!

15th October

A beautiful day. Pilot Officer Lucas and Sergeant Pilot Drummond were scrambled for two Fw 190s which had made brief landfall over Brixham. They were vectored south to Bolt Head when at 8,000 feet saw two enemy aircraft diving down to 1,000 feet heading south.

The section dived after them overtaking very easily. Pilot Officer Lucas selected one enemy aircraft and had a bit of a turning match with it, but it then obligingly straightened and he was able to get in several good bursts from dead astern. The enemy aircraft's starboard undercart dropped and after another burst the pilot baled out, his parachute was seen to open.

Meanwhile, Sergeant Drummond took the other enemy aircraft which after turning a bit flew straight on and Sergeant Drummond fired a number of long deflection bursts at it seeing strikes and smoke. The enemy aircraft started turning again and after some deflection shots Sergeant Drummond ran out of ammo. He told Pilot Officer Lucas and he chased after it and in one short burst the enemy aircraft blew up and crashed in the sea. He did not know it at the time but he also used all his ammo.

Claiming one and a half Fw 190s destroyed by Pilot Officer Lucas and a half Fw 190 destroyed by Sergeant Drummond. The cine gun cameras of both our pilots are very good.

Pilot Officer Lucas climbed and told Ops that the Hun pilot had baled out and transmitted for a fix. The Huns evidently heard this and a little later on operations ordered four aircraft, Squadron Leader Le Fevre leading, to patrol the area where the Hun baled out. Unfortunately, two aircraft had to return as the engine of one gave trouble when about 15 miles out. The two remaining, Squadron Leader Le Fevre and Flight Sergeant Hulley, when approaching the area at zero feet saw six enemy aircraft apparently searching. Immediately all the enemy aircraft turned and belted for home.

The two Typhoons chased the six Fw 190s and it was nearer France than England too, Squadron Leader Le Fevre overtaking slowly was just about to fire on the rear aircraft when he had to break as another enemy aircraft had at last turned to attack him. He managed to get a very short burst in at this attacker without results. However Flight Sergeant Hulley was able to close in on the COs original quarry unmolested and fire several bursts at him, starting from long range and closing to 200 yards.

THE STABBER OF THE SKY

He saw a strike, but had to break off the combat as he very rightly considered that he must rejoin his Number 1. All the enemy aircraft continued to belt for home, Guernsey by then being only a few miles ahead.

If the other two of our patrol had been there it seems probable that we should have been able to make a good 'bag', it is said that today's victories are the first by any aircraft taking off from Harrowbeer. Claiming one Fw 190 damaged by Flight Sergeant Hulley.

16th October

A howling, pouring wet day. 193 Squadron adopted by the Brazilians, poor 193, they all got soaked to the skin, taxied a Typhoon into a car, the Ambassador's wife's hat blew off in her speech, and at the lunch claret was served in liqueur glasses and drunk as port.

18th October

Having received long range tanks (45 gallons each) most of the aircraft are to be fitted with these and tested. Flight Lieutenant Deall and Pilot Officer Miller made first flights with these tanks.

23rd October

Eight aircraft took off from Bolt Head with eight Bomphoons of 183 Squadron and flew to St. Malo estuary and diving from 10,000 feet the Bomphoons bombed three destroyers and several other smaller ships in St. Malo estuary mouth. We saw one certain and one possible hit on destroyers and many near misses. The final score being: one destroyer hit and one smaller tanker destroyed. No enemy aircraft seen and slight inaccurate flak.

24th October

Eight aircraft took off from Harrowbeer to sweep over

Lezardrieux estuary to see if any ships there. Flew southwards to railway then turned west to Forlaix near Forlaix airfield which was deserted and then northwards home.

All this was at 2,000 feet yet no flak and no enemy aircraft. Lezardrieux was not adequately covered and we offered to do the trip again. In the afternoon four aircraft flew to Cherbourg harbour to spot the damage done to a large merchant ship which was bombed a few minutes earlier by eight aircraft of 263 Squadron. All our pilots saw that the ship was well on fire. Considerable light and heavy flak but none really near our aircraft.

25th October
Eight aircraft acted as top cover with eight aircraft of 193 Squadron to Mitchell bombers bombing Landveoc airfield. Saw burst on southern side of airfield. The CO had to return early with engine trouble and Flying Officer Mollet and his No. 4 returned from Landerneau as one Mitchell shot down by flak. Flight Lieutenant Wright led after CO returned.

In the evening there was a very rowdy party starting in the Mess, then at the Rock Hotel, continued again on return to the Mess and finished off by shaving moustaches off in the billets, Pilot Officer Miller's being a complete write-off, the others repairable.

3rd November
No flying today as weather unsuitable. Pilots went to Plymouth on a liberty bus, most went to the pictures then fed and then danced a bit, but the evening was not a great success.

8th November
Flying Officer H. A. Cooper posted to No. 5 PDC.

9th November

Four aircraft led by Flight Lieutenant J. D. Wright did a Rhubarb intending to attack Gael airfields, but as there was insufficient cloud cover it developed into an attack on railway engines. Flying Officer N. J. Lucas shot up some trucks and he and Mollett fired bursts at an engine shed into which an engine had just gone. This was thought to be at Combourg on the Rennes - St. Malo railway.

On the way out a fishing vessel type fired rifle gun at our aircraft so it received a short burst of fire for its spiteful behaviour from Flight Lieutenant Wright.

10th November

Eight aircraft led by Squadron Leader Le Fevre acted as anti-flak squadron to eight aircraft of 183 Squadron to bomb some 'M' Class minesweepers previously reported in Lezardrieux estuary. 193 Squadron were the escort.

266 Squadron led and saw the ships straight in front. Most pilots fired at ships and then 183 Squadron came in and dropped their bombs. We obviously took the ships by surprise. 183 Squadron claim one escort vessel Cat. 111, one 'M' Class minesweeper Cat. 1V.

11th November

A fair day with good visibility. Four aircraft led by Flight Lieutenant J. D. Wright went on a Rhubarb to railway east of Granville. Beat up two locos and freight train and continued eastwards, but as cloud was down to the deck turned about and attacked the same target a second time.

Flying Officer J. H. Lucas was hit in his port LR (long range) tank that was knocked off. As he was running on this tank his engine immediately cut, not knowing the cause he jettisoned his hood and doors to bale out, but just before doing so he tried switching over to main tanks, the engine picked up and all was well. Claiming two locos damaged, one German AA gunman killed and one light AA post damaged.

Fifteen pilots did dive bombing practice off Dawlish, this is the first practice we have had doing dive-bombing.

This next section of the ORB is hand written and is quite difficult to read in places. Flight Lieutenant Collcutt, the Squadron Adjutant since March 1941, and the first of the Rhodesians, posted to 44 Squadron - the Rhodesian Bomber Squadron. In future our (unreadable here) 'Adj's' work is to be done by one of the aircraft pilots.

12th November
Sergeant E. Palte posted as pilot to the Squadron.

15th November
Sergeant Pilot E. Palte did his first flight in a Typhoon. (This next section of the ORB is again hand written and difficult to read in places.) Party in the Officers Mess as farewell to their 'Colly' Collcutt who of the officers has been longest with the squadron and was looked upon as 'The father of the Bezas'.

See 11th of November entry. It can be assumed that 'Bezas' is taken from the Squadron's motto.

16th November
Cold, but visibility good. Four aircraft loaded with bombs, this being the first occasion that bombs have been carried on an operation by the Squadron. Went to bomb Poulmic airfield, but weather over target unsuitable so bombs jettisoned and operation abandoned.

Flying Officer Sanders takes on the duties of Squadron Adjutant.

17th November

Four aircraft on early shipping recco area Lezeardrieux estuary.
When saw and attacked a small armed trawler, seeing many
strikes. A second recco to same place later saw but did not attack
the same boat in the same position.

26th November

Seven aircraft, together with seven aircraft of 193 Squadron
escorted eighteen Boston bombers from St. Catherine's Point
over Barfleur to special target south of Cherbourg and then back
to base. Considerable flak over peninsular. Did not see bombing
results as 8/10 cloud over target. No enemy aircraft.

In the afternoon eight aircraft - two returning early - with
six of 193 took part in a Ramrod making five runs east-west line
over the target area of special target at 13,000 feet, saw bombers
making run and smoke from bombs in target area. Intense
accurate heavy flak throughout. Many other friendly fighters
seen.

A patrol was done by a section from the Lizard to Bodman
Point. A cruiser type ship which was passed several times on the
patrol suddenly started firing at Flight Lieutenant J. H. Deall
otherwise there was no incident.

Pilot Officer H. C. Ballance posted as pilot to the Squadron.

27th November

No flying so the Squadron is released from duty. Pilots went into
Plymouth and to the Moorland Links Hotel in the evening for
quite a hectic party.

1st December

Eight aircraft took off from Predannack with four aircraft of
193 Squadron and one Mosquito on Roadstead to attack a motor
vessel of 4,000 tons near Groix Island. Flew out at zero feet and

when approaching Groix Island saw the large merchant ship and several armed trawlers or minesweepers.

193 Squadron as anti-flak attacked the ships but the Mosquito dropped its bombs a bit short then hit the sea itself and went in. At this moment Red Section (Squadron Leader Le Fevre, Flight Sergeant Hulley, Flying Officer Mollett and Flying Officer Blackwell) saw a Ju 52 fitted with mine detecting ring flying at 300 feet.

Flight Sergeant Hulley and Flying Officer Mollett attacked. The enemy aircraft was seen to hit the sea, claiming one Ju 52 destroyed shared by Hulley and Mollett. Red Section continued flying east around the island coming out to the south and getting a lot of flak from ships and the island.

Blue Section went to the south of the island, attacked two minesweepers, then turned about for home and were now some miles ahead of Red Section. As Blue Section approached Cap Chevre with two aircraft of 193 Squadron they saw two Ju 88s. One escaped into cloud but Pilot Officer Pressland of 193 Squadron attacked the other setting its starboard motor on fire and then Flight Lieutenant Deall and Pilot Officer Miller each fired at it from close range and sent it into the sea. Flying Officer Sanders also fired at close range and saw strikes but he is not claiming as the enemy aircraft had already had it, claiming one Ju 88 destroyed, half to Pilot Officer Pressland of 193, quarter to Flight Lieutenant Deall and a quarter to Flying Officer Miller.

As this combat was taking place Blue Section flying near Glenan Islands saw another Ju 88. Flying Officer Blackwell saw and attacked it, first pressing his attack home to very short range. The other pilots of the section saw strikes on the enemy aircraft and then Blackwell broke away. This was the last seen of Flying Officer Blackwell and it is assumed he was hit by the enemy aircraft's rear gunner.

Squadron Leader Le Fevre attacked firing until his ammo

ran out, then Flying Officer Mollett attacked followed by Flight Sergeant Hulley who also ran out of ammo. All saw strikes and then Flying Officer Mollett attacked twice more and enemy aircraft crashed into the sea, claiming one Ju 88 destroyed shared by one quarter each to Flying Officer Blackwell, Squadron Leader Le Fevre, Flight Sergeant Hulley, Flying Officer Mollett.

Red Section and Blue Section were attacking their respective Ju 88 at almost the same time. Blue Section heard Red leaders attack instructions just as they were themselves about to attack and Pilot Officer Eadie heard someone say "I am getting out", this is thought to have been from Flying Officer Blackwell, so possible he baled out and may have been rescued.

Four aircraft were about to take off again to search for him but as there were no fixes and really very little idea where he might be, there did not seem much chance and then it got too late and it had to be called off. Pilot Officer Pressland of 193 had to bale out, but was quickly rescued.

2nd December

Four aircraft flew to Ushant and Raz Point searching for Flying Officer Blackwell but saw nothing.

Seven aircraft escorted twenty-four Bostons with eight aircraft of 193 Squadron to bomb special target south of Cherbourg. Bombing looked good. Moderate flak. All returned safely.

5th December

A vile day, strong wind and freezing, visibility fair. Eight aircraft, two returning early, flew with six of 193 and eight of 257 Squadron to a point on the south coast of Brest Peninsular to meet with 240 Fortresses and together with various Spitfire Wings, escort them home. A few minutes before the R/V (rendezvous) a large unescorted formation of Liberators was seen at the same time, height 12,000 feet, as the Fortresses were going to be. These were escorted home. No Fortresses were seen.

7th December
No operational flying so the Squadron was released from duty in the afternoon. Most pilots played rugger and some went into Plymouth later.

12th December
The airfield was attacked by ground troops and mock attacks were carried out on them by two aircraft on a practice scramble. The ground personnel formed pockets of resistance round the 'drome till wiped out.

14th December
Squadron formation flying and cine gun, then flight formation and a bouncer to attack them. Twelve pilots in dispersal till 10.30 hours for night flying, but it was washed out by weather.

16th December
No flying. Afternoon spent clearing up the ground around our dispersal area. All got very wet and dirty. As it was Dingaan's Day most of the Squadron went to the London Inn at Horridge and had a wild party.

Dingaan's Day - initially the 16th December was celebrated by Afrikaners as Dingaan's dag (Dingane's Day.) This was in celebration for what Voortrekkers viewed as a 'victory' over Zulu warriors near the Ncome River in KwaZulu Natal. On that day an estimated 10,000-20,000 Zulu warriors led by Dingane's Generals Dambuza (Nzobo) and Ndlela kaSompisi attacked about 470 Voortrekkers at dawn. With the advantage of gunpowder Zulu warriors were repelled with an estimated 3,000 warriors killed. The blood of casualties flowed into Ncome River turning its water red earning it the nickname "Blood River". This earned the confrontation between Voortrekkers and Zulu regiments the name "Battle of Blood River". December 16 remained a rallying point for the development of Afrikaner nationalism, culture and identity.

Day of the Covenant. During their trek into Natal Afrikaners were led by W. J. Pretorius and S. A. Cilliers, "to enter into a covenant with God". Thus, when the Voortrekkers repelled the Zulu attack, it was viewed as a confirmation of God's ratification of that covenant. This resulted in the establishment of Day of the Covenant. For instance, in 1864 the General Synod of the Afrikaners' Natal Churches agreed that the 16th of December would henceforth be celebrated as an ecclesiastical day of thanksgiving by all its congregations. The following year the Executive Council of the South African Republic declared that the 16th of December must be a public holiday in this Boer Republic. In 1894 the Government of the Free State also declared the 16th of December to be a public holiday.

After the South African War the unification of the Cape Colony, Natal and the two Afrikaner Republics of the Transvaal and Orange Free State, an act was passed by parliament in 1910 enacting the 16th of December as a National Holiday (Dingaan's Day) throughout the Union of South Africa with effect from 1911.

In 1952 the name of the day was changed from Dingaan's Day to Day of the Vow. (Day of the Covenant.)

18th December

Eight aircraft were to make R/V with six torpedo carrying Beaufighters off Congarnmau Harbour and the Beaus were to attack the Piettro Orsealo, a 450 foot long motor vessel. On arrival the ship was seen but the Beaus were 20 minutes late. We swept over area and returned landing at Predannack via the Brest Peninsular. No enemy aircraft, no flak. We heard that the Beaus scored two torpedo hits later but boat is still afloat. The eight pilots got weather bound at Predannack and had to spend the night there, much to their annoyance as there was to have been a party at Harrowbeer.

21st December

Flight formation flying in which Flight Sergeant McElroy's engine cut out when at 3,000 feet but he brought off a successful crash landing near Tavistock.

Aircraft smashed but pilot unhurt. Cause was lack of petrol to engine, reason not yet discovered. If this is a failure on the part of the aircraft it is the first for a long time.

24th December

Fine and frosty. Eight aircraft took off from Predannack escorting six Bomphoons of 183 Squadron on Ramrod 116 to bomb Guipavas airfield. Results of bombing appeared to be very good, but no enemy aircraft seen on ground or in the air.

A large-scale party in the Officer's Mess to which ladies were invited. Dancing and much singing. A very good party.

25th December

Christmas Day and weather unfit for flying and all squadrons released from duty. Sergeants invited to Officer's Mess and then Officers served dinner in Airman's Mess. An extremely good dinner too. 'Tusky' Howarth upset a heaped plate of dinner slap on a WAAF's head.

A party in the Sergeant's Mess and then gentle parties for the rest of the day. A good time was had by all.

26th December

Weather unsuitable. Visited the Moorland Links Hotel before lunch and then continued a very amusing session in the Mess until late afternoon. Five of 'B' Flight have bad colds but they are bearing up still.

27th December

Unsuitable for flying most of the day. Squadron released in

afternoon. Nearly all pilots attended the dance at the Moorland Links when some of the better type danced.

28th December
A pilot from 193 Squadron crashed at the end of the runway. One long-range tank came off and exploded causing a large fire. His aircraft went a few yards further thus getting out of the worse of the fire, but it was burning slightly upside down with the pilot trapped in cockpit.

Corporal Hosie and LAC MacMaster got there first and somehow got the jammed door open and they pulled the pilot out not too badly hurt. A good effort on their part.

30th December
Eight aircraft took off from Predannack and flew west towards Kerlin Bastard and onto Ile de Croix when a Ju 52 with minesweeping ring was seen flying west at zero feet. Flying Officer Lucas and Flying Officer Mollett attacked and it fell flaming into the sea. The rest of the Squadron were lined up behind waiting to take their turn. Claiming one Ju 52 destroyed, shared by the two pilots.

Returning to base when Lucas had to make a wheels up landing as his hydraulics had been damaged by being hit by a piece of debris from the Ju 52. Evidently the range was really closed on this occasion. We heard later that as the Squadron had returned by the sea route we should have met several Fw 190s off Brest. A pity, but still the Ju 52 is something to be going on with.

31st December
Seven aircraft took part in a big operation as fighter sweep. Intention was to fly to Kerlin Bastard but operation was abandoned when 20 miles inland of France as the leaders radio

transmitters could neither send nor receive.

A second sweep by six aircraft to Guipavas and St. Brieuc was done and the returning Fortresses seen. No enemy aircraft, no flak.

In the evening a number of pilots went to the Moorlands Links Hotel and had an excellent evening and saw the New Year in great form.

Summary of 1943

The move to Exeter in January wasn't a popular move for the pilots, as it took them temporarily away from any action to and over occupied Europe. Flights over Europe, mainly Holland, were against rail targets and shipping.

The Typhoons were still proving to be troublesome; throttle linkages were still failing; engines were problematic and cracks were even discovered in the tail units resulting in the squadron being grounded during March.

However, everything was not all 'doom and gloom' for the Squadron. Two engagements in April and two weddings (both on the same day) to follow, one was the CO, Squadron Leader Green, to Miss Betty Bowden.

In July a new Mk of Typhoon arrived at the Squadron capable of carrying long-range tanks and bomb racks.

On the casualty side; one pilot missing in France, four pilots killed in flying accidents, two killed in action and four listed as missing in action. On the plus side, nine Fw 190s, two Ju 52s and two Ju 88s claimed as destroyed. Nine Fw 190s claimed as damaged.

1944

3rd January

Three anti-Rhubarb patrols eastwards from Bolt Head to cover
large practice landing exercise taking place at Slapton Sands.

The CO and Rogers crash-landed the Tiger Moth near Old
Sarum, neither hurt, caused by engine failure.

4th January

Beautiful day, visibility unlimited. Three anti-Rhubarb patrols
in the morning as yesterday. Four aircraft took off with four
of 193 Squadron to bomb NOball target No. A/A10A. Found
target area covered with 7/10 cloud. Our four aircraft think they
located the village of Flottemanville 500 yards south of target so
bombed just north of it. No results seen. Not very satisfactory.
Moderate flak.

'NOball', and sometimes 'Noball' or 'no ball', is the RAF code
for German V1 launching sites. Target references are given now
in place of a specific named location, which is frustrating as the
named target is missing. I have endeavored to investigate the use
of target references to discover the actual location. At the time
of writing I have not been successful. Wing Commander Baker
DFC and bar arrived to be Wing Commander Flying.

6th January

Eight aircraft detailed to attack NOball target X1/A/10B while
193 and 183 were attacking other NOball targets. Our target
was obscured by cloud so leader decided to attack target number
X1/A/10A which was visible. Dived from 7,000 feet to 3,000
feet and saw bursts in target.

Later eight more aircraft took off again to bomb X1/A/10A,
but target was not definitely recognised as this particular one,
though it was a target and craters from previous attacks seen in

it. Squadron dived from 10,000 feet to 5,000 feet but were not able to see results. No enemy aircraft, fairly heavy flak.

7th January
Eight aircraft took off with eight of 193 to bomb two NOball targets, but as they were both covered by cloud both squadrons instead attacked and bombed Maupemtus airfield. Many bursts were seen in and near southwest dispersal and two in centre of airfield. No aircraft seen however on the airfield. Intense flak.

In the afternoon eight more aircraft took over to bomb Noball target number X1/A10/B, but actually target number X1/A26B attacked from 8,000 to 4,000 feet. Several bursts seen in target area when old bomb craters seen. No flak from target but much from Cherbourg.

10 January

Air/Sea Rescue search in Channel, but cloud base was falling so the aircraft had to return after 15 minutes.

Flight Sergeant Paul and Sergeant Shepherd, McMurdon and Mitchell arrived from OTU.

13th January
No flying today. Sergeant Donne arrived from OTU.

14th January
Eight aircraft of 266 with 183 and 193 detailed to bomb target No. 11/A/6. Twelve of our aircraft flew, four being with four from 193 who were short of aircraft. Our eight followed 183 by two minutes, with 193 two minutes after us. Nearly all the bursts for all three squadrons appear well in the target. This must have caused a considerable amount of damage. No difficulty was experienced in finding the target.

Later six of our aircraft following six of 193 led by Wing Commander Baker again attacked the same target and again put their bombs well into it. Altogether the three squadrons have dropped 20 tons on this target, most appear to have hit it, a most satisfactory effect.

16th January

Wing Commander Baker led four aircraft on a small Ramrod operation. The target was a store, being four large sheds beside a railway at St. Theggonnec, four miles east of Landivisiau.

The attack was low-level using eleven-second delay action fuses in the bombs and was highly successful. At least four bursts seen slap in the target shattering parts of buildings and one burst right on two trains standing in the siding. Bombing height 150 feet, rest of trip at zero feet. No flak.

19th January

Flight Lieutenant Cook, the Squadron doctor since January 1942, is posted away. A pity as he hoped to be with us for the invasion.

A party at the Rock Hotel before lunch as farewell to him, this resulted in the Squadron being comatose all the afternoon.

21st January

Rodeo 65 with eleven aircraft which was a sweep with five aircraft from 193. Dinnard-Rennes-Gael-St. Brieuc-Lannion while 183 did the sweep in the reverse direction, we met them as we crossed the French coast. The formation flew at below 2,000 feet which was cloud base. Got some accurate flak from Rennes. Flew past Gael then turned north.

When approaching Lannion saw two Me 109s apparently commencing to land, one with its undercart down. Squadron Leader Le Fevre detailed 193 Squadron to attack one and he attacked the wheels down one. He fired just 20 rounds per cannon from 200 yards closing to 100 yards, saw a lot of strikes and the enemy aircraft flew on at an angle of 25o to the horizontal as though it were going to land but continued and hit the perimeter track and exploded. One Me 109 claimed destroyed. Nice shooting.

Flying Officer D. C. Borland, his Number 2, with his finger hovering over his firing button saw the enemy aircraft explode and realised that his services were not required and got quite a dose of flak as he flew at zero feet over the airfield.

Meanwhile Flying Officer Meyer flying with 193 Section overtaking the other enemy aircraft too fast had a squirt, but saw no results. He says he could have slowed up and had another squirt but thinking that 266 pilots were following him he broke away and Flight Lieutenant Cassey and Flying Officer Inglis of 193 between them came in attacking and the enemy aircraft exploded in the air and crashed in flames. The formation formed a defensive circle very smartly and returned to base.

23rd January

Violent storms today, but visibility fair and improving. Eight aircraft did a fighter sweep as part of Ramrod 12a. When flying east, 2 - 3 miles south of Gael airfield, one enemy aircraft seen at 3,000 feet just north of the airfield, presumably coming into the circuit. The squadron turned 180o to port and attacked.

In all six pilots had squirts at this enemy aircraft, an Fw 190, which kept turning into our attacks. From the gun camera film it has been decided to share this between Squadron Leader Le Fevre, Flight Lieutenant Deall, Flight Lieutenant Sanders and Pilot Officer Eastwood. Flight Lieutenant Wright and Flying Officer Mollett also had squirts, but had awkward angles and do not think they hit enemy aircraft. Flight Lieutenant Sanders had a good burst at rather long range, then the CO then Eastwood had a really long burst and finally Deall shot its wing off while

Sanders took a cine of it. Three enemy aircraft destroyed by this station in three days. Very lucky encounters.

New pilots flew familiarisation experience on Typhoons.

24th January

No flying, pouring with rain all day with visibility less than a mile. 'Barney' Wright, 'A' Flight Commander is to leave and become a test pilot. He joined the squadron in August 1941 at Collyweston and has been on every operational flight that he could wangle himself onto; he has bags of guts and the most charming personality. The Squadron will miss him.

News has been received that Johnny Small, identified by the number of his aircraft shot down near by, has been buried at Le Ftgoet near Legneven. Barney Wright said at the time that he saw Small bale out and his parachute open, he also said that enemy aircraft flew round the parachute. We all thought that Johnny Small had got away with it.

Several pilots attended a party at the WAAF Officer's Mess, and a very hectic party.

26th January

Air Marshall Hill visits the Station and was introduced to each pilot at dispersal and chatted with us for a while. The Squadron was released in the afternoon when several pilots went to Plymouth.

29th January

Wing Commander Baker with ten aircraft went to Beaulieu at first light with 193 Squadron. Flight Lieutenant Deall crash-landed near Hurn, cause was a petrol blockage, pilot unhurt, aircraft badly damaged.

Trip to Exeter in the evening where pilots spent the night, and twenty ground crew went in the evening from Harrowbeer by road, taking long-range tanks to service the aircraft the following morning. New pilots did local flying.

30th January

Ten aircraft including the Wing Commander took off from Beaulieu to sweep Paris area, but on reaching the Needles they were recalled as fifty enemy aircraft were reported operating and our formation was considered too small, landing back at base.

A telephone call to the Officer's Mess in the evening announced that 'Blackie' Blackwell (Pilot Officer Blackwell) was speaking from London. He has just arrived back in England after being shot down south of Brest on December 1st. This is a terrific show.

1st February

We have just heard that Mrs. Vernon Sanders had a baby girl on January 25th, thus Vernon wins the maternity stakes. (The wife of Flying Officer A. V. Sanders.)

4th February

Pilot Officer Blackwell arrived back with squadron and told us of his really remarkable experiences when he baled out south of Brest.

6th February

The Wing CO and one other aircraft were on a weather recco, then eight aircraft with 250lb bombs followed eight of 193 anti-flak aircraft in an attack on an 'M' Class minesweeper. 193 plastered the boat with cannon fire then we bombed, and it is thought that one direct hit was obtained and two near misses.

The boat was covered in smoke during attack. Considerable light flak from the boat. Squadron Leader Le Fevre said he was hit and was seen to bale out about three miles out to sea. He had insufficient height and his chute did not fully open. He was seen motionless in the water. We're afraid there is not very much hope that he can have got away with it.

He has been a damn good CO to this Squadron, keen as mustard and a really experienced leader in the air. His incredible slang and expressions have come into general use in the Squadron. As can be seen from this book (the ORB) he flew on practically every offensive operation in which the Squadron was engaged since the day he arrived. Four aircraft went out and searched for any signs but saw nothing.

9th February

A sweep with 193 Squadron near Isigny. One aircraft was seen and Pilot Office Erasmus being nearest turned and attacked. The enemy aircraft was either a Me 109 or a captured Mustang, anyway, it had large black crosses on it and Erasmus sent it crashing in flames after a short burst.

Continuing the sweep when west of Dreux a Dornier 24 flying boat was seen and Flying Officer Lucas and his cousin attacked and saw it crash in flames. Two enemy aircraft destroyed, only three of our aircraft on the do!

Our new CO Squadron Leader J. Holmes DFC arrived. All who know him like him, and we are very pleased to have him as our CO. May he lead us to success.

10th February

Five aircraft with two of 193 and Wing Commander Baker to carry out a sweep east of Port on Bressin and to go 10 - 15 miles north-east of Paris. Crossing the French coast at 8,000 feet and then, down to the deck, swept east. Two aircraft flown by Pilot Officer Baillie and Flying Officer Ballance returned to base with engine trouble.

The formation swept south and attacked Etampes Mondesir

airfield. Flight Lieutenant Deall attacked first and set on fire a Ju 88 with the help of a pilot from 193. Flying Officer McGibbon set an He 111 on fire. After this little do the formation reformed and steered east still at zero feet. The Wing Leader then detailed aircraft to attack Brestigny airfield. Only one enemy aircraft was seen on this airfield - a Do 217 which had belly-landed and had men working on it. Flight Lieutenant Deall attacked and destroyed it, probably doing the working party a little no good. The Wing Commander and his Number 2 during this attack became separated, as Flight Lieutenant Deall reformed his section and proceeded independently.

Steering northeast he then saw a Ju 88 flying east at 1,000 feet. He destroyed it without help from the rest of the section. Then seven training aircraft similar to our Harvard were sighted all attempting to land at an airfield. Pilot Officer McGibbon waded in and shot three down in flames with a minimum of ammunition expenditure. Pilot Officer Haworth damaged another as it was landing. Flight Lieutenant Deall again reformed his section and brought them safely back through very bad weather landing at Tangmere.

Meanwhile Wing Commander Baker and his Number 2 struck very bad weather and became separated from each other. To round off this memorable day the Wing Commander (flying a 266 aircraft) just saw and destroyed a Do 217 and then destroyed a Fw 190 both flying round about Paris.

The total for the Squadron this day is thus eight and a half destroyed and two aircraft damaged, or for the station 10 aircraft destroyed and four damaged.

Our old CO Wing Commander Charles Green visited us for two or three hours, unfortunately he left before we knew what a day we had had.

13th February
Another baby for the Squadron! Mrs. Bob Menelaws comes second in the maternity stakes with a baby boy born on the 12th of February. (The wife of Pilot Officer R. Menelaws.)

14th February
Heavy rain all day. 193 Squadron are leaving. This seems strange when we have just got a Wing Leader and have done very well in the short time he had led us.

A party in the Officer's Mess to celebrate the Paris show and as farewell to 193 Squadron.

15th February
A rush to briefing for an operation to intercept some Ju 88s which had attacked a Sunderland in the Bay and which we hoped would be landing back at Merlin Bastard or Poulric airfields. Nine aircraft were to take part but the Wingco could not get his engine started and took off four minutes after the others and could not catch up due to the poor visibility, Flying Officer Lucas thus led. Land fall was made about 8 miles east of track and although original plan was to climb rapidly to 8,000 feet for crossing the coast, as cloud base was 1,500 feet, the formation crossed in at zero feet and by a piece of rotten luck suddenly found themselves crossing slap over Morlaix airfield. The flak must have been warned, as it opened up instantaneously with appalling results.

Denis Miller's aircraft became a sheet of flame and crashed. Drummond was also on fire and last seen heading for the deck. Mollet's aircraft was hit, he climbed, said he was hit and wished the lads cheerio. Lucas had a big hole in his rudder. The remaining five avoided by getting right down on the deck and both Eastwood and Holmes hit trees with their leading edges but without damage. The formation flew down to Merlin Bastard and then back home without seeing any Ju 88s. A disastrous day. Mollet should be alright, but there is practically no hope for the other two.

16th February
Flying Officer Norman Lucas posted to 59 OTU for rest. Norman has been with us since Kingscliffe days, a quiet, efficient pilot who always managed to bring his aircraft home despite having it badly shot up on several occasions. A most popular member of the Squadron and one who has steadily done his job and done it very well indeed. Saw combat films from the 10th. They are excellent.

19th February
Mention today of new pilots under going training but no names given.

20th February
Very cold, windy and 8/10 cloud. 193 Squadron at last managed to take off, leaving the base. Good old 266 now at standby all day.

22nd February
263 Squadron arrived, were briefed and took off here for a sweep. It was abandoned early and on the way home near Guernsey Squadron Leader Warns DFC, ditched, and his Number 2 seeing him in difficulties in the water baled out to help him. This is surely the most amazing effort.

Six aircraft to search area at Guernsey for Squadron Leader Warns and his Number 2 and another pilot of 263 who was also reported to be in the drink. Saw nothing.

27th February

Poor weather had curtailed any operational flying for several days now. We hear that Wing Commander Baker is posted. Saw 266 Squadron film in the evening.

28th February

Formation flying by new pilots. In the evening we were amazed to hear Mollets voice on the telephone. He is back in England 13 days after being shot down - see Feb 15th. What a show!

2nd March

Flight Lieutenant Healy led five aircraft from Beaulieu to sweep Verneuil-Dreux-Bretigny airfields. It was intended only to fly four aircraft, but at the very last moment we were told to take five.

Formation climbed to cross the French coast at Cadbourg then dived and flew the rest of the way at zero feet, and this was really low. At Ramouillet Flying Officer Erasmus in avoiding another one of the section struck a tree and severely damaged his wing and radiator cowling. His temperature rose and so the formation about turned for base and could only fly at 230 ASI.

Before crossing out formation attempted to climb to clouds but Erasmus was unable to do this, formation went down to zero feet again and then about 15 miles inland of French coast Flight Lieutenant Healy said that he had also hit a tree and doubted if he would be able to get back.

Formation suddenly flew towards a town - Gabourg - so broke Hulley and Bailey to the left, Sanders, Erasmus and Healy joining out to the right and so crossing the coast separated. Almost immediately Flight Lieutenant Healy said that "he must get out", he got a good fix and sent out the Air/Sea Rescue boys. Flight Lieutenant Sanders at once orbited and transmitted for a fix, but could see no sign of Healy. This was four - five miles west of Havre.

Erasmus still with high temperatures made straight for home. Sanders orbited for eight minutes then set course for home about six minutes later heard May Days given in a sing song voice, this was also heard by Hulley and Baillie. If it was Healy then he had evidently kept flying quite long after his original message. Air/ Sea Rescue was laid on but nothing seen. Flight Lieutenant Healy is missing. Flight Lieutenant Sanders managed to get back to Friston and brought off a successful landing. Sanders landed and the other two also at Friston.

5th March
Flying Officers D. Borland, Howarth and McGibbon posted to OTU. This seems to leave us very short of operational pilots.

6th March
Twelve aircraft and servicing party are to move at first light to Bolt Head tomorrow.

7th March
Fine and clear. Eight aircraft flew at first light to Bolt Head, seven more following later as they become serviceable or had their rocket firing rails removed.

Flights to Bolt Head. Road party of fifty-five arrived at Bolt Head and started to get dug in. Weather is marvellous, though cold, and the men are content. All available pilots are here, seventeen. We are here in a defensive role while various large transports and landing craft pass on their way to an exercise taking place on Slapton Sands. If the Hun reacts we will be scrambled to shoot them down. Here's hoping.

On 27 April the Germans did indeed attack a practice D-Day landing. Using high-powered launches - E boats - they attacked the American troops on various landing craft killing several hundred.

9th March

Beautiful day, but haze all a.m. Flight Lieutenant Deall, Flying Officer Eadie and Flying Officer Ballance arrived from leave and sick leave, thus helping the Squadron strength.

Signal received that Flying Officer Peter Blackwell has been awarded the DFC for his escaping from the enemy. Good old 'Blackie'.

10th March

Party at the local for 'Blackie's' DFC. Everybody played rag football and had more fresh air and exercises than usual.

11th March

One scramble to lead home a Dakota, and one on which there were Huns, but they were below cloud and we were above, so we did not see them, and two convoy patrols without incident. This brings our stay at Bolt Head to an end. As regards Huns it has been disappointing, but everybody has enjoyed themselves.

Flight Lieutenant Allen DFC arrived to be 'A' Flight Commander when Flight Lieutenant Deall leaves. Flight Lieutenant Deall has been with the squadron since Colley Weston days. He has a score of destroyed and is one of the Old Guard. A hell of a nice bloke, he deserves his rest, but we all hope that he will be back again in the squadron at some future date.

12th March

Whole Squadron moved back to Harrowbeer in the afternoon to hear that we are to go up to Acklington for a gunnery course for about 10 days and shall then move to Thorney Island to an airfield in 20 Wing.

Flying Officer Lucas and Flight Lieutenant Deall have been awarded the DFC. They both thoroughly deserve it, having been on a great number of hops, and this will sweeten the pill of their leaving the Squadron for rest.

13th March
We were supposed to go to Acklington but just before take off it was cancelled. No flying. A large and noisy party in the Mess.

15th March
Seventeen aircraft took off in two flights and flew to Acklington via Hutton Crenswick. Squadron Leader Holmes had already arrived at Acklington having completed his course at Millfield. During the move to Bolt Head and back and to Acklington Flight Lieutenant Sanders has acted as CO, Flight Commander, and Adjutant and deserves great credit for having successfully coped with the work.

Flying Officer Tidmarsh posted to airfield for duties with 266 Squadron. Flying Officer Borland will in future keep this diary.

20th March
Gunnery and bombing sorties, but South Range closed by police owing to landmine exploding and killing two children.

Flying Officer Doug Borland, Howarth and McGibbon flew across from Annan to look us up. Flying Officer Borland and Howarth stayed two days. We were all very pleased to see them again and much beer was drunk.

21st March
Section and individual training attacks on lorries and tanks in the morning. The afternoon was free. Everyone preparing to leave for Tangmere. Our training complete we said cheerio to 3043

Echelon who have serviced us so very well since the Duxford days.

22nd March
The Squadron left Acklington in two flights each of nine aircraft led by Flight Lieutenant Sanders, the CO having left the day before bound for the Palace to receive the DFC. The Squadron flew direct to Tangmere through some rotten weather, arriving there one and a half hours later. This brought 266 Squadron into 146 Airfield, 20 Wing TAF. (Tactical Air Force.) The afternoon was spent getting straightened out.

24th March
Weather good, slight ground haze. Six of 266 plus Wing Commander Baker bombed Noball targets south east of Crecy Wood.

26th March
Eight aircraft bombed Noball targets in Abbeville areas. An aircraft of 257 Squadron was damaged by flak and was escorted home by 266.

31st March
Wing Commander Charles Green and Flight Lieutenant Barney Wright paid us a visit. We hear Barney is engaged to a girl in the Senior Service (Royal Navy), what!

3rd April
The whole Squadron moved under canvas in the morning, from this day the Squadron personnel ceased to have any glamour.

6th April
Six aircraft led by Wing Commander Baker went on a Ranger.

Rennes - Gael in the afternoon. On approaching Rennes a Ju 88 was sighted by the starboard section, this section Flying Officer Eastwood and Flight Sergeant Hulley attacked and made short work of the Hun who was making a wide circuit of Rennes aerodrome. The Ju 88 was last seen heading for the ground in a mass of flames.

Considerable light flak came up from Rennes, no one being hit. No further aircraft sighted and the formation landed at base having opened the score sheet for 146 Airfield. (Tangmere.)

9th April

Weather clamped in the a.m. clearing p.m. Ten aircraft took off at 19.00 hours on a Military train recce. Sergeant Shepherd forced landed in France owing to engine trouble.

Non-operational flying. Four aircraft took off for practice formation, the weather clamped down, visibility 200 yards. One aircraft landed at Ford, two after great difficulty landed at base. Flight Sergeant Harrold after an excellent attempt to get in, considering his lack of experience, overshot and took half an armoury building with him. He was uninjured.

10th April

The Squadron moved with the Wing to Needs Oar Point, our airfield and Base until the second front opens, we look forward to our next move -France!!

16th April

Everyone went to Lymington this evening to have a bath and beer. There are no bathing facilities here and no beer, poor show indeed. BO is prevalent! (Body odour!)

18th April

Flight Lieutenant Sanders and Flight Sergeant Dodd detailed

for Exercise Smash could not locate their target and returned to base, during this time several aircraft were vectored onto a Hun in the vicinity. Flight Lieutenant Sanders and Flight Sergeant Dodd on entering the circuit at base, and not knowing an enemy aircraft had been reported in the vicinity, saw flak concentration on a particular spot and proceeded to investigate and found a Ju 188 stooging around at 200 feet. Sanders with ball ammo and Dodd with war load attacked, despite the enemy aircraft firing two reds. The Ju 188 soon crashed in flames about 3 miles from base.

On investigating the crash it was found the aircraft carried a crew of seven and must have lost its way in bad weather. Flight Lieutenant Sanders and Flight Sergeant Dodd thus destroyed the first Hun on English soil for 266.

21st April

Eight aircraft went to Thorny Island to give a show from there, this did not come off. While at Thorny Island, Dwight D. Eisenhower paid this station a visit. He met the pilots and had an informal chat with them.

24th April

Fine weather. Eight aircraft bombed the marshalling yards at Amiens amidst both light and heavy flak. The target area was well and truly pranged. Bomber Command efforts were clearly visible, the place being a mass of craters.

25th April

Lovely day. Eight aircraft paid Baupte Bridge a return visit; the bombing was a lot better. One direct hit was claimed and some near misses.

27th April

The Squadron moved to Snaith, Yorkshire, for week to britch (brush) up smoke laying. Our CO who comes from the district was able to lay on some wizard sorties after a day's work. The Black Swan at Holsmanton was the favourite, never have we tasted such fine beer as Tetleys. Mrs. Holmes and Mrs. Armitage really showed us what Yorkshire hospitality can be like, they kept open house for us.

28th April

Fine day. Exercise Kate (smoke screening) in conjunction with the Army carried out successfully. Exercise Tetley in the evening!

30 April

Typhoons affiliated with Halifaxes to give them practice evasion. Exercise Tetley in the afternoon. By the way, since being at Sneath we have been living like normal people, sleep in beds, have a tin roof over our heads and a bath everyday.

Ist May

Industrial haze in the a.m. Exercise Kate carried out and local practice flying. Flight Lieutenant Deall and Flying Officer Burland paid us a visit from Great Orton where they are on rest. Flight Lieutenant Collcutt and Flying Officer Lucas also arrived. It was great seeing the 'old boys' again, they were persuaded to stay the night which was spent at the Black Swan in Normanton, much beer flowed and finally wound up at the COs home.

6th May

A fine day. The Squadron left Snaith and returned to Needs Oar Point. Flight Lieutenant Nesbitt of Salisbury ex 237 Squadron joined us.

7th May

Another fine day. Eleven aircraft from 266 together with 197, 257 and 193 Squadrons went to Manston to bomb Arras; operation was abortive with cloud over target area. The operation was successful later in the day and fair bombing results were observed.

9th May

Eight aircraft in the morning to bomb what was supposed to have been an ammo dump, the bombing was excellent but unfortunately the dump wasn't there. Flying Officer Baillie had engine trouble over the target area and was last seen heading inland having called up saying he was going to bale out. He has an excellent chance of being safe.

In the afternoon eight of our aircraft plus 193, 197 and 257 Squadrons bombed the marshalling yards at Rouen. The results were excellent. Sergeant McMurdon was possibly hit by light flak and headed south at 6,000 feet with glycol streaming from his engine. Two in a day! A bit much.

10th May

Cloudless day and very fine. Eight aircraft went to Tangmere in the morning and from there bombed a No ball target with good results.

In the afternoon eight aircraft of 266 together with 193 and 197 Squadrons bombed a bridge on the Seine near Rouen; one direct hit and several near misses were scored, a convoy of barges passing under the bridge also took a pasting.

Flying Officer Cunnison joined us. He has had a very hectic time in the ME (Middle East), shot down three times. He walked back to his unit once, returned by camel, and once by Air/Sea Rescue.

11th May

Fine weather. Eight aircraft of 266 plus 193 Squadron operated from Manston. Bombing the marshalling yards at Cambrai, the bombing was excellent, trains and buildings became airborne.

In the afternoon eight aircraft with 193 Squadron took off from Thorney Island and bombed a radar station at Le Touquet, two bursts were seen near the apparatus, close enough to cause severe damage.

12th May

Another fine day. Twelve aircraft plus 193 Squadron operated from base to bomb a bridge near Lilliers, both the bridge and a train received direct hits. The formation landed back at Tangmere.

In the afternoon eight aircraft together with 193 Squadron attacked a radar station near Cherbourg, bombs were seen to land in the target area and the results considered excellent though hard to access through bomb smoke in the area.

13th May

Weather very good. Eleven aircraft, one as spare, and four aircraft of 193 Squadron attacked a motor transport in a wood near Rouen, bursts were seen in the area. The formation dived low and flew through light flak to use their cannon fire.

14th May

Squadron Leader Holmes and Wing Commander Baker plus thirty other aircraft attacked a radar station at Caen. The bombing was good, two direct hits obtained.

18th May

Fine day but no ops. Sir Godfrey Huggins, Prime Minister for Southern Rhodesia paid the Squadron a visit and presented us with a new aircraft bought with funds collected by the Matabele tribe. He spent an enjoyable morning with us and listened to several grouses. The Squadron put a formation of eight aircraft to fly past.

19th May

266 took off at 10-minute intervals with 257 and 197 Squadrons on a No ball operation in the Cherbourg area. The target was bombed but most of the bombs overshot. Target was difficult to identify owing to excellent camouflage which blended perfectly with the ground. Flak light and heavy was intense and accurate. When returning, Flight Sergeant A. O. Holland was seen to lag and when 40 miles from English coast was loosing height and apparently tried to ditch but dropped a wing at 50 feet, and crashed into the sea, and burst into flames. The position was orbited but nothing seen.

20th May

The Squadron was operating from Tangmere. The No ball target in the Maison/Pontieu area was located and dive-bombed. Several bursts seen among the buildings - eight bombs overshot the target. There was poor light flak in area and visibility was poor.

25th May

266, 193, 197 and 257 Squadrons led by Wing Commander Baker attacked railway marshalling yard concentrations at Armetiers which contained at least 200 wagons. Results were good, all bombs in target area. Also attacked Hazebrook railway yard with good results. No flak at Armetiers and light and medium flak at Hazebrook.

27th May
Attacked radar station at Predefin. Took off with aircraft of 197 Squadron and dive-bombed from 2,000 feet. One probable hit on Eastern Warzburg (German radar) and two near misses. Remainder of bombs on buildings and many cannon strikes seen.

28th May
The intended target was a road and rail junction west of Yvetat but the squadron made the wrong landfall and could not locate target. Opportunity target attacked near Etretat, railway/road intersection. One hit was observed on rail track west of intersection and the remainder fell in fields.

Took off in the afternoon with four aircraft of 257 Squadron from Manston. Could not locate No ball target so finally attacked rail sidings at Wallon-Chappel. Three bomb hits observed on sidings and two on adjacent railway buildings.

2nd June
The target today was a radar station at Cap d'Antifier. The target was dived bombed from 8,000/1,000 feet. All aircraft strafed target with cannon during dive. General results were hard to access owing to large number volumes of smoke and dust covering area.

Two English lads joined us today, Flight Sergeants Morgan and Bell.

3rd June
Clamp (low cloud) all morning, clearing midday. Operational flying with 257 Squadron carried out, the target another radar installation at Cap Grie-Nez. The target was dive-bombed from 8,000/2,000 feet, bursts being observed between radar masts and a light AA post. There were many bursts amongst buildings round the North Freya, two bombs straddled the Southern Freya.

Boys all awaiting D-Day with eagerness. (The first reference to the Normandy invasion of Europe landings that took place on the 6th of June.)

5th June

A day full of operational sorties and surprises for the boys, briefed for the big event we have all been waiting for.

Targets today were radar stations at Fecamp and Vandric Urt. Both targets were dive-bombed and strafed. Sergeant Ted Donne baled out and landed safely in 'No Man's Land' (France.)

6th June - D-Day

D-Day everybody tense, boys over the beaches when first landings were made, a wonderful sight.

The target was a rocket gun post near Bayeux. Nothing was seen at the target except bomb craters. Several flashes similar to a rocket gun seen at position. Target bombed from 1,500/100 feet and strafed with cannon. Bombs were well concentrated in target area and a building hit. There was medium light flak from the Bayeux area. Sergeant Mitchell crash landed on the beachhead.

No activity during the afternoon. In the evening an armed recco near Caen was carried out. Military transports were seen and bombed, strafed - three being left in flames. Some armoured cars were then attacked and two damaged. Bombs cratered the road. Sergeant Dunne successfully baled out five miles northwest of Caen.

Later in the evening another armed recco near Caen. The squadron split into two sections. One section attacked two motor transports and destroyed four motor transports that were parked. Stationary armoured cars were strafed and bombed - three parked together were observed by smoke. 150mm gun attacked and many strikes observed. The other half of the squadron destroyed two full open troop carriers and one empty. Troops were de-busing at the time.

7th June
A fine day, our aircraft on operational sorties all day, change from dive-bombing to armed recco, boys are happy strafing.

An armed recco near Lisieux. Four aircraft taking part swept the area Pont Eveque - Lisieux and saw nothing. Another four attacked a light armoured car and six motor transports on the Moult - Vimont road. There was a near miss on the motor transport and many strikes on the armoured car. One of the crew was killed. When returning to base Flight Sergeant Mitchell crash-landed near St. Aubin as his petrol tanks were punctured. Hugh Ballance baled out successfully into the drink, picked up by boat 40 minutes after event happening.

In the afternoon a section of four aircraft were diverted by the control ship to attack tanks S. W. of Bayeux. One was left in flames near Balleroy - three were bombed and seen to burst into flames that rose 100 feet. They were claimed as destroyed.

Early evening and an armed recco in the Lisieux area at 3,000 feet, but could not find a target. There was very thick haze over the whole area. Road and rail junctions were bombed with fair results.

8th June
Another glorious day, boys went swimming. Operational flying, and stooge flying for the new boys.

Dive-bombing and strafing at Fligny area. The majority of the bombs fell in the target area. The remainder fell south of the river in the centre of a village and blocked the main road. A fire and much smoke was observed in the target area.

In the afternoon an armed recco south of Caen. On crossing the French coast Baldwin (Air Controller) instructed section to go to Longues to attack a battery. Went there and saw nothing so challenged Baldwin. Correct answer received 10 minutes later. In Villiers area saw motor transports widely dispersed on roads. Attacked with bombs and cannon. Got two flamers (set on fire) and strikes on others. In a nearby wood one flamer and another damaged. Intense light flak from wood. Flying Officer Ballance baled out 40 miles north of Caen and was seen in dinghy.

Early evening, five aircraft went on an armed recco to the south of Caen with four aircraft of 193 Squadron. Three of ours turned back, two with engine trouble and one with finger trouble. Area was searched but no motor transport was seen so a radar station was bombed - two direct hits. Railway line cratered.

Boys went out on 'Night Ops' at the Mayflower.

10th June

After yesterdays bad weather it was clear again. Operational and stooge flying. Ted Dunne arrived back from France intact with a German rifle and helmet. Flight Lieutenant Sanders spoke on behalf of the Squadron and 'Chimbo' Hulley gave his impression of D-Day over the air on the B.B.C.

Late evening and eight aircraft on an armed recco to the Falaise area. Attacked Air/Sea Rescue with three flamers and two damaged. A direct hit with a bomb on SP guns (self propelled) and a direct hit on a tank that left it overturned.

11th June

Boys all fighting to get all the operational trips, but no ops owing to bad weather.

12th June

Military transports were attacked today in the Argentau - Caen area with bombs and canon. Two near misses with bombs, but many canon strikes seen and one vehicle left in flames. Flight Lieutenant Nesbitt was seen to crash in flames. Lost Paddy Nesbitt today, no hope. Put the boys back a little, usual odd operational sorties.

Late afternoon and an armed recco south of Caen. The squadron split into two sections over the target to provide cover for each other. Many single motor transport targets were attacked with excellent results. Petrol bowsers, ammo truck and an eight-wheeled lorry left in flames.

Two Me 109s sighted, chased, but lost them when they dived to deck level. Bombs were dropped on a road, but the results were not seen.

13th June

Army close support north east of Caen. The target was dive-bombed from 3,000 - 1,500 feet with 90% of bombs in target area. Target well strafed with canon. A farmhouse was left in flames and the area showed evidence of previous heavy bombing.

Another close support operation at Tilly-Au-Seul. The target briefed was not attacked as no red smoke was seen. (Red smoke is used by the Army unit requesting the strike to clearly identify the target. If none seen the attack is aborted.) Rocket projectile Typhoon squadrons were seen to go into La Lenaudiere area so squadron followed up their attack. All bombs except two were seen to drop in target area. Sergeant Mitchell landed on a strip as he was short of petrol.

In the evening an armed recco in the Caen area. Attacked tanks on road. Two direct hits and near misses on four. Many cannon strikes on motor transport and personnel.

Boys making good use of the strips in France. Flying Officer E. T. Cunnison down today but OK.

14th June

Operational and stooge flying. Close support operation at Couerville with 193 Squadron. Bombs were seen to burst in outskirts of village and in the main street. The target was well strafed with cannon during dive. Many explosions were thought to be land mines.

Early evening Wing operation to Fontenay - le - Pesnel. The target was dive-bombed from 6,000 - 1,500 feet and all bombs were seen to burst in target area. Number of buildings received direct hits and one large explosion observed in target area. Intense light and heavy flak was experienced.

Boys entertained by nurses and Wrens in the Mess, fair show.

15th June

Flying Officer Erasmus posted away on rest, loathe to leave us. Two of the new boys Flight Sergeants Love and Wheeler on their first ops today.

16th June

CO returned from leave today. The Wing lost a good man in Wing Commander Baker "lost in France." There are no details recorded here other than that Wing Commander Baker led the Squadron with 193 and 257 to an unspecified target.

Dive bombing a strategic bridge in the early evening. A canal bridge north of Caen was bombed and all bombs dropped in the target area. Three very near in water and two direct hits on eastern approach road. Bridge appeared undamaged after attack. Squadron Leader Holmes awarded the Air Force Cross.

17th June

Armed recco south of Caen. Took off with 257 Squadron, but separated from them at Vire and split into two sections of four aircraft. As no satisfactory targets were seen the one section bombed a rail bridge at Virserx and another section a road junction and bridge.

20th June

In the morning a bridge and No ball targets near St. Omer were attacked, the squadron being led by Wing Commander Baldwin. Owing to low cloud the target was difficult to find and the results of the bombing not seen. A similar target in the Bavior area was attacked in the afternoon. Target not located so bombs dropped on new excavations on the edge of a dummy aerodrome.

Late evening the target was a railway embankment. There were two direct hits on the embankment, two amongst 15/20 trucks in a small siding at the southern end of the target. The remainder fell on the western side of the embankment. The trucks were strafed with cannon fire in the dive.

22nd June

Armed recco to the Bernay area. Attacked small isolated targets. Two HDT (High Definition Targets?) probably destroyed. Two large Met (or MET - Motorised Enemy Transport) bombed but results not seen. A large motor transport, thought to be a fire engine probably destroyed.

23rd June

A very early morning armed recco to the Bernay area. Sundry targets attacked. Dive-bombed from 6,000/2,000 feet on one AMC (Armoured Military Convoy) and one motorised enemy transport. Near misses and damage by cannon fire. Two staff cars were left in flames and one large motor transport left smoking.

24th June

Wing Commander Baldwin led the Squadron. The first section did not locate target so bombed railway lines east of target.

Second section bombed tunnel, one bomb seen to burst inside tunnel and one on the track.

An armed recco in the early evening to the Lisieux area. Attacked tanks in village. Four tanks badly damaged. A convoy of Met and tanks on road with bombs and cannon. Four flamers.

27th June
Took off with 193, 197 and 257 Squadrons to dive-bomb Army Headquarters. Half of the main building was destroyed and all the outbuildings entirely razed.

28th June
Squadron packing up for move to Eastchurch for conversion to rocket projectile Tiffy's. (Rocket projectile Typhoons.)

29th June
Leaving Need Oar Point. Formation flying, saying farewell to the airfield.

30th June
At Eastchurch. Weather clamp. Boys have Squadron party in the village; everybody nice - thank you, a nice break from living in luxury, but all would like to be back on the job.

lst July
Squadron on rocket projectile course at Eastchurch. Doug and Tasky (unfortunately no surnames given) have come back to the squadron, GOOD THING.

2nd July
Weather clamped. Squadron party at the Harps, a good start for the course.

4th July
Rocket projectile practice during the day, another party at the Harps. Boys enjoying 48 hours off.

5th July
General flying practice. One unfortunate prang to aircraft. (No further information given.)

10th July
Dagwood Eastwood and Scott Eadie posted to GSU. (Ground Servicing Unit?) A loss to the Squadron. General flying.

11th July
Squadron Leader Holmes to leave us, replaced by Squadron Leader Barney Wright, one of the old boys.

12th / 13th July
A move to Hearn to join 136 Airfield. Squadron farewell dance at Eastchurch, enjoyed by all.
The Appendices for the period 1st of July through to the 14th of July are not recorded. There is however a comment in the Appendices prior to the 15th of July simply stating "Eastchurch. 1st July 1944 to 14th July 1944 at RAF Eastchurch. Carried out rocket projectile training."

17th July
A move to France, great day for all.

18th July
Squadron now operating from B8. Armed recco to St. Pierre Dives. Horse drawn vehicles and two motor transports damaged and destroyed. Later in the day - Pranged convoy of six vehicles - damaged. Later Pilot Officer Forrester destroyed a tank.

19th July

During an evening armed recco the Squadron was bounced by twenty-five Me 109s north of Lisieux. Dogfight ensued. Pilot Officer Forrester destroyed one. Three pilots missing from this operation, Pilot Officer Meyer, Flight Sergeant Harrold and Flight Sergeant McElroy.

22nd July

Bad weather prevented any activity, although the airfield was bombed by Jerry every night.

24th July

The Squadron led by Squadron Leader Wright took off at 19.45 to attack motor transports in an orchard T825605. Target located on time, no red smoke and no attack made.

25th July

An early morning Army support operation led by Squadron Leader Wright. Located target area but no guns seen. First section attacked orchard near River Orne. Light flak. Section Two attacked target area. Results not seen owing to thick haze. All rockets in respective area however.

Later in the morning another Army support operation west of Thury Harcourt. A rocket projectile attack on twenty motor transports four miles west of Thury Hardcourt in a wood. All rockets fired into wood. Slight dark brown smoke from wood afterwards. Flight Lieutenant Bob Allen's Typhoon went straight in at T887486. Fate of pilot not known, he may have baled out in time.

26th July

In the afternoon an armed recco with 257 Squadron north of River Seine area, 257 acting as cover throughout. Attacks made on motor transports at Flamanville. Twenty trucks, one direct hit, many damaged. Railway line, Les Fouches, several trucks damaged. Railway line Pavilly. Rocket projectile attack on trucks two direct hits. Light flak.

Early evening and the Squadron was briefed to attack a stronghold three miles south of Bourguebus. No red smoke seen, and no attack carried out. Moderate heavy flak on target area.

The first indication in the ORB that the Squadron has moved to airfield B3 at St. Croix in France as part of the 146th Wing.

27th July
Poor weather. Army support in the morning near Raqancourt to attack tanks and guns. Six tanks destroyed. The target was attacked again in the afternoon. Fires seen. Slight heavy flak from south of target area.

28th July
Armed recco with four aircraft from 257 Squadron to Vire - Domfront - Alencon. This operation abortive due to weather. Lost Pilot Officer I. H. Forrester, engine failure, crashed into building. A good man gone.

Flying Officer Ken Rogers back with squadron. 'Blackie' (Flight Lieutenant S. J. Blackwell) takes 'B' Flight. Vernon back on rest. Don McGibbon takes 'A' Flight.

29th July
Doug Shepherd rejoins us. Vernon and Rastus visit us again. (No further details of which these two pilots are.)
30 July
Close Army support west of Villier Bocage in the afternoon. Attack made on mortars in wood west of Villier Bocage. Area well pranged. Dive became too steep so remainder attacked wood 860584; all bursts in target area.

Two hours later the target was attacked again. Four aircraft attacked with rockets. 24 rockets seen to hit target area. Eight rockets overshot and hit pinpoint 852590 producing black smoke. No flak.

In the evening an armed recco to Thury - Aunay. Motor transport and tanks parked on road Cauville - Valles. One tank, one Staff car, two motor transports attacked. Results not definitely seen, a further tank attacked, but dust obliterated target.

31st July

Really lovely day. Bags of flying and sunbathing. Boys enjoying life in France. Armed recco with four aircraft from 193 Squadron as escort to Aunay - Vire - Essay. Three motor transports attacked on Conde behind goods shed. Direct hits on two sheds. Results on motor transports not seen. Accurate heavy flak Thury.

In the afternoon another armed recco to Falaise - Argentaun - Domfront - Vire. Four ambulances seen, not attacked, no other transport. 10 railway waggons attacked near Damblainville. One flamer. Railway waggons attacked near Briouze, five damaged. No flak.

Early evening and an attack on strongpoints near Tilly La Campagne consisting of MDV (Men Deployed with Vehicles possibly) and tanks in houses and MDV and tanks dug in. No red smoke seen, no attack made, very disappointing.

1st August

Four aircraft attacking from 8,000 to 2,000 feet on AOP (Army Observation Post) 076525. Results difficult to observe owing to dust and smoke. Two salvos hit base of wall, one salvo 10 yards short. Building still standing. Flak moderate to light.

Shortly afterwards eight aircraft on an armed recco to Virg - Mortain - Domfront - Conde with four aircraft of 193 Squadron as escort. One motor transport at 8415 attacked by three aircraft using total rockets. Claimed damaged. One stationary tank attacked by five aircraft, no claim. Many ambulances moving south Flers - Domfront and east Mortain - Domfront.

Two of 266 Squadron landed at an American airfield. They claimed Volkswagen damaged at T8716. One tank smoker at 9704.

2nd August

Boys are all flak happy. Armed recco to Flers - Domfront - Argentan - Falaise areas in the afternoon. Claims as follows: one tank flamer at T7004, one Staff car destroyed by a direct hit at T8415. One six wheeled troop transport lorry destroyed by direct hit at Q3025 and four motor transports also damaged.

Early evening and another armed recco to area north of a line Falaise - Flers with three aircraft of 257 Squadron as escort. Very little movement seen. One AFV (Armoured Fighting Vehicle) attacked, flamer. Intense heavy and light flak from Theisy, Hareort and Bretteville.

An hour later and eight aircraft were briefed to attack tank concentrations at 8639 and 916357. Circled each target but NMS (possibly No Military Seen) so carried out armed recce Conde area and south.

Three aircraft attacked one motor transport, flamer at target 945337. One motor transport strafed, cannon strikes seen, claim damaged at 9734. 10 tanks seen stationary 880460 to 880470. Six or eight motor transports and one tank seen at 870458 to 880460. 16 rockets fired. Intense light and medium flak.

3rd August

An early morning armed recco by eight aircraft to the Falaise area. Four motor transport attacked and destroyed after several attacks at U0432. One tank flamer at 9320. One six wheeled motor transport destroyed at 0333. Two motor transports destroyed at 9617. Many ambulances seen south of Falaise - Putanges, not attacked.

In the afternoon eight aircraft on an armed recco to Flers - Briouse - Falaise area. Flew to Flers and swept eastwards. The two sections became separated due to cloud after sweeping several times and seeing no movement. One section returned without firing rockets. Two aircraft of rear section fired two pairs of rockets at tank, near misses. At U0829, one motorcyclist destroyed by cannon. Accurate intense heavy flak. One aircraft slightly damaged.

Early evening and an armed recco to Flers - Falaise - Mezidon. Flew to Argentan - Briuge at 10/10 cloud over area ordered. Attacked four motor transports at T9613 with rockets and cannon, all damaged. Attacked one AFV near Briouze - flamer. One of three motor transports attacked T9313 - smoker. 45 rockets fired. Moderate light flak from Argentan. On returning boys carried out a recco for wine etc. for coming party.

4th August

Weather duff in the morning. Wing Commander Baldwin led attack by eight aircraft on railway gun at Beuvron en Augue 227610. Winco scored direct hits and covered target in smoke cloud. One pilot hit house adjacent that burst into flames. Target considered destroyed. Moderate light flak from target area.

The party in big swing, incapable all round. Wing Commander Green on visit.

5th August

Fate is in our favour. Weather clamped until early evening. Armed recco Conde - Falaise - Brettville. Swept area making several attacks with following results. Four motor transports at 9428 destroyed. One motor transport 9426 destroyed. 20+

motor transports on road Falaise - Putengas conveying troops. Eight aircraft attacked with rockets and cannon. Many hits, five flamers. Six to eight motor transports at T9025 attacked with rockets and cannon. Strikes observed. Intense light flak at T9428. Intense heavy flak at Vassy.

Late evening and eight aircraft on an armed recco to Argentan - Bitanges - Brevege - Flers with four aircraft from 257 Squadron. Visibility poor due to haze. Three motor transports damaged by rockets and cannon at 41816, also one tank in same area. Scattered motor transports seen. Intense heavy and light flak at 8,000 feet from woods at U3222.

No life in Squadron until late evening. Bob Shaleton and Colin visit us in their 'recce' car. (No more details as to which these two men are.)

6th August

Eight aircraft briefed to attack tanks at U0750 but nothing seen, so recce Falaise area. Four aircraft damaged car at U210384 and two motor transports at Danblainvitle village. One aircraft destroyed a half-track at 1737. One Staff car damaged by cannon fire. Four aircraft rocketed two armoured fighting vehicles at Matigny, one turned over, the other in ditch damaged. One Staff car damaged and one motorcycle destroyed by cannon fire.

7th August

Break in weather early afternoon. Boys kept very busy on operations. Briefed on motor transport reported on road St. Pierre Conde at 863405. No motor transport seen on pinpoint, but scattered motor transport elsewhere. 20 rockets fired.

Flight Sergeant Wheeler forced down in our lines after being hit by flak, good effort. His aircraft was badly shot up.

Attacked ten tanks in the late afternoon, five miles east if Vire, target area 704336. A very successful show, all rockets in tank area. Two tanks seen in attack claimed destroyed. A large explosion and an orange flash seen. Target area left enveloped in smoke and flame.

8th August

Late morning and twenty tanks attacked in orchard at Fontaine le Pix at 053449, none seen, but one motor transport among AA guns on pin points attacked by three aircraft - guns ceased fire. Five aircraft attacked wood at 087445. Smoke and sheet of flame 30 feet high after attack.

Early evening recco at Argentan - Alecon - Flers area carried out and only scattered motor transports seen. One armoured fighting vehicle damaged. Twenty motor transports seen south of Vassy, but identification uncertain and no attack made.

9th August

Bad luck hits us again. Flight Sergeant Green down in enemy lines. CO crash-landed on return. Flak happy.

Morning armed recco for motorised enemy transports. Reported Conde Falaise road, six tanks attacked 41632, one damaged. Elsewhere scattered MET, one destroyed and four damaged. Moderate to intense flak south east of Falaise.

Later that morning eight aircraft led by Wing Commander Baldwin carried out an armed recco in Falaise area. 30+ tanks seen moving into Falaise from southwest, south and southeast. Results, tanks 1-2-0, (possibly means one flamer, two smokers, zero damaged) armoured fighting vehicles 1-0-0, motor transport 3-3-1. Mechanical excavator destroyed. Two rockets. Direct hits. 20 infantry in ditch. Convoy of 20 motor transports strafed by all aircraft. Strikes along whole length, claims not included above.

Early afternoon. Led by Wingco (Wing Commander), carried out armed recco in Falaise area. Only scattered motor transport seen in area, all attacked. Claims, AFVs 2-0-0, motor transports 3-1-3, and two horse drawn guns damaged.

Flight Sergeant Green force landed about 10 miles north east of Falaise. Squadron Leader Wright crash-landed at base, both due to flak.

Late afternoon and led by the CO, attacked rocket mortars north of le Moncel. Seven aircraft of 266 attacked target. All rockets in the target area.

10th August
Weather clamped in morning, good afternoon. The Squadron complimented on good Army support by the Army.

In the afternoon a successful attack on HQ near Montboint U126449 jointly with nine aircraft of 263 Squadron. Numerous strikes seen on main buildings also minor buildings. Chateau seen to be destroyed after attack. Red flames and column of white smoke.

11th August
Weather fine. Armed recco carried out in the Falaise area, the Flak Valley for the squadrons. Destroyed two tanks and half a dozen motorised enemy transports. Also carried out successful attack leading the Wing in on radar station at Beauvais. Rockets fired followed by 500lb bombs, all in target area except four bombs. Very good prang.

A late evening Wing show led by Wing Commander Baldwin flying with 266. Target infantry and mortar at 750565. 266 attacked red smoke with rockets, large fire started. Remaining rockets and bombs followed resulting in fires and explosions, thought to be ammunition. One exceptionally large fire, smoke to 3,000 feet.

12th August

Another fine sunny day. Very successful attack on Jerry (German) HQ at Epanay and troop concentrations resulting in a very good explosion of rockets around Chateau. Area covered in black smoke early in attack and volume increasing, some flashes seen. Moderate light flak in target area.

With seven aircraft of 193 Squadron. Briefed for attack on tank transporters near Argentan. Searched at 5,000 feet but nothing seen. Possible tanks at Donfront, forty transporters seen in wood 43120 but no attacks made. Barrage of heavy flak at 10,000 feet T8032 - T8932. Considerable haze.

'Ticky' Baggot came to visit us today, with the usual party being the result.

13th August

Boys very busy. Again success on chateau southwest of Lounguy. Was reported to be a Jerry HQ. Complimented by the Army on success of blowing up observation tower that was causing them trouble. Few of the boys damaged by flak.

Led by the Wingco the squadron attacked an observation post at 175643, east of Caen. Four salvoes obtained a direct hit causing explosion. Target area covered in smoke and remaining attacks not observed. From the distance the target appeared to be collapsed after completion of attack. The Wingco forced landed at aerodrome, one wheel down. Unhurt.

A Wing show in the early evening. Attack on HQ and troop convoy at 52417 and 1939197. All squadrons carried bombs. Sixty-two rockets fired. One direct hit on buildings in village, 80% in village north of wood.

193 Squadron dropped 16 x 500lb bombs, fourteen in the target area. Probable hits on chateau, remainder in wood. 197 Squadron dropped 80% in target area. Intense medium and light flak in target area at first.

14th August

More successes for the Squadron. Completely destroyed SP gun, two tanks and four heavy guns at St. Pierre, few of our aircraft hit by flak.

Together with eight Bomphoons of 193 Squadron attacked guns in orchard at U142431. Sixty-four rockets fired, half in orchard 144428 and half in another 142431, also strafed. 193 Squadron dropped 16 x 500lb bombs as above and strafed. Black smoke after attack. Twenty mortars were seen firing at River Valley 2346 and 2340. Released in the afternoon giving the lads an enjoyable afternoon at the beach.

Early evening attack on troops and guns at 267474 together with 263 Squadron. 'Rockphoons' (rocket firing Typhoons) fired 128 x 60 rockets all in target area. Direct hits on houses, and probable hits on hillside. Moderate light flak in target area. Meagre accurate heavy flak at St. Pierre.

15th August

Morning armed recco to the Falaise area. Considerable movement at Falaise - Argentan - Flers area. 62 x 60lb rockets fired. Claims in area 2837. One tank flamed, one tank damaged. U1422 going east. (Went west!!) Two large motor transports - smokers. Column of troops and stationary motor transports strafed on road 41028 - 1231. Area T9825 Argentan Flers worth rocket attack.

Bad luck hits us again. Flight Sergeant Wheeler believed killed by direct flak hit during armed recco in Falaise - Argentau area. Seen to crash in area 41423.

Early afternoon and an attack on troops moving east on Truan - Dozule road. Little movement seen. Forty-six rockets fired. Half-track troop transport destroyed 175727. One staff car flamer, one motor transport damaged. Another motor transport attacked, no results seen.

A few hours later and a Wing operation. Tanks in woods south east of Falaise. 266 fired fifty-six rockets on target. Flames from target area. 263 Squadron – sixty-four rockets fired on target, a few troops seen but no tanks. 197 Squadron dropped 24 x 500lb bombs on target area with heavy strafing. 193 Squadron dropped 16 x 500lb bombs on target, flames seen.

Wing Commander reported flames or smoke on all targets. Army reported a very successful show. Flak very heavy on these trips.

16th August

No flying until the afternoon. Armed recco on trains. Forty-eight rockets fired. Fifteen stationary tanks attacked at 41322. Four flamers. Fifteen tanks and motor transports seen 41124, one large gun moving south approx. 41230. Twelve motor transports and two HDT seen going north U1434. HDT damaged.

Late afternoon attack on bridge over River Risle attacked and holed. Road movement light except ambulances in area of field hospital, not attacked. Two motor transport flamers, one damaged. Ammo dump suspected in wood one mile east of Montfort.

Attack on tank convoy later at L128340. Rockets fired on seven tanks in wood U2328 also 70+ motor transports in area stationary at heading east. One tank flamer U2428, three motor transports destroyed at U2533 2633 and 2329. Two motor transports damaged U2428. All aircraft strafed with cannon.

These reports from the Appendices contradict the ORB report that simply states that "Quiet afternoon spent sunbathing and indulging in a little French wine." In can be assumed that some pilots were on rest from operations.

17th August

Boys have a field day on the Seine and Falaise area. Four tanks destroyed, seven tank smokers and two motorised enemy transports.

Bounced by 70+ Fw 190s. Flight Sergeant Love missing. Flight Lieutenant McGibbon and Flight Sergeant Palte damage two 190s. Flight Sergeant Luhnenchloss badly shot up by Jerry.

From the Appendice. Afternoon attack on barges by sixteen aircraft from 263 and 266 Squadrons (8 + 8 in 4's) on barges in River Seine, Les Audely's to Quilece Boruf. 266 attacked four barges on River Risle, one destroyed, three damaged. Ten barges south side of River Seine and six barges north side all attacked and strafed. One barge destroyed, several damaged.

Early evening armed recco of Vimoutiers (Gap) area. A very successful Wing operation led by Group Captain Gilham flying with 193 Squadron. Other squadrons were 263, 266 and 197. A skirmish took place with 15+ Fw. 190s resulting in two being damaged by Flight Lieutenant McGibbon and Sergeant Palte. Flight Sergeant Love was not seen again after dogfight. Other claims, one tank damaged, three motor transports flamers, one motor transport damaged.

An hour after landing and an armed recco to Vimoutiers - Orbec - Livarot. Before being re-called the squadron got one tank flamer and one motor transport damaged.

The reader should be aware that not all Squadron pilots took part in all sorties. The Squadron was flying at least three sorties each day, to expect the same pilots to fly continuously was not acceptable. Sorties were 'shared' between pilots to enable nonflying pilots to catch up on sleep and rest.

18th August

Another field day for the Squadron. Jerry on the run. Attack on 1,000 MET, tanks, Staff cars and many METs destroyed.

The German Army was now attempting to escape from

the Falaise Gap where the Allies were attacking in an effort to destroy or capture a large proportion of the enemy en-masse.

A morning armed recco to Conches - Brionne - Cormeilles. Three stationary tanks attacked, one destroyed, one smoker. Two Staff cars destroyed, one motor transport damaged, one DR (possibly Dispatch Rider) destroyed. Twenty ambulances seen in area Q8379 east.

An afternoon attack in the Falaise Gap in bombing area U2825 recce. Claims - two tanks flamers, five motor transports flamers, seven motor transports probables and 4 - 5 damaged at U3223. 300+ motor transports seen in area.

Returning to the Gap area later in the late afternoon. Saw considerable motor transport on roads, all stationary. Attacked mostly between Boissiere and Motbllerie. Two tanks flamers, one tank smoker, five motor transports destroyed, three motor transports probables, three motor-transport damaged. One ammo lorry of six parked close, violent explosion, all destroyed.

German Army under constant attack. Early evening recco led by the Wingco. Vimoutiers - Brouglie - Orbec areas. One motor transport flamer, three motor transports attacked. Two motor transports damaged two miles south of Orbec. One tank smoker, one motor transport damaged, two motor transports seen flaming the result of Spitfire attack. Moderate light accurate flak.

Flight Lieutenant Blackwell DFC on rest, Flight Lieutenant Erasmus DFC has taken over his place.

19th August

Early morning operational flying to Orbec - Broglie - Bernay areas. Five tanks - flamers, four tanks - smokers, two motorised enemy transports destroyed, Eleven damaged. One tank covered with white sheet and two red crosses. Unidentified aircraft shot down in dogfight west of Bernay.

Late morning and an armed recco to the same area with 193

Squadron. We claim five tanks destroyed, one damaged, one armoured fighting vehicle damaged, all in area of patrol. Most tanks and motor transports stationary. Many ambulances seen all morning moving east. 193 Squadron saw parachute wires in operation at Bernay.

20th August
Very little activity due to heavy rain. A lull in the battle, the Squadron's time mostly spent in sunbathing and catching up on correspondence.

An infantry and tank attack in the afternoon. We did not attack however as no red smoke seen. Six Sherman tanks with white stars and cerise stripes going east on road Q4154. Yellow stripes seen at Q4455.

In the evening we were briefed to operate with VCP (Vehicle Command Post) but no reply on radio so recce Bernay area. Two motor transports destroyed and one AFV damaged. One pilot reports roads entering Bernay blocked with wrecked motor transports.

22nd August
A pleasant day. Lull in operational flying, two armed reccos carried out in Bernay area, destroying four motorised enemy transports and troop concentrations.

23rd August
Further operational successes in the Brionne area on motorised enemy transports and troops. Very little enemy activity, but plenty of flak to welcome the boys.

In the evening attacked motor transports and tanks near Brionne. Saw 18+ motor transports and tanks northeast Brionne. Destroyed two motor transports One smoker and one damaged. Twenty motor transports and tanks going southeast, no attack.

Very accurate moderate light and medium flak east and west off Brionne. Flying Officer Rogers crash-landed on return to base due to flak action on the trip out.

24th August

Local flying only, and a visit paid to us by Wing Commander Davidson of Rhodesia House. The lads enjoyed an afternoon of sunbathing and swimming on the beach.

25th August

The Squadron again comes into its own, destroying barges and other traffic on the River Seine and roads.

One barge attacked, no results observed. One tank flamer, two motor transports flamers at L9815. One motor transport flamer at L9505, one motor transport flamer at M0080. Stores park seen on south bank of Seine. Tents seen in clearing surrounded by numbers of light guns.

Returning early afternoon sixteen rockets fired. Staff car going east destroyed, and several occupants hit. Two direct hits on three barges, one ship beached. One ship and three barges seen but not attacked. Moderate light and heavy flak from area.

Later that afternoon two aircraft at various intervals patrolling the Seine area. First patrol. One barge sunk, corpses in water. Sixteen rockets fired. Second patrol with two aircraft of 197 Squadron. One barge ferry midstream hit and exploded. Another salvo hit jetty causing explosion. One tank damaged. Third patrol. Five barges damaged, plus three steamers. Two stationary barges near misses. Patrol number four. Rocket attack on cable ferry barge moving north. Direct hits on stern. Claimed as probable. Light flak. Fifth patrol. One motor transport bearing white stripes attacked. Sixteen rockets fired, no results observed. The final patrol of the day. No claims. Twenty to thirty motor transports moving NL9818. Eight - ten moving onto ferry and attacked. NRO. (No Results Observed.) Seven rockets fired on South Rouen as ordered.

27th August

The Squadron had a very successful shipping strike, destroying two destroyers and one minesweeper, damaging one other. Unfortunately these were Royal Navy ships, ordered, by mistake of the Admiralty, to be attacked and destroyed. The Admiralty took full responsibility.

The Appendice Report. Five ships attacked off Etretat, six ships located sailing southwest, four probable destroyers, two MVs (motor vessels.)

Owing to doubt as to identity the Controller was asked four times whether to attack and told that ships had fired correct colours of the day. Controller said that no friendly ships in area and ordered attack to proceed. 263 Squadron claim rocket salvos on two ships, 266 on three ships. Also strafed. The ships were actually our own.

This attack on friendly forces resulted in two destroyers and other ships being sunk and others damaged with the loss of 78 killed and 149 wounded Royal Navy personnel.

Later that afternoon another armed recco to the Seine. One ferryboat destroyed with a vivid flash. One barge damaged and smoking. Ten steel barges attacked with rockets and cannon. Many strikes observed. One motor transport attacked, no results seen. Moderate light flak from target areas.

28th August

Weather very poor, but armed recco again to the Seine carried out. Tanks and motor transports on Seine, no ferry seen. Burning motor transports Six undamaged motor transports attacked, one smoker. Small boats and dinghies from this point to 98016. Cannon strafed and fifty-five rockets fired.

A troop attack on a Seine river crossing. No barges seen just fifteen small rafts at waterside, left bank. Heavily strafed and attacked with rockets. Two fires seen with thick black smoke.

Group Captain Gillam and Squadron Leader Wright carried out AR. (Armoured recco.) Small armoured car destroyed, large lorry destroyed and scattered motor transport seen in all of area. Squadron complimented on successful strafing of enemy troop movements by the Army.

29th / 30 August
Weather poor, continuous rain, no flying. The lads visited the forward area by jeep.

31st August
Armed recco to areas 'A' and part of 'C' by eight aircraft. Scattered movement only. Twelve HDT destroyed. Large explosion seen at wood at L8847.

1st September
Squadron still based at B3 St. Croix le Mer. Weather fine. Due to the enemies hasty retreat we do normal flying only. Flight Commanders get the boys down to cleaning aircraft.

2nd September
Squadron carries out long range armed recco over Calais - Lille area, refueling and rearming at Manston. Three motorised enemy transports in flames and many destroyed. Pranged three horse drawn vehicles. Weather not too good, and a little flak. Armed recco carried out in the same area en route to base, weather very poor, 9/10 cloud and squalls. No attacks made.

3rd September
Battlefront now out of range. Squadron carried out local flying

only.

4th September
Weather clamped. No flying activity so boys visited Rouen and enjoyed many a liberation party with the French.

6th September
Squadron breaks camp, moving to B23. Excellent Squadron fly past of twenty-two aircraft. Weather at B23 was poor, continual rain. We slept in barns and ground shelter due to ground party not arriving.

7th September
Weather clamped, continual rainstorms, runway bogged. Squadron visits the sight of previous bombing by the Wing - self-propelled gun and tunnel at St. Andre. Entertained afterwards by a French family at their chateau.

8th September
Another quick move. The Squadron prepares to move to Abbeville, strip unserviceable, landed at Manston, (England) no further activity.

9th September
Squadron take off with Wing consisting of 266, 263 and 197 Squadrons, led by Wing Commander Baldwin on a shipping strike at the Channel Isles, no enemy shipping seen, landed and spent the night at Tangmere.

10th September
Squadron returns to Manston. Pilots carrying out their own daily inspections on their aircraft. Shipping recco in afternoon to Dutch Islands with 263 Squadron. We attacked one large, two

medium and five small barges in harbour at Middleharnis. Direct hits on barge and medium barge and all strafed with cannon. Moderate inaccurate light flak from Middleharnis and position D4321. Intense heavy and medium from area D3424. Heavy evacuation traffic Breskens to Flushing.

IIth September

Eight aircraft on Army support targets well pranged by both flights at village and orchard west of Boulogne, very little flak. Target attacked out of the sun with twenty-four rockets, all but two in area. Also strafed with cannon after getting permission from Longbow (Air Controller.) Building well hit and Huns ran into trenches, running zig-zag east and west. Inaccurate light flak. On return we refueled and moved to Lille Aerodrome.

At the same time another eight Squadron aircraft attacked guns and tanks in wood three miles south west of Boulogne. Obtained permission from Longbow to attack. Proceeded inland to Foret de Boulogne. Turned north and attacked target, wood, orchard and houses, with thirty-two rockets and cannon from 7,500 to 2,000 feet. Intense accurate light flak

I2th September

Back in operational distances. Squadron carried out three sorties. Early morning attack on shipping and motor transport in the Flakkee area. One motor transport destroyed moving east. One large and eight small boats attacked going into Terneuzen. Direct hit on large and one small vessel, both in flames. Intermittent light flak from boats. Suspected rocket sites in woods southeast Rooendaal, two parallel concrete ramps, and slight activity.

Mid afternoon shipping attack to Dutch Islands. Two ships in harbour attacked, one flamer, one ship going southeast attacked and left sinking. Fifty-six rockets fired. Nothing more seen on roads.

An early evening attack to Ghent. Attacked guns and motor transport in woods together with 193 Squadron. Eight aircraft fired sixty-four rockets into woods from southwest to northeast, all bursts in wood. Target also strafed by both squadrons. No results observed. Slight light flak.

13th September

Army support at Boulogne, bags of joy, direct hits observed. Marshalling yards attacked at Dunkirk but only a few trucks in the yards. Sixty-four rockets fired into the engine sheds. 100% hits, explosions, several fires with smoke up to 800 feet. Results considered very good.

Final sortie of the day. Late afternoon. Attack on guns casement. Twenty-four rockets in target area. One external gun and one large lorry received direct hits. No claims on casemate, intense light flak in target area. Flak happy, weather very hazy, no further flying activity. We were released and visited Lille.

14th September

Weather fine, slight haze. Army support on gun positions at Hulst, no red smoke to indicate target area. Carried out armed recco of Dutch Isles instead. No joy.

15th September

Weather clamped, no operational flying, so the boys carried out a sector recco of the local countryside for eggs etc!

16th September

Clamp until midday, sky clear, operational flying. Loose Army support missions carried out on Boulogne and Dunkirk against strong defence position.

First operation against strong point near Boulogne. Target located and attacked with sixty-four rockets. One salvo undershot, but remainder in target area. Two salvos direct hit on cross roads.

Army support target was a defended village near Boulogne. Sixty-four rockets fired 80% in target area. Trenches seen but no results observed although later grey smoke was seen.

Attacked strong point and gun position at Dunkirk, bags of light flak. Fifty-one rockets fired. Two salvos overshot in moat, remainder in target area. Concrete construction in centre hit. Three of four guns at western end of target area believed hit. Moderate light flak at 7,000 feet.

Last operation of the day. Defences at Dunkirk attacked. Sixty-three rockets fired. One salvo each end of island. One salvo near miss on gun position and considered worth repeat attack. Moderate light flak from target area.

17th September

Fine day. Very little air activity. Squadrons carry out an attack on barracks at East Dunkirk. Sixty-four rockets fired all in target area. Many direct hits claimed.

Attack on two outer lock gates at Wemelflinge. Sixty-four rockets fired and direct hits obtained by complete section and put out of action. Inner lock gates not attacked. Moderate inaccurate light flak.

18th September

Industrial haze and low mist, no flying activity, Squadron was released. Held a party in Lille, which was enjoyed by all.

19th September

Weather clamped. No operational flying. The lads make use of an old rifle range and rugger ball to break boredom.

20th September

Weather clamped until evening. Dusk attack carried out on Calais on gun positions, welcomed by concentrated light flak. Silo south east of Calais. Silo not identified, but rockets fired at pinpoint. 90% seen to burst between canal and railway support. Area appears to have been previously devastated.

21 September

Clamp. Boys visited the local towns in the vicinity and Belgium by jeep. Finished off by a party that night.

22nd September

Weather hazy and uncertain. Two Army support missions. One on Dunkirk, the other north of Antwerp allocated to squadrons. Returned on both occasions, weather unsuitable over target area.

Weather poor, bad industrial haze. Carried out two Army support operations at Dunkirk and north of Antwerp. Both very successful, bags of light flak. Pilot Officers Hully's aircraft hit.

24th September

Continual rain. The jeeps did a trip to Theims for champagne, successful trip. Squadron party followed.

25th September

Very misty. We set out on attack on three railway guns near Knoke, returned due to low cloud over target area. No further activity all day.

26th September

Clear weather at last. Squadron prepared for a busy day. Guns attacked north east of Antwerp. Red smoke seen and three aircraft fired twenty-four rockets. Salvos burst in south of wood. Red smoke seen at another target and thirty-two rockets concentrated on this point. A very successful prang.

An attack on guns and observation post in a church. Four minutes over target then trace of red smoke seen. Sixty-two rockets fired all in target area. Church hit but still standing.

Guns at Calais attacked. Sixty-four rockets fired into area of casemates, but owing to low cloud and haze impossible to say if casemates were hit. Area well strafed with cannon. Moderate light flak from target area.

27th September

Weather holds good. Army support on strong point at Fort de Shoder, successful show. Silo targets destroyed near Andres. Seventy-two rockets fired with direct hits in several salvos on silo. Smoking after attack. Strikes seen on sandbags during strafing. Attack praised by French civilians.

Attacked mobile guns and heavy flak positions at Antwerp and Calais, heavy and accurate flak encountered. Congratulated by the Army.

28th September

Attacked and destroyed blockhouse at Cap Griz-Nez and guns at Merxplas. The lads are very flak happy. Attacked two church steeples being used as an observation post near Calais. Direct hits on both, steeples still standing though. Both were strafed with cannon. Congratulations from the Army.

Guns attacked near Merxplas. Forty-eight rockets fired all in target area. Area strafed with cannon, after which guns ceased fire on Army.

29th September

Weather duff. No operational flying due to fog.
30 September

Squadron has a very successful day destroying strong points in Calais and a German HQ building north of Ooatsburg.

Led by the Wingco. Attacked without smoke six minutes early. Sixty-two rockets fired all appeared direct hits. Most of the buildings demolished, persons seen in buildings at start of attack. Moderate medium flak from a four-gun battery.

A strong point near Calais attacked. Five direct hits on large white house. One aircraft landed with wheels up with burst tyre. Pilot unhurt.

A heavy gun position and strong point in a house four miles north of Antwerp. Very near misses from thirty-one rockets, also strafed with cannon. Black smoke observed from roof of target. Inaccurate medium flak from target area.

1st October

Squadron move from B51 base imminent. Only one show during day and that a combined effort, but with the majority of pilots from 'A' Flight. It was directed against radar installations at Berkenbosch in the Dutch Islands and was very successful despite heavy and intense light flak. All three targets claimed as destroyed. Flash and explosion from target attacked by Wing Commander Baldwin's section. The attack was made with cannon only from a height of 2,000 feet down to zero feet. Gun pit in target area hit by cannon. Weather beginning to deteriorate and becoming wintry.

2nd October

Squadron moves to Antwerp - Base B70. 'A' Flight flew there direct, but 'B' Flight carried out a shipping strike on the way during which Squadron Leader Wright force landed north west of Rotterdam. He led the attack on a fair sized ship and was the only one to fire his rockets, for the vessel became 'airborne' in front of him and in flying through the debris must have holed his radiator. He flew north leaving a white trail. 'Skid' McAdam the CO's Number 2, returned with 18 holes or dents in his aircraft.

'Doug' Borland obtained an excellent cine-film of the whole attack and the huge pall of smoke - all that remained of the ship. The CO has since been reported prisoner of war. In the afternoon 'A' Flight carried out an armed recco in the same area and claimed a number of barges.

Although we moved into static quarters at B70 we were getting rather well organised at Lille, what with electric light, beds and mattresses, tables, armchairs, mirrors and what - have - you, for most of these amenities we have the Bosch to thank!

Some members were too particular to dine at the mess, preferring their own eggs, chips and tomatoes, varied occasionally by the inclusion of partridge on the menu. Grapes, apples, pears etc. were not plentiful but could be obtained. A wireless building craze seized the squadron, led by Geoff Henderson, but at B70 the 'building' changed to 'buying'!

It was quite common at B51 to have Spits taking off on one runway and Typhoons at the same time on another - very interesting - to onlookers. To complicate the matter, Bowser Liberators started operating to and from the aerodrome, bringing in fuel, in there hundreds. They were out of control...from the ground, except by Verey pistol, with the result that occasionally we were entertained to wizard fireworks displays.

Flight Lieutenant Haworth posted as Flight Commander to 257 Squadron.

3rd October

Weather not too good providing the necessary breather in which to get settled down in the new surroundings. Everybody out scrounging stoves and light fittings for their houses and making themselves comfortable. Squadron allotted two adjacent houses as aircrew billets and the Orderly Room situated in one of the ground floor rooms. Occasional shells whistled eerily overhead.

4th October

Weather cloudy and only one operation possible, this being an attack on a railway bridge north of Utrecht, led by Wing Commander Baldwin. His navigation was superb and he brought the Squadron dead on target after flying above cloud. The railway bridge was well hit.

Flight Sergeant Paddy Culligan arrived with 'S' ('S' is the aircraft code letter) that had been unserviceable at Lille. 'A' Flight flew an air test only. Flight Lieutenant McGibbon taking 'E' up.

5th October

Quite a busy day of ops. Led by Wingco 'A' Flight carried out a successful attack on tanks and guns near Hoogstracten. Later 'B' Flight also gave Army support in an attack on machine-gun and mortar positions at Zeebrugge. Four of 'A' Flight did the last show, the briefing being for an attack on a train transporting 100 tanks near Utrecht. They had no joy there, so attacked barges on the Rhine, "No claims being made through flak" to quote Flight Lieutenant McGibbon.

6th October

A good days work, quite up to B3 standard. 'B' Flight started the ball rolling with an armed recce of the Rhine mouth at 08.30. Barges and transports were attacked, Flight Sergeant Dodd claiming three of the latter. Next 'A' Flight also carried out an armed Recce for V2 sites in Schouwen Islands. Attacked transports, railway trucks and barracks, thought to be connected with V2.

'B' Flights show was to be another armed recce, but as a ship was seen west of Rotterdam this was attacked. Accurate flak which got Warrant Officer Paul, he baled out and was seen to land on a sand bank in the mouth of the Rhine.

'A' Flight finished the day with an Army support show led by Flight Lieutenant McGibbon. Target was gun position two miles south of Tilburg. Smoke was in wrong position so no attack made. Congratulated by Army for not attacking wrong smoke position.

7th October

'A' Flight first off on Army support target. Abortive due to weather. The next show was Squadron Leader Deall's first as CO and the squadrons first over Germany. Attacked road over railway bridge at Bedburg near Cleve. Bombs well concentrated with several direct hits cutting the line. Very good shooting. Slight medium flak over target area. It was on this raid the Me 262 jet fighter trails were seen, as noted in the Appendices.

Last show again with 'A' Flight, successful attack on railway bridge two miles east of Utrecht. Fifty-five rockets fired. Two salvos direct hits on western end of the bridge, and several direct hits on the track west of the bridge. Photographs of damage requested.

8th October

Weather recce flown by Flying Officer Borland and Flight Sergeant Dodd to the mouth of the Rhine - Utrecht - Deventer - and base. Very adverse weather report.

'A' Flight flew a number of air tests getting their operational machines up to strength. Late in the evening 'B' Flight took off in appalling weather conditions to disorganise an enemy counter attack south of Bergen - Op - Zoom, area well pranged. Plenty of light flak. Congratulated on this operation, counter attack was disjointed and easily repelled. It was necessary to use navigation lights coming back. Flying Officer Borland burst a tyre taking off as spare - slightly shaken up, otherwise OK. A spare aircraft was used in case one of the attacking aircraft had to return to base for any reason.

11th October

Originally twelve aircraft, eight from 'A' Flight and four from 'B' Flight were to attack shipping off Flushing. Actually four aircraft, Squadron Leader Deall and Flying Officer Ballance with their Number 2s were successful, pranging shipping in Breskens Harbour. Thirty-two rockets fired at three small and one big barge. One probable hit on big barge and eight hits on dockyard claimed. The weather was shocking.

Later when the weather had improved 'B' Flight paid Breskens a return visit with rockets and cannon against barges in the harbour. A direct hit on one barge, left smoking. Two others seemed to be waterlogged after attack.

The next operation, a cannon attack on the radar station at Walcheren was abandoned due to very bad weather.

The days last show was an armed recce in the Tilburg, Zaltbrommel, and Dordrecht area when barges and motor transports were successfully attacked leaving two flamers, three smokers and several others were undoubtedly hit. Five tanks probably hit parked in barn and farmyard. The barn was set on fire. Intense light flak experienced.

Flying Officer McAdam had engine trouble and was losing height with bags of flak coming up at him. Engine picked up and he made base OK.

Squadron Adjutant ceased course at Admin. School and proceeded to Loughborough Hospital for treatment of fibrositis.

12th October

Weather recce flown, Breskens area. OK over target. 2,000 - 3,000 ton ship attacked in East Schelde by 'B' Flight. Bags of light flak. Ship appeared to be deserted and aground and almost on its side.

Another shipping 'do'. Pink Section only successful, attacking barges on return from west of Rotterdam where main target observed sunk already. One Red Cross ship being towed by barge was seen going westwards in Oosterschelds. Not attacked.

Radar station near Domburg successfully attacked with cannon, although installations difficult to identify. Another Wuerzberg appeared not to be there. Light flak.

Last show as armed recce of area 'C' by 'A' Flight was successful and barges at Bergen were pranged. One motor transport strafed near Rosendaal.

13th October

A big day. Wing visited by His Majesty King George and Field Marshall Montgomery. His Majesty spoke to Squadron Leader Deall, and Monty remarked upon Flying Officer Cunnison's Africa Star and Rhodesian Wings

German HQ south of Breda successfully attacked. 'A' Flight participated. The King was present at the briefing. Two squadrons took part, 197 went in first. They dropped 22 x 500lb bombs together with eleven-second delay bombs in low-level attack. Twenty fell in target area.

266 followed firing fifty-five rockets all in target area. As a result of these attacks all buildings were seen to be destroyed. Area also strafed with cannon fire. Typhoon flown by Flight Sergeant Morgan, was hit in the main tank by rifle fire. Pilot Officer Hulley's aircraft cut out on take off and made good effort to force land near fort at end of runway.

'B' Flight took off to attack pillbox in support of Army, but as there was no smoke although requested, attacked target in Breskens Harbour instead. 'Longbow 6' (Controller) transmissions were weak and distorted. Saw Spitfires attack and set a haystack pillbox on fire at Breskens.

The Germans were attempting to disguise their pillboxes by camouflaging with hay to give the appearance of haystacks.

14th October

'A' Flight had a rest while 'B' operated twice, both operations being Army support attacks on hedges and haystacks, against which bullets were observed to bounce off! This phenomenon was mentioned in the papers. German troops seen running from haystacks into cover under hedges. Suggest rocket attack on haystacks.

'B' Flight returned later and after second attack target was well pranged and burning, with each haystack taking at least eight direct hits. Second strafing attack on hedges and trenches in the vicinity. Nothing much seen. The position was near Biervliet, south east of Breskens.

15th October

'B' Flight rested today while operations were carried out. The first a successful attack on train east of Dordrecht following a report of tanks on wagons but no tanks were seen but thirty railway trucks in station east of Dordrecht attacked, many strikes on trucks with cannon.

A shipping strike but no shipping found apart from two hospital ships at Dordracht which were not attacked. Inland and ten - fifteen trucks attacked in siding. Eight direct hits and many cannon strikes.

An attack on tanks in a wood between Tilburg and Breda. No tanks seen, weather very poor but attack carried out from height of 2,000 feet down to zero feet. Ten rockets fired and the area was thoroughly strafed.

16th October

Only one operation carried out, and that an Army support attack on a three-gun position in Breskens area. The wrong target area was fired upon, then the correct pinpoint recognised and strafed three times with cannon. Heavy strikes seen on gun position. Identifying red smoke was six minutes late. Flying Officer Cunnison destroyed a machine gun.

17th October

'A' Flight carried out a low level attack against a convoy north of Tilburg with cannon only, destroying three motor transports and killing many German soldiers.

Second section returned to scene of previous attacks. No motor transports seen at pinpoint. Strafed small body of troops hauling a light four-wheeled vehicle, many strikes seen.

In an Army support attack, 'B' Flight attempted to knock down an observation post in a church tower, but a strong wind spoilt the rocket shooting. However the target was well strafed with cannon. This was at Huitbergen.

18th October

Wing visited by Air Chief Marshall Leigh - Mallory, who said the Typhoons had had a considerable effect on the outcome of the invasion so far. He told us that he was going east and hoped to see us there.

'B' Flight made repeat attack on yesterdays observation post in the church tower with fourteen aircraft flying in pairs and attacking at 15 minute intervals. Despite many hits at the base and on the steeple it remained standing. Experienced light flak.

On 'A' Flight only operation. An interdiction target.(To prevent the movement of an unspecified target, probably an enemy train.) Flight Lieutenant McGibbon was hit by flak and baled out and landed near Grubbenvorst. Rails cut at Haldern. Was not sure if flak was aimed at his parachute or not.

An Army support operation on casemates at Schoondyke.

Many slit trenches and three gun emplacements seen in target area. Direct hit with one salvo on one emplacement and one building seen to explode violently with hits on other buildings. The area also strafed.

19th October
'A' Flight taken over by Flight Lieutenant Ballance. An observation post in a church on south point of Beveland Island. Eight aircraft attacking in pairs. First section attacked with sixteen rockets with eight direct hits on roof of church at base of the spire. Much smoke and debris seen.

Second pair, one salvo hit church but did not destroy steeple. Third pair had one direct hit on base of tower and flames seen from subsequent cannon strafing. Steeple still obstinate. Fourth pair scored sixteen direct hits on base of tower and steeple. Church furiously burning and large hole observed in tower. Steeple is tottering.

20th October
'B' Flight on Army support. Attack at Eschen. 'A' Flight carried out an attack on heavy gun emplacement west of Breskens. Very successful. Repeat of first attack. Counter attack at Eschen.

21st October
Successful attack made by 'A' Flight on heavily defended HQ west of Breskens. 266 and 193 took eight aircraft each. 266 fired sixty-four rockets into area, several direct hits on large red building roof which was seen to be holed after attack.

'B' Flight gave Army support in attack on gun emplacements south west of Breskens. Flight Sergeant Cambrooke was killed when he attempted to force land after being hit by flak. His aircraft was seen to be smoking after pulling out from attack and so he was told to make for base. His aircraft was later seen burning on the ground.

The day was ended by 'A' Flight attacking barges in the Oooseteschelde. 266 with 263 Squadrons led by Squadron Leader Rutter attacked barges three deep with 124 rockets resulting in an estimated twenty-seven or twenty-eight smokers. Ten bombs fell in and amongst barges, but failing light made assessment of damage impossible. Intense light and medium flak in target area.

At the same time the Group Captain with Flight Sergeant Palte as Number 2 did a special armed recce of Dutch Islands and north of Breda. Two ten ton motor transport vehicles going south to Oudenboasch attacked with four rockets and machine gun and left fiercely smoking.

Flying Officer Cunnison awarded the DFC. Big celebration!

22nd and 23rd October

Wing visited by Lord Trenchard who autographed flag. He talked mostly about the state of Belgium and France in the winter war conditions.

Air Officer Commanding Brown said goodbye and wished us the best of luck. He said that he felt, having this Wing under him, that he had realised the height of his ambition.

The weather clamped and no flying for two days. Pilot Officer Dix, our Intelligence Officer, posted to 263 Squadron, and we welcomed back Flying Officer Tidmarsh as Squadron Intelligence Officer.

24th October

Quite an important day in the Wing's history due to the outstanding attack on the German 15th Army HQ at Dordrecht. We were the first squadron to attack.

According to information received through underground channels, the HQ and staff were virtually wiped out, and the resulting funeral was the biggest ever seen in Dordrecht. Some bombs went slightly astray also did useful damage in a motor transport yard. The attack had noticeable effects on the fighting qualities of the 15th Army. Two Generals, seventeen senior officers, fifty officers and 200 other ranks were said to have been killed.

Next 'A' Flight attacked shipping in Hellevoetsluis harbour with some success. Eight direct hits were seen on two barges in harbour, both smokers. Intense light very accurate flak in target area.

25th, 26th and 27th October
A spell of very rough weather with flying absolutely nil. A V2 landed at Radio and Instrument Section killing five and injuring eleven. Corporal Offley-Shore and Leading Aircraftman Gold among the injured.

28th October
'B' Flight took off very early to attack gun position south of Goes with rockets and then again with cannon. This was in the south Beveland peninsular. No guns were seen in position. One house seen to be already pranged.

Meanwhile 'A' Flight carried out some air tests in preparation for their operation, an attack on huts and dump at Wilhelminadorp. This was successful. Wizard. One building left blazing and one large motor transport seen moving in target area.

Officer's Mess party and dance with lots of everything but women.

29th October
'A' Flight flew to Zuid Beveland again to strafe road between Goes and Wilhelminadorp, results fairly successful. Next operation directed against ferry at Willemstad, mouth of the

Rhine, well pranged with rockets and then roads to south of Rhine as far as Mardyk Bridge recced, when large transport was pranged.

Following this 'A' Flight carried out an attack on radar installations at Domberg which was very successful. Heavily hit and holes seen in Freya. Flak gun pit also strafed.

DFCs awarded to Flying Officer Haworth and Flight Lieutenant McGibbon - another big celebration.

30th and 31st October
Weather very poor and flying nil.

1st November
Weather improved in the afternoon. Flight Lieutenant Sheward, an old friend of squadron members who were at TEU (Tactical Evaluation Unit), Ashton Down, made a very welcome addition, but for all too short a period.

2nd November
'A' Flight and four aircraft of 'B' Flight took off to attack two different targets at Walcheren. The former on gun emplacements in support of the Army, north of Nieulands, and the remaining four on another gun position nearer Middleburg. Both were successful.

Later eight aircraft of 'B' Flight went to silence machine gun nests at Stampersgat. In error rockets fired east of Steenbergen which was heavily defended by the Huns. Leader then proceeded to correct target at Stampersgat which was strafed with cannon.

3rd November
First show to Eindevandenhout in Army support to attack mortars and buildings, aborted owing to a layer of low cloud. 'A' Flight attacked successfully Huns massing for a counter attack

using heavy guns in position south of Willemstad.

4th November
Twelve aircraft supported Army in attacks on observation posts in three churches at Dinteloord. Each section of four aircraft attacking one church. One church and steeple demolished and others badly damaged. Although weather over area was bad, 'B' Flight recce south of Rotterdam for Big Ben activity, (this code phrase unknown unfortunately,) but nothing seen. Proceeded to vicinity of Utrecht above cloud. Descent was made through gap in cloud, when Pink Section cut a railway line, and Grey Section pranged two transports.

Last operations of the day. One was an attack on Gestapo Head Quarters at Rotterdam led by Flight Lieutenant Ballance. Eight direct hits in target area causing severe damage, but exact location of building not certain so a photo recce was requested. This was successful.

The other was with 'B' Flight who finished off with a successful Army support attacking dug in tanks at Zeuebergen together with six aircraft of 197 Squadron who went in first. Target well pranged with bombs and cannon fire. 266 then attacked firing sixty-four rockets and also strafed which helped to increase fires from previous attacks.

5th November
Weather duff and flying nil, but 'fireworks' by no means absent! V1 and V2s plentiful!

6th November
'A' Flight started off with an attack on train in Gouda station firing sixty-four rockets which ripped into twenty trucks in marshalling yard. The 1.30 p.m. which was successfully pranged.

More successful train busting by 'B' Flight south of

Amersfoort, with bags of light flak. Unfortunately Flight Sergeant Laing's aircraft was giving trouble on way out to target. He turned back to base but his engine cut out and force landed in friendly territory eight miles south of Gilze Rijan Airfield, he managed to call up reporting he was OK, and was soon back.

7th November

Weather poor and a strong wind blowing. Improved sufficiently by the afternoon for 'B' Flight to get a show to Dunkirk on an army billet. Owing to the high wind shooting was rather erratic and large percentage of rockets overshot although numerous cannon strikes seen on buildings with one building just west of canal on fire. Squadron Leader Deall had to turn back owing to radio failure. 40mm flak a nuisance coming out.

Flight Lieutenant 'Colly' Collcut, 'Tickey' Baggott and Squadron Leader Joe Holmes arrived from England to pay us a social visit, but what a shout went up when it was discovered that they hadn't brought across any BEER. Nevertheless, during the days they spent with the lads, one party especially was a huge success.

8th, 9th and 10th November

Very considerately the weather clamped for the duration of our visitors sojourn and then remained operationally unfit for a further day, to give people time to recuperate!

11th November

'B' Flight went in search of V2 trains in the Utrecht area, but finding none, attacked a railroad bridge obtaining numerous hits on bridge and rails which was considered to be cut.

A rail and road bridge was also attacked on 'A' Flight's trip west of Gouda, hits being observed to road and railway bridge. This last show was more successful.

12th - 16th November

A very bad spell of weather, considerable amount of rain which played havoc with the aerodrome surface and made it necessary to move some dispersals.

Model plane building being a popular pastime during the poor weather. Numerous wireless sets brought in Antwerp, very necessary with long winter nights approaching.

Very sorry to lose Derek Erasmus to 193 Squadron as their CO. Doug Borland now commands 'A' Flight. Nice work both of you. A number of air tests flown during the few days.

Group Captain Gillam with (then) Flight Lieutenant Erasmus flying as Number 2 carried out tests with phosphorous heads to the rockets. Weather shocking.

17th November

Before the weather had chance to deteriorate - it was far from perfect - 'B' Flight took off to give Army support by attacking observation post in church steeple, village three miles east of Groesbeck, just this side of the German border. Church received direct hits, but steeple still stood. Attacked a second time with cannon. We heard the bell ringing so low were we flying!

18th November

'A' Flight airborne to recce area north and north west of Arnhem, but forced to return by numerous layers of cloud from 1,500 feet upwards.

'A' Flight flew a number of air tests while 'B' Flight carried out another show in Army support on heavy gun positions east of Ede; a section of four took on each emplacement, followed in by four bombers. Wing Commander Wells pinpointed the guns situated in wood with phosphorous rockets for benefit of bombers; a large explosion was seen in this position during attack.

Cloud was 10/10ths at 6,000 feet and light flak bursting at this height, looked very dicey.

19th November
A train of twelve wagons was caught east of Gouda by 'B' Flight and well pranged. Flak effectively silenced by cannon fire. Flight Sergeant Laing had to force land behind enemy lines unfortunately, with engine failure, thought to have been brought about by debris from attack. He called up on the radio to say he had landed safely, figures seen running towards turned out to be members of the Resistance Movement who organised his safe return. He returned to us on the 14th December, nice work 'Zombie'.

Combined 'A' and 'B' Flights show led by Wing commander. The operation to attack Gestapo HQ at Amsterdam aborted due to weather, so various squadrons did interdiction attacks. 266 attacked railway bridge over canal, at least one salvo hit bridge.

20th November
Low cloud and rain, no flying. Flying Officer Cunnison and Flying Officer 'Killer' Miller (Australian) jeeped to Brussels and were presented with a Citroen saloon car by Squadron Leader Alex Gibbs, who salvaged the car from the Falaise Gap. Very welcome too.

21st November
Weather improved in the afternoon and four aircraft of 'B' Flight gave Army support in an attack on a dug-in tank. This was very successful with direct hits on tank. Tank crew running away towards a bomb crater were picked off.

22nd - 24th November
The slight improvement in the weather didn't last and it closed in

again for another three days. We had rather a good a good game of rugby - once we discovered a ground to play on - and this not without a very comprehensive search in jeep and Citroen.

It was pilots versus ground staff and some of the latter had to be briefed on how to play the game. Nevertheless the score, three all, was very fair. Afterwards we all proceeded to the swimming baths which all enjoyed.

Before returning we had a beer on Flying Officer Cunnison, who had been grounded, pending posting home.

25th November

Although the weather was very poor and target area covered by 9/10ths cloud, in some places as low as 1,000 feet, 'B' Flight managed to find a gap and dived through to attack a railway line and bridge, before pulling up above cloud again. This was in the vicinity of Hilversum.

A most satisfactory operation was 'A' Flight's in Army support, directed against an observation post in a windmill south of Arnhem. Report from front line stated windmill burning well. A V2 rocket trail was seen going up north of Tilburg, distance away unknown.

Flight Lieutenant Merrick Heath from 44 Squadron visited us and was well entertained in Antwerp. We were sorry to hand over Flight Lieutenant 'Shoeie' Sheward posted to 263 Squadron so soon - it was grand having him with us.

26th November

Given Army support target. Rocket gun projectiles near station at Kronenburg north of Leichswold Forest. Seven aircraft participated. Five of 'A' Flight and two of 'B' Flight. Originally intended to be four from each, but two of 'B' Flight's didn't get off. Target area well pranged with cannon and rockets. Quite a lot of light flak and several guns observed firing.

The next show, mostly 'B' Flight, was a very big operation, the Gestapo HQ and mess south of Amsterdam. It was scheduled to take place at about mid-day to catch staff at lunch. As there were schools in the neighbourhood this would also have been the best time had it been a weekday.

After the Group Captain had marked the target with phosphorous rockets, 266 with the Wing Commander leading, were first to attack the furthest building i.e. the Mess. The port side of the HQ was left on fire. Photographs of the attack were taken by Flight Lieutenant Enton of 257 Squadron.

During this time, two squadrons were dive-bombing flak positions to the west and flak ships in the harbour. We saw not a single burst of flak. Unfortunately, documents which it had been hoped were kept in the HQ were elsewhere, but an eye was being kept on their movements.

In the evening 'A' Flight made a successful interdiction attack on the marshalling yards at Gouda. During the attack a V1 flying bomb flew behind Flight Lieutenant Crydermans aircraft, striking the slipstream and crossed just north of Antwerp. A lucky escape.

27th & 28th November
Weather again unsuitable for flying.

29th November
Wing attack on Gestapo HQ in Rotterdam. 266 played the role of anti-flak diversion, dive attacking marshalling yards to the north east of city. Flying Officer Dodd flew Number 2 to Wing Commander marking HQ with phosphorous rockets. 193 attacked buildings at low level with delay action bombs, few of which exploded. Other squadrons also did anti-flak diversion on west side of city.

The operation was successful in that it enabled eleven

prisoners to escape, who would otherwise have been forced to divulge valuable information. Under German methods it is not an insult to say that almost anyone would eventually talk.

Eight aircraft of each flight attacked with success an observation post in church at Kranenburg. The target was found and plastered with sixty-four rockets plus cannon fire. Many direct hits on all parts of church, but spire still standing.

While this operation was in progress another panic Army support target of a strong point, five miles east of Nijnegar, came through and four aircraft - two from each flight - took off with four (actually there were three) bombers as top cover during an attack and vice versa. Rockets and four bombs were concentrated in target area which was well strafed afterwards by all aircraft.

Later an armed recce to the Amsterdam - Amersfoort area. Attacked train consisting of ten trucks and engine in marshalling yard at Bussum. Sixteen direct hits on trucks left blazing. Flak car silenced and cannon strikes on all trucks.

30th November
Combined 'A' and 'B' Flight operation which was very successful. Train in marshalling yard at Bussum well hit.

Pilot Officers Hulley and Palte posted to Technical Evaluation Unit having completed their first tours.

1st - 4th December
Bad weather, cloud and extremely poor visibility prevented any operational flying. Some air tests were carried out, but nothing much else.

5th December
A busy day for both flights. 'B' Flight started off with a most successful show on gun positions in a house west of Strijen. All rockets in target area and everyone emptied their cannon

magazines. Twenty-four direct hits on gun positions and farmhouse set on fire. Ammunition seen to explode from target area.

'A' Flight went out and knocked down a chimney east of Nijmegen which was an enemy observation post with their rockets. The chimney collapsed leaving a short stump. We were congratulated during the day by the Army for the show.

After lunch 'B' Flight went for two targets, a pillbox at Erelkom and an observation post in a church steeple east of Groesbeek. Rockets and cannon on target but the church steeple, although hit, was left standing. 'A' Flight attacked and destroyed this same observation post after 'B' Flight attack. The church was left a smoking heap of rubble. Flight Sergeant Brooks lost himself, but landed at Valenciennes and returned to base later in the day.

6th & 7th December
The weather was too clamped even for air tests and local flying. 'Scottie' Eadie and Noel Borland arrived back to the squadron to replace 'Chimps' Hulley and Ellis Palte who were posted on rest 1st of December. A big party was staged in the Officer's Mess.

10th December
The weather was duff in the early part of the day and a few aircraft tests were done. After lunch 266 excelled itself by having sixteen aircraft at one time airborne.

'A' Flight had a successful show using their rockets and cannon, they demolished two houses - HQ's - and some haystacks north east of Groesbeek.

'B' Flight also had an Army support target and had to attack strong points in houses east of Groesbeek. The area was well pranged by rockets and cannon. Flight Sergeant Ewan turned his Typhoon over on landing, but he was uninjured.

11th December

The weather enabled 'B' Flight to get away to a fairly early start. They carried out a four aircraft armed recce. On this show one Staff car moving south near Hilversum was claimed destroyed. Rail line also attacked and cut.

'A' Flight then had a successful sortie on an observation post in a church steeple in the Hyemegan area. All rockets on target. Flight Sergeant Howell force landed safely behind our lines.

12th December

Because of very bad weather no flying today. Cunnison sailed for Rhodesia today.

13th December

Today the news that Bob Allen was a Prisoner of War was confirmed. Owing to weather no flying was done at all.

16th December

Dingaans Day draws with no sign on the weather abating. No flying possible. The lads get busy and turn the stores room into a bar. The bar just reeks of Rhodesia by the time we have finished - Rhodesia landscapes adorn the walls and the Squadron Crest, the Rhodesian flag hanging up with Dingaan written under it. A large quantity of good cheer (beer) was consumed, not forgetting the potent loving cup of Dingaan's blood.

17th - 22nd December

Adverse weather conditions. No flying on some days, with only local flying on others. 'A' Flight attempted an armed recce on the 22nd, but this was aborted due to bad weather conditions.

23rd December

Both flights did armed recces of Enschelde - Munster -

Dortmund area and had some joy with rail traffic. One motor transport attacked and a large covered trailer, a flamer. One aircraft attacked motor transport south of Enschede with strikes seen. Railway bridge near Ledger attacked and two direct hits claimed.

Warrant Officer Philips, Flight Sergeants Anton, Clack and Mole arrived on the squadron.

24th December

'A' Flight started off by attacking trains in the Dulmen - Geldern area, an armed recce. A stationary train comprising of thirty trucks and engine attacked. Four near misses, the rest overshot the target. One aircraft attacked a 40mm gun near the train. A big explosion seen and the gun silenced. 25+ soldiers strafed on the road by one aircraft. Flak inaccurate at trains.

The CO force landed after having been hit by flak near Derne. His Number 2, Flight Sergeant Howell, landed away from base short of fuel.

'B' Flight did an armed recce of Amersfoort - Ewolle - Appledoorn. No movement observed except a stationary loco and four trucks in Amersfoort station.

Flight Sergeant Hayworth arrives on Squadron.

25th December

'B' Flight went off on an armed recce in the Duigden - Dortmund area. Just after they had destroyed a train they were attacked by 150+ enemy aircraft, Me 109s and Fw 190s. Flying Officer Scott Eadie shot down and Flight Sergeant Green failed to return from this show believed to have been hit by flak. 193 Squadron who were in the vicinity and were acting as top cover claimed one enemy aircraft destroyed and one damaged.

In the afternoon after having served the 'erks' (airmen) their Mess diner, 'A' Flight unsuccessfully attacked a V2 site near

Steenversen. Three cylindrical objects seen by pilots who could not attack with rockets as their long-range tanks would not drop.

The Appendice only records one pilot taking part in this attack - Pilot Officer E. H. Donne - flying Typhoon MN739. It would be very unusual for a lone aircraft to take part in any attack, so it could be assumed that there were other aircraft, but for some reason they are not listed.

In the evening the officers and sergeants had their Christmas dinner which was a first class meal, and the remainder of the evening was spent in the bar drinking the Christmas quota of beer.

26th December
'A' Flight together with four 'B' Flight pilots successfully attacked V2 site near Steenrijk. Railway and suspected V2 activity. Nothing at railway station, but long metal objects attacked alongside new track. Attacked with 46 rockets, two were left smoking, whole area strafed

27th - 28th December
Adverse weather conditions, so no flying of any type took place over these days.

29th December
'B' Flight participated in a Wing show together with 193, 197 and 257 Squadrons on a German HQ in Bilthoven, east of Utrecht. Bombs and rockets falling in target area leaving house severely damaged. This was a successful show.

30th December
'A' Flight went looking for shipping off Overflakee and successfully pranged 5/6 barges with rockets and cannon in harbour. Barges seen burning.

31st December

The morning started by 'B' Flight doing a most successful armed recce of the Louda Zwolle area. One section got rocket and cannon strikes on five coaches in a siding while other sections cut a rail track between Auires Foort and Appendocur.

'A' Flight then went looking for shipping north of Dordrecht where they found a concentration of barges on which salvoes of rockets were directed plus cannon fire. Two salvoes of rockets struck a floating crane in the middle of same barges. Warrant Officer Phillips was hit by flak.

'B' Flight ended the day by pranging a German occupied village, Neeunen, well with rockets and cannon fire. 20mm anti aircraft fire from area of a windmill about 1/4 of a mile away from target area.

Flying Officer G. Eastwood returns to the Squadron after completing his rest. Confirmation that Flight Lieutenant McGibbon is PoW arrived today. Good show.

Summary of 1944

A busy year for the Squadron. Covering the D-Day invasion, the Squadron's first offensive sweeps into Germany, attacks on motor transports, V1 and V2 sites, radar stations, rail marshalling yards and canal transports, Army close support operations, just to mention a few of the targets.

Tragically though there was the attack on Royal Navy ships that resulted in many casualties. No fault of the squadrons that took part however, as the Navy took full responsibility for the tragic error.

Visits to the Wing and squadron by His Majesty King George, Field Marshall Montgomery and General Eisenhower.

Tally of German aircraft were - one He 111, two Ju 88s, one

Do 24 flying boat, two Me 109s, two Ju 88s, two Fw 190s, one Ju 188, one Do 217, another possible Me 109, which is thought to have been a captured Mustang, and three unidentified trainers, all claimed as destroyed. Claimed as damaged were - four Fw 190s plus one unidentified training aircraft.

Sadly the Squadron did not get away scot-free. Losses were - Eight pilots killed in action, ten missing in action, and five crashing in France, although one of these was 'picked up' by the French Resistance, the remainder becoming prisoners of war, some eventually to return to the Squadron.

1945

1st January
New Year's Day starts with fifty odd Jerry 109s and 190s strafing the drome. This resulted in us losing one aircraft - fortunately the most 'clapped' out one in the squadron.

'A' Flight pranged barges with rocket's and cannon at Sliedrecht which were locked in frozen water and unable to move. 'B' Flight then demolished German barracks in a factory at Keizersveer with rocket's and cannon. Very successful show is reported later by the Army who said the target area was burning furiously.

'A' Flight took off after 'B' Flight and again gave the barges at Sliedrecht bags of punishment with rockets and cannon.

2nd January
Not even local flying because of the weather.

4th January
'B' Flight took four 'A' Flight pilots with them and pranged a village near Zierkzee on the Schouwen Isles with rocket's and

cannon. Three fires seen to start among these houses. No sign of activity in village.

5th January
'A' Flight made a successful rocket and cannon attack on some buildings housing German troops near Lierikzee. 'B' Flight were detailed to look for some big white ships near Rees sailing along the Rhine moving towards Emmerich, these were not seen so they cut a railway line with their rockets.

6th January
Escorted four Spits of 145 Wing. Operation abandoned through bad weather and intercom; unsatisfactory due to language difference - Polish 'v' Rhodesian.

7th - 15th January
No operational flying due to adverse weather conditions, but some local flying was possible occasionally.

16th January
'B' Flight attempted to reach an embankment west of Gouda, but no luck due to weather, so they attempted their first bombing attack for ages on a railway line near Woered and got some very near misses. Line cut in two places. 10 x 1,000lb and 6 x 500lb bombs dropped.

17th - 21st January
Very poor weather conditions again with more snowstorms. Some air test carried but mainly no flying at all. On one of these flights Flying Officer Borland crashed on landing (NDEA) but was unhurt. (NDEA. Possibly Not Down to Enemy Action.)

22nd January

An Army support operation for 'A' Flight. The village of
Heinsberg was bombed most effectively. One Me109 and a 'jet'
job were seen lurking about, out of range, as the flight went on
an interdiction operation and were about to attack target.

'B' Flight went out on an interdiction and attacked a railway
line east of Amersfoort with 500lb bombs. Two direct hits
observed.

23rd January

'B' Flight went on an interdiction show. The target was a bridge
at Leiden, but weather prevented reaching the target so they
bombed a railway at Sleidrecht; two direct hits with 1000lb
bombs observed.

'A' Flight then got an interdiction target and bombed Utrecht
- Arnhem railway line getting some close hits and one direct hit.

'B' Flight finished the day by an interdiction attack on a
railway near Appledorne - some near misses observed. On
the way back they saw several transports on the road west of
Appledorne and attacked these with cannon - claimed one
flamer, four destroyed and two German soldiers definitely shot.
Much flak was encountered on this attack.

24th January

'A' Flight was sent out on interdiction and completely demolished
a small railway bridge east of Haage; also bombs were seen to
burst on the railway line. 8 x 1,000lb bombs dropped

25th - 31st January

Weather very bad and condition of the 'drome not very good.
Everyone brassed off with the consistent bad weather.

2nd February

The Squadron started the day by sending a pair of machines on a weather recce. The weather was pretty duff, but later on 'B' Flight set off to bomb the line northeast of Appledorn. No direct hits were claimed, but on the way back they saw some motor transport, they attacked and claimed one Staff car destroyed, one truck destroyed and another damaged.

3rd February

'B' Flight set course to bomb a bridge near Deventer but owing to cloud over the target they bombed the railway line 10 miles east of Deventer. The line was not cut.

In the afternoon a mixed flight took off to bomb a bridge near Leyden, no hits were scored but on the way back two Staff cars were seen north of Gouda, they were both destroyed - flamers.

Flight Lieutenant Harrison led the next show against a railway yard at Lommen. This was very successful. Later Pilot Officer Dodd led a section to bomb a bridge at Oudewater. No results were observed.

6th February

'B' Flight set out to bomb a railway bridge east of Gouda. The bridge was missed, but five transports were destroyed east of Utrecht. 'A' Flight then set course after lunch to bomb the railway line between Gouda and the Hague. This was successful.

Flight Sergeant Pascoe's aircraft was damaged, but he made a good job of landing it on one wheel.

7th February

Flying Officer N. V. Borland and Warrant Officer Phillips set out in the evening for the new strip, B89, which was at Mill. Billets were Nissen huts and were quite comfortable. Taxying the aircraft was made difficult by the fine dust on the 'drome. No operational flying.

8th February
The Squadron set off for the new strip B89. 'B' Flight started operations and set course to bomb the village of Niel. There was 10/10th cloud over the target, so they bombed the railway station and village of Leuven.

After lunch 'A' Flight had a go at MRCP, the squadron led by Flying Officer Hughes. Hughes bombed a village west of Cleve. This was successful. It was the first time the squadron had done MRCP and it went off quite well.

Later in the afternoon 'B' Flight attacked enemy positions on the Materhorn near Cleve, this was successful.

9th February
'A' Flight did a second MRCP. They were sent against Calgar, apparently it was successful, though no results were observed by the pilots. 'B' Flight did the next show. They could not make their original target so they bombed the village of Hess.

10th February
'B' Flight did their first MRCP against the town of Mareinbaum, they were successful. Flying Officer Hughes then took a section to bomb the railway line at Bedburg, this was also successful.

14th February
The CO led 'B' Flight against Brunen, they dropped 1,000lb bombs on target successfully. About the same time Flight Lieutenant Harrison led a mixed section of 'A' and 'B' Flights against Brunen, a section of 257 Squadron led the attack which was very successful. Many direct hits were scored with 1,000lb bombs.

The CO then lead 'A' Flight against Schloss-Calbeck, this was a rest home for German soldiers from the Front, it was situated east of Goch, this was very successful.

Flight Lieutenant Borland led 'B' Flight on the next show, this was against a target at Zutphen, there being 10/10 cloud. They cut a railway line near Zutphen and later attacked transports north and south of Harde.

Later in the day the CO led 'A' Flight against some tanks in a wood near Offerden, this was successful.

16th February
The first show was done by 'B' Flight, and set course to dive bomb Asperden with 1,000lb bombs. 100% hits were scored. Later 'A' Flight took off to bomb the same place and was very successful. Asperden fell to our troops without any defence being shown.

Flight Lieutenant Borland led 'B' Flight against some pillboxes on the outskirts of Goch. This was a successful show.

19th February
'B' Flight did the only show of the day against Calcar. The bombing was successful and several large houses were left burning. Pilot Officer Dodd led the flight.

21st February
Squadron Leader Deall led by 'A' Flight did their first show against Calcar. This was an MRCP show and was successful. 'A' Flight also did the next show and dive-bombed the same target, this was a great 'prang' the bombing well spread. Pilot Officer G. Henderson flew a photo recce a few minutes after the attack.

22nd February
'B' Flight led by the CO set out to bomb Kepplen, the bombing was good. Flight Lieutenant Hughes led the next 'A' Flight show

against some buildings south of Calcar, the result being good bombing and the buildings flattened.

The CO then led 'B' Flight against Kepplen and left the place burning well. The show by 'A' Flight was against the village of Sonsbeck, this was successful.

24th February

Leading 'B' Flight, the CO attacked a drawbridge at Leiden, but the target was covered by cloud, so they bombed the railway line between Woerden and Utrecht. Three cuts were claimed.

'A' Flight led by Flight Lieutenant Hughes set course to attack a bridge east of Gouda, they attacked the line between Amersfoort and Zwolle. 'A' Flight later set out to attack the Amersfoort - Zwolle line again, which was successful.

25th February

'A' Flight left early for an interdiction near Zwolle, the CO leading. A train was seen southwest of Zwolle and promptly attacked, a direct hit was scored on the train by the CO and the train was left burning, quite a lot of flak.

27th February

There was only one show on this day, and that was MRCP on Winnekendonk. The weather was poor but the show was carried out successfully.

28th February

'B' Flight led by Flight Lieutenant Borland did the first show against Winnekendonk, they dive bombed it successfully. 'A' Flight then proceeded to liberate Winnekendonk again and were successful.

'B' Flight attacked some guns and troops near Weeze, though

they encountered much medium and light flak they were successful.

'A' Flight then proceeded to attack a factory southwest of Xanten. It was a beautiful show, the building was left burning. A lot of heavy, medium and light flak was met. Pilot Officer Shepherd was hit and was forced by flak to steer south where he later baled out in the enemy lines. He was captured and made a PoW.

7th March

No flying weather, duff all day. Wing Commander Davidson, Air Liaison Officer paid us a visit after seeing the AOC who discussed with him our future CO. We consider the squadron very fortunate in having Squadron Leader Sheward as our CO. He hails from the Argentine and is well known to 266.

Wing Commander Davidson was taken by jeep into Germany sightseeing, visiting Asperdan and Goch. Squadron Leader Sheward was 'initiated' in the evening!

9th March

Eleven aircraft of 'A' Flight on interdiction followed by eight aircraft of 'B' Flight also on interdiction. Both were successful and cut rail lines in north Holland.

It came as a very sad blow to 146 Wing to lose Squadron Leader Derek Erasmus, CO of 193 Squadron. He was carrying out a low level bombing attack on a railway line in north Holland when he was seen to crash and explode soon after his bombs were released, the causes are yet unknown. It was a sudden end to a most promising career. His gay cheerful nature and ready answer to the call of duty will long be an inspiring memory to all who knew him. He was just 22.

10th - 12th March

Weather unsuitable for any flying, very duff, but two sections of four aircraft managed to get airborne (on the 12th), each carrying out attacks for the RAF film unit which took movie pictures.

13th March

Eight aircraft of 'A' Flight on interdiction but primary target was not located, so pranged a rail line west of Arnhem. At least two direct hits, line and sleepers were seen airborne! The Wing was released for 24 hours from noon.

15th March

This is the first day of this year that the sun has shone all day and had any bite in it. Things are very quiet, limited flying obviously working up for something really big, once and for all we hope.

16th March

Weather duff all day, unsuited for any flying. The sergeants came across to the Officer's Mess in the evening. A very fine party ensued!

17th March

No operations, weather unsuited. Stood by for a 'Tit' show. A few air tests carried out. The meaning of 'Tit' show has sadly been lost to memory. (No amount of research has come up with a possible meaning for this word. Possibly a word simply used by this Squadron.) Flying Officer D. Quick of Bulawayo joined the squadron.

18th March

The long awaited 'Tit' show came off at 3.30pm, the weather eventually clearing. Nine aircraft of 'A' Flight together with 193, 197 and 263 Squadrons took off. Wing Commander Deall led the show; Group Captain Wells flew as 'Master of Ceremonies'.

The target was a HQ south of Deventer, said to house three Generals and staff. All the buildings were dealt with in the thorough 146 Wing manner. Photos taken afterwards proved the bombing more successful than thought at first.

19th March

A very successful day's operation. 'B' Flight represented 266 on another 'Tit' show. The Wing led by Wing Commander Deall clobbered a big motor transport repair works at Doetinchem. It was a beautiful target and was left under a pall of smoke which rose to 3,000 feet. The flak was plentiful but was avoided.

'A' Flight sent off four sections of two aircraft at 15 minute intervals on armed recce up to north Holland, resulting in five vehicles destroyed, five damaged and thirty plus troops attacked while marching down a road, many casualties observed. Pilot Officer Donne who carried out this attack, reports that aerobatics such as theirs is seldom seen.

21st March

Yet another 'Tit' show. Eight aircraft of 'B' Flight together with the rest of the Wing pranged the HQ of the General and his staff who dealt with the withdrawal of troops and equipment from Holland.

The show went off at first sight, and it is considered that the big hotel in which the HQ was situated was completely wiped out. The HQ was situated on the outskirts of Bussum. A hell of a lot of flak came up from Hilversum, it was intense but inaccurate.

Four aircraft of 'A' Flight led by Flight Lieutenant 'Killer' Miller (Australian) did an interdiction on a bridge north east of Zwolle. Near misses were scored.

A composite eight aircraft, 'A' and 'B' Flight, went after a fuel dump in some woods south east of Deventer. All bombs went into the target area, but no fires observed. This was a Wing show.

This is the first day of spring and the day itself couldn't have been lovelier.

Flying Officer Neil Borland (Black Section) pranged his troublesome 'H' for hard luck on landing in a 20mph crosswind. Pilot shaken but unhurt.

22nd March

Interdiction was the order of the day. Weather perfect. 'A' Flight and seven aircraft set out to cut the line from Amersfoort to Buarnevelt. The bombing wasn't up to the usual standard and no cuts were claimed.

'B' Flight's eight aircraft later got two cuts on a line north east of Deventer. They went after a bridge, but cut the line either side of the bridge.

One motor transport was pranged through fear. Flight Lieutenant Doug Borland went down after it, but before he could open fire the vehicle broke hard to starboard pranging itself among trees lining the road.

A really beautiful cloudless day, we are still on limited operations waiting for the last big push, we hope.

23rd March

Four aircraft of 'B' Flight went off at first light and pranged an ammo factory southeast of Deventer, all bombs in target area, most successful.

Four aircraft put anti-personnel bombs on Enschelde and eight aircraft plastered Stelewigh, both are aerodromes, lots of flak but no movement seen.

Eight aircraft of 'A' Flight liberated Heldern three miles east of the Rhine. All bombs - incendiary – hit in the town, left a lovely fire, hard luck 'Heldern'.

24th March

D-Day for the crossing of the Rhine today. 'A' Flight was rudely awakened at 04.30 and proceeded with eight aircraft to attack the village of Kundenburg, east of Wessel. The attack made with eight aircraft of 193 was successful and the target was left in flames.

Our next detail was an anti-flak patrol to cover airborne landings. Eight aircraft of 'B' Flight and four aircraft of 'A' Flight forming Pink, Grey and Blue Sections took part. The sortie was successful, 'B' Flight getting some transports and the section of 'A' Flight a large flak position which was attacked three times and left with a decided twitch.

The next detail, eight aircraft of 'A' Flight and four aircraft of 'B' Flight held plenty of excitement for 'Dusty' and 'Killer' Miller. 'Dusty's engine packed up on the way out and he forced landed east of Goch. 'Killer' was hit by flak in the port aileron which jammed. He had sufficient control to make a right hand circuit and pulled off a good landing. Good show the 'Millers'!

The sortie itself was successful. Several flak positions were attacked and hits with bombs and cannons seen. 'Killer' finished off a dispatch rider just before he was hit.

A mobile radar control post was laid on for the next show to be done by 'B' Flight, but the weather was too bad and they did not take off. A very good day's work.

25th March

Eight aircraft of 'B' Flight led by the CO attacked a HQ at Auholt very successfully. Three direct hits were scored. The building was adorned with a large Red Cross and protected by batteries of light AA guns. The Hun up to his tricks again.

Bad weather prevented further sorties over the battlefront, but Dave Hughes, 'Killer' Miller and Ted Donne wrecked their constitutions by doing a tail-chase and some fancy formation flying.

26th March

In the middle of a great offensive we are released for the day to do 'Practice Bombing'! A truly amazing war! In the morning four sorties were flown by 'A' Flight, 'B' Flight taking over in the afternoon.

After lunch four aircraft of 'A' Flight and four of 193 made a very successful attack on some SS Headquarters south east of Rhenen. The four buildings containing the HQ were all flattened.

Pilot Officer Paddy Culligan met with a fatal accident, burst a tyre on take off and cartwheeled. Paddy was most popular on the Wing, his death is a sad blow to all who knew him.

28th March

The weather cleared for a while and enabled eight aircraft of 'A' Flight led by the CO to get off on an armed recce in the Coeorden area. The Hun transport proved as elusive as ever, but the boys found two motor transports both of which were well pranged.

31st March

Weather cleared after two days of no operational flying. 'B' Flight went off in pairs at 30-minute intervals on armed recce in the Almelo area. Four pairs collected six motor transports destroyed and four damaged.

1st April

Though the cloud base was only 1,000ft we were sent off in pairs on armed recces. The first pair turned back early owing to engine trouble, our second pair, Pilot Officer Donne and Warrant

Officer Phillips, set off and found some motor transport which they beat up, in the process of which Ted Donne was hit by flak and seen to gain height and then stall and spin in, something was seen to leave the aircraft before it spun. It is considered that Ted has a chance, only time will tell. Ted Donne was a "hell of a good bloke", it's a pity there aren't more like him.

This suicide low recce was stopped at midday after the Wing had lost two pilots in the Group and nineteen pilots all told.

7th April

'A' Flight started the day by an interdiction on the Amersfoort - Appledoorn line. One cut was scored. There were also several near misses.

After a weather recce by Flight Lieutenant Borland and 'Skid' McAdam, 'B' Flight set off to cut a line in the Zwolle area. They were successful. Another section of 'B' Flight went for a road and railway crossing at Epe, north of Appledoorn. Near misses were scored. 'A' Flight later went for the same line; they attacked in the morning. They were again successful. Later 'B' Flight dive-bombed the railway between Nursfeet and Hardewyk. Four cuts were scored.

At 17.30 a section of 'A' Flight led by the CO set out to attack a train south of Assen, they found the train and trucks and attacked those. Two direct hits were scored on the train and one cut on the line north of the train, the train blew up after the attack and smoke rose to 3,000 feet. It was the busiest day we had for a few weeks.

8th April

'B' Flight started the day in the afternoon by sending two sections on armed recce. The first led by the CO went to Grontingen area and destroyed three motor transports. The second led by Flight Lieutenant Borland were more successful, they scored three flamers, one smoker and damaged another six motor transports. This was particularly good, as there were only two pilots, Flight Lieutenant Borlad and D. Dodd. The other two had returned earlier owing to mechanical trouble.

'A' Flight then set out and the first section led by Flying Officer Noel Borland scored four, all damaged. The other section was led by Wing Commander Deall.

9th April

At 13.35 the CO and a section set for an area west of Emden, this was very successful, for they scored five flamers, four smokers and an unknown quantity damaged.

The effect was dampened considerably by the loss of 'Numpie' Phillips whose engine packed up and he had to force land in the Leuwarden area. After his plane came to a stop he was seen to leap out and run for it. The aircraft then proceeded to burn furiously.

The other section was not very successful, but scored on horse drawn transports. 'B' Flight then went out, one section led by George Eastwood proceeded to search for suitable targets between Emden and Bremen. Their effort was rewarded by getting one flamer and two smokers, these being motor transports, and also horse drawn vehicles. Flight Lieutenant Borland's section went farther afield towards Groningen for the gain of one large motor transport which was destroyed.

In the early evening a section of 'A' Flight led by Pilot Officer Luhnenschloss proceeded to an area north west of Oldenburg, very early on a Staff car was spotted, the driver spotting the aircraft took cover in a front garden. However the cars days were soon numbered, the pilots' satisfied that it was finished after seeing a large tree fall on it. Later four trucks were breeched up on a cross roads, three damaged claimed, again north of Oldenburg some trucks were spotted and was reported, 197 attacked these and found engines on them. Jerry sending up flak and more came from a lake west of Oldenburg.

10th April

'B' Flight started the day by complaining of the earliness of the hour and by having two sections make abortive sorties. 'A' Flight sent out two sections in the afternoon, the first led by Flight Lieutenant Borland which was lucky in that they managed to destroy two motor transports and one horse drawn vehicle, the horse frantically trying to jump the hedge.

Its such a pity the Germans use horses to draw their vehicles. They, like civilians, are the innocent victims of the war.

11th April

This day started very early, after a long wait 'A' Flight set off at 12.00 for north east of Leer, some fun was had, three motor transports on side of road were set upon and left totally unserviceable. Whilst flying north of Leer at a place named Bagband some flak encountered. Inaccurate at first but improving at end of attack. It appeared to come from a flak battery near a factory, this was reported.

The other section led by Flying Officer Noel Borland were not successful. One section of 'B' Flight next took off and proceeded to Leenwarden - Emden via Groningen. Flight Lieutenant Borland's section claimed four flamers and motor transports. Another section led by Flying Officer Eastwood had similar claims. Flying Officer Borland again took off and returned with a score of two ammunition buses and one Staff car destroyed.

The CO and section left for an aerodrome north-east of Cloppenburg and promptly 'clobbered' one Fw 190 and one Ju 88 on the 'drome, they also damaged a 109, this was confirmed when our troops took the 'drome.

12th April

'B' Flight took off for the Bremen - Emden area, they spotted some Ju 188s on the Ardhof aerodrome and proceeded to the attack. They claimed one probable destroyed and another damaged, on the roads they destroyed one three tonner and damaged another, the other four saw transports, destroying one Staff car and petrol lorry and a three tonner.

The CO led a section of 'A' Flight for the Leer area; one motor transport and two trailers were destroyed. Later at a nearby aerodrome five motor transports were seen, one smoker and the rest damaged, spraying 20mm amongst personnel.

The other section saw eight motor transports and came away after destroying six and damaging the other two. Only one more section went off that day which was led by Flight Lieutenant Gray. Between Emden and Wilhemshaven they destroyed three motor transports and better still damaged two Ju 188s. This was a successful day.

13th April

Geoff Henderson started the day by doing a photo recce. The next show was a Wing 'Do'. This took place at Den Haldern and consisted of two batteries of coastal guns which were firing at the Dutch Resistance Movement on Teael. Two sections led by Wing Commander Deall attacked the target, and flak was in plenty, heavy and light which followed them out into the Zuider Zee. The other section led by Squadron Leader Sheward attacked guns further south and were also successful. Den Haldern used to be one of the hottest spots in Holland.

At 20.00 hours two sections of 'B' Flight set course to bomb a strong point north of Arnhem. The barracks were well pranged with 500lb bombs.

14th April

The day was an easy one. Four aircraft of 'B' Flight led by Flying Officer Eastwood set out for Leuwarden - Groningen area. Only one motor transport found and that was destroyed.

16th April

Tactics were changed and the Squadron went out in pairs. Flight Lieutenant Borland did a weather recce and armed recce. He and Flying Officer Gray struck heavily at Jerry's fuel supply destroying one three tonner and small bowser, both were carrying petrol and burnt well, another motor transport vehicle caused another bonfire. Geoff Henderson and Moll then had a try, but only claimed one truck and trailer smoking.

Flying Officer Eastwood and Flight Sergeant Mitchell set out, but his Number Two did not get off. Flying Officer Eastwood carried on undeterred and got himself one armoured fighting vehicle destroyed and damaged three trucks, this was carried out near Amersfoort.

Flight Lieutenant Hughes set the 'A' Flight pairs going, setting for east of Amersfoort and attacked enemy transports. Noel Borland and Mitchell patrolled west of Arnhem and Deventer and claimed two horse-drawn and one motor transport. 'Killer' Miller and Godley had a score of two motor transports destroyed and one damaged.

Joe Luhnenschloss and 'Skid' McAdam set course for northwest Holland. A 'Queen Mary' was spotted and pranged, the flak gunners then got a bit anti, they were forced to leave the area, they made for Amersfoort and attacked a small convoy of motor transports and horse-drawn, claimed two motor transports and one horse-drawn destroyed. Roy Gray and Ian Anton were very successful, having one five tonner and one three tonner, one van and three small motor transports were also damaged.

George Eastwood and Johnny Moll had the luck with two

280

trucks destroyed and one damaged. All pilots then proceeded to the refreshment bar, and got ready to take off to the new airfield at B105 led by Wing Commander Deall, on arrival it was discovered to be a grass 'drome north east of Lingen and went by the name of Drope. The Squadron returned to a life in tents.

17th April

The Wing Commander led 'A' Flight to attack a stores depot west of Oldenburg. This was flattened and proved by photographs. 'B' Flight then did a show, a factory housing motor transport vehicles, bombing was good, part of the buildings destroyed. This was considered a good Wing effort.

Later in the evening Flight Lieutenant Hughes led 'A' Flight on an artillery HQ south of Oldenburg, but unfortunately the target - cross roads - was mistaken for other cross roads.

18th April

'B' Flight started off for some thirty-eight barges in the Bremen - Wilhemshaven estuary. They were successful. 'A' Flight led by Wing Commander Deall set out to bomb a HQ south east of Leer. 193 Squadron also went along. It was a low level show. After the attack one building was completely demolished.

In the afternoon 'B' Flight led by the Wing Commander set out to bomb a fort south of Utrecht, this was also successful.

In the evening 193 and 266 Squadrons set out to bomb a wood east of Amersfoort. 193 took the southern half and 266 the northern half. The bombing was well dispersed and thoroughly strafed, a good show.

20th April

Shipping recces was the order of the day. Flying Officer Eastwood and Flight Lieutenant Miller did the first one round the Emden - Wilhemshaven area, they saw no enemy shipping, but destroyed one motor transport. Flight Sergeant Wheeler and Mitchell set out but saw nothing. No further flying was carried out until the 23rd. Pilots carrying out ground recces obtaining several radios at Delmenhorst.

23rd April
Flight Lieutenant Hughes led a section and took off for southeast of Stade to attack a train. Cannon strikes were seen on the train and on nearby barracks. Later Flying Officer Borland and 'Killer' Miller carried out a shipping recce. On the way back some motor transport were seen and attacked. Flying Officer Borland was hit and went straight in. He did not call up. His loss was a blow, for he was very popular. Sympathies were extended to his brother Doug. It was later found that he had been buried near the crash and later his body was removed to a nearby village cemetery near Leer. Further flying was delayed until the 25th.

25th April
A real Wing show. Twelve aircraft of 266 took part, eight of 'A' Flight and four of 'B' Flight, barracks being the target north of Bremen and they were well pranged. Later Flight Lieutenant Gray and Flight Sergeant Moll did a shipping recce. Pilot Officer Henderson and 'Dusty' Miller then took off to photograph the results. Doug Borland and 'Skid' McAdam doing some Auster flying to Antwerp.

No more operations were done up to the 27th. The squadron packed up to go to Fairwood Common and left at 11.00 hours. The CO led two sections of 'A' Flight, the rest of the Squadron was led by Doug Borland and Dave Hughes. The weather was not very good and the ceiling being about 150ft, Doug and Dave turned back but the CO and two sections forced on and landed at Courtrai. The weather was bad over the Channel so they stayed the night at Courtrai. They forced on the next morning and landed at Manston in time for lunch. After lunch they set course for Fairwood Common passing over London, they landed later in the afternoon.

The rest of the Squadron left Drope on the same day and spent the night at Manston. They reached Fairwood Common on the following day. The boys immediately began to indulge in good British beer with real enthusiasm.

30 April

Now back in the UK. We started a course with air to ground and rocket firing practice. Eleven sorties being carried out for the day. Squadron settled down to the new surroundings.

1st - 7th May

This week saw bad weather and limited flying. What flying there was is more air to ground, dive-bombing and low level bombing practice.

8th May

VE Day. No flying carried out. The day was spent in celebrating in no mean manner. Wing Commander J. H. Deall visited the squadron. A good day was had by all.

9th May

V1 Day. Still celebrating. Completed the day with a grand dance in the NAAFI (Navy, Army, Air Force Institute.) Everybody enjoying them selves immensely.

10th - 13th May

More practice flying, weather permitting.

14th May

The pilots took part in a Victory Parade through Swansea.

15th May

One sortie of dive-bombing and two of rockets were done before weather clamped. Flight Lieutenant Borland arrived with Flying Officer Scott-Eadie, Pilot Officer Shepherd and Flying Officer Dodd. These pilots had just returned to England after being released from PoW camps. Shepherd was a bit thin, but all three had interesting experiences to tell.

16th – 22 May

More practice flying. On the 22nd Squadron Leader Sheward did a beat up in Army maneuvers, co-operation exercise with the Black Watch.

23rd – 26th May

More practice flying. On the 25th Pilot Officer Henderson pranged his aircraft.

27th May

The Squadron was released. Nil flying. Several of the pilots again visit their old haunts. Others playing a leisurely round of golf. A few attended a dance at Langland Bay.

28th May

Fourteen sorties of dive-bombing and rocket firing carried out. The Squadron packed up early in time for a strenuous and exciting foursome, the contesting parties being the CO and Adjutant versus Flight Lieutenant Borland and Flying Officer Ford, with a win for the latter. Other pilots played singles. There is no indication of what they were playing.

29th – 31st May

More practice flying – dive-bombing, strafing, rockets, and air to ground attacks. After lunch they set course for Gilze where the Squadron were to refuel, but there was sufficient fuel to continue so they flew to Alhorn B111 which was now base.

7th June
Four sections of 'A' and 'B' Flights took off for cross-country flights. Most flights were over Wilhemshaven, Bremerhavern, Cuxhaven, Hamburg, Bremen, Kiel and Flensburg.

8th June
The Wing moved today for Hildersheim. 'B' Flight left in the morning and 'A' Flight followed after lunch. The 'drome was a grass surface with only one runway, the surface being a bit rough. Settled down into the new billets which were very good.

9th - 25th June
This period was taken up with various cross-country flights over Allied occupied Germany, air tests and formation flying.

26th June
'A' Flight under the Wing Commander led the fly past over Wunstorf for the departure of the AOC. The Wing was congratulated and Group Captain Baldwin of the rival 123 Wing did not stint his praise. Flying Officer Henderson took photos of the fly past in a photo-reconnaissance Typhoon.

30th June
One section of 'A' Flight took off for local flying and formation. Warrant Officer Becks flew the leave Anson to Lasham.

'B' Flight set out with two sections for a practice fly past which was to take place over Copenhagen on the next day. The weather however prevented this.

1st July

Seven sorties carried out consisting of local flying. Squadron pilots played pilots of 263 Squadron at cricket, unfortunately weather stopped play.

2nd July

One sortie carried out by Flight Lieutenant Hughes. Resumption of cricket match in afternoon resulting in a draw.

4th July

Eight sorties consisting of local flying in formation and air tests. A football match was played in the evening against the ground personnel of 193 Squadron, several pilots taking part, resulting in a win for the Squadron. The Squadron was visited by Flying Officer S. Eadie, late PoW.

5th July

Squadron left for Gilsey preparatory to fly past in Brussels area next day. Ground personnel played 413 RSU at football in the evening, result win for the Squadron.

6th and 7th July

Thirteen machines took part in fly past in Brussels area which was to mark the departure of the 2nd Tactical Air Force from that town. A letter of congratulations by Wing Commander (Flying) for a good show. Also unstinted praise from CO of a rival Wing.

8th July

The Squadron returned to base. Pilot Officer Mitchell had to force land in home circuit. Pilot uninjured but the aircraft a write off. Ground personnel with some pilots busy practicing for the Wing Sports.

11th July
Air Chief Marshal Tedder and Lady Tedder visited the Wing in the morning and stopped for lunch. Cricket match played in the evening versus 193. A very close game resulted in a win for the Squadron.

12th July
Busy day flying. Local formation, cross-country, map reading and navigation. Warrant Officer Haworth pranged prior to take off due to a burst tyre, fortunately he escaped injury.

14th July
A busy day of flying. Eleven sorties were flown which were made up of local flying only. In the afternoon a cricket match was played against Radio & Instruments, resulting in a win for the latter, the Squadron losing the first match of the season.

15th - 21st July
Some flying when thunderstorms allowed. More local flying, cross-county and aerobatics. Cricket and tennis were played.

22nd July
Nil flying. Day spent on practice for Wing Sports. A launching ceremony took place of the motorboat made by pilots of the Squadron, this was a great success.

28th July
In the afternoon the Wing Sports Day was held, the Squadron being placed 2nd in all events. The sports were a great success.

30th July
Nineteen pilots informed of their posting to the UK pending repatriation. The Squadron held a party in the evening for a

farewell party to the ground personnel. An excellent time was had by all.

31st July
A sad day for the Squadron. The pilots left at 17.00 hours bound for 14 PTC en route for England.

Summary for 1945

Targets during 1945 were becoming much harder to find. The Third Reich was 'on its' knees', and the end of the Second World War in Europe was rapidly approaching.

Coastal guns, German Army barracks, rail lines and motor transports were all attacked. The crossing of the mighty River Rhine, the last line of defence for Germany. Then VE Day and a return to the United Kingdom for the Squadron. Various Victory parades and five captured Squadron pilots find their way back to the Squadron after release from PoW camps.

Back to Europe and Western Germany briefly before pilots were repatriated to England for discharge. The ORBs do not describe in any detail what the feelings were amongst either the pilots or ground crews, but it must have been one of relief for surviving the war and yet great sadness that, although they were returning home, they possibly would never meet each other again.

The losses for 1945 were - one pilot killed in action 2 missing in action, one PoW and one killed in a flying accident. Claims were - one Fw 190 and two Ju 88s destroyed. One Me 109 and three Ju 88s damaged.

Epitaph

And so we come to the end of No. 266 (Rhodesian) (Fighter) Squadrons wartime diaries.

The squadron disbanded on 31 July 1945 but was reformed again on 1 September 1946, but that is for another book. As a fitting conclusion I offer to the reader The Squadron Song! The tune and composer is sadly unknown. Kindly sent to me by Michael Biggs, ex 266 Squadron.

"Out on the strip the Riggers are a working.
Out on the strip the armourers are working too!
The Pilots come out.
We're rushing about.
To the cry of 266. See them fly by.
Loaded up, Loaded up.
See them Return Loaded up twice.
They couldn't find it! Fuel them up.
Fuel them up there Flapping.
Then off once again for the Target."

193 & SQUADRON 266 PILOTS, HARROWBEER 10 FEBRUARY 1944.
3RD TO 6TH FROM LEFT ARE WING COMMANDER E. R. BAKER,
FLIGHT LIEUTENANT DEALL, FLYING OFFICER HAWORTH AND
FLYING OFFICER MCGIBBON, ALL 266 SQUADRON PILOTS.

AIR MARSHALL SIR HUGH DOWDING WITH BATTLE
OF BRITAIN PILOTS. 266 SQUADRON PILOT R.
H. GRETTON IS ON THE FAR RIGHT.

GODFREY HUGGINS, PRIME MINISTER OF SOUTHERN RHODESIA, VISITS NO. 266 (RHODESIA) SQUADRON, MAY 1944. THE PM IS SITTING IN A DINGHY SURROUNDED BY AIRMEN OF THE UNIT.

HURRICANES OF NO. 1 SQUADRON FOLLOWED BY 266 SQUADRON SPITFIRES. POSSIBLY THE FACTORY FLY PAST FOR FACTORY WORKERS 26 SEPTEMBER 1940.

PILOT OFFICER J. F. SODEN FLYING TOMAHAWKS
IN THE WESTERN DESERT. (STANDING THIRD
FROM LEFT WITH JUST HIS FACE VISIBLE.)

NO. 7 OTU SPITFIRE CONVERSION COURSE,
HARWARDEN 1 JULY 1940. SUB LIEUTENANT
GREENSHIELDS IS SEATED FIRST ON THE LEFT.

THE HARROWBEER WING IN 1944.

266 SQUADRON IN 1944 PHOTOGRAPHED WITH 6266
SERVICING ECHELON. COURTESY OF MICHAEL BIGGS.

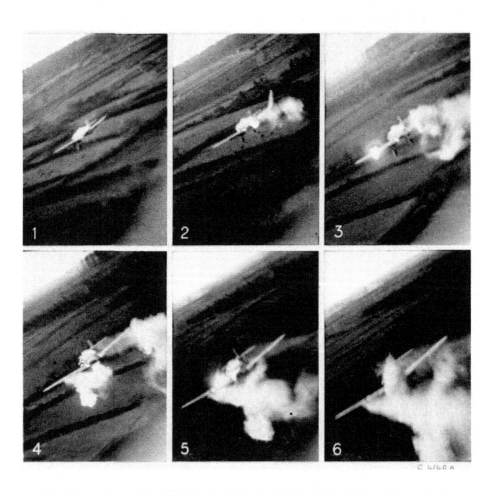

CAMERA GUN FOOTAGE FROM FLYING OFFICER BORLAND'S
TYPHOON SHOOTING DOWN A ME 109, 21 JANUARY 1944.

GUN CAMERA FOOTAGE FROM A TYPHOON FLOWN
BY FLIGHT SERGEANT ERASMUS 15 AUGUST 1943.

FROM FLYING OFFICER W. V. MOLLET'S CAMERA GUN
OF 30 DECEMBER 1943, RECORDING SHOOTING DOWN
A JU 52 MINESWEEPER AIRCRAFT. CANNON SHELLS ARE
STRIKING THE SEA AND AIRCRAFT FUSELAGE. HE SHARED
THIS CLAIM WITH FLYING OFFICER N. J. LUCAS.

(13) 266 SQUADRON SUPERMARINE SPITFIRE. JANUARY
1940 – JULY 1942 IN SQUADRON SERVICE.

266 SQUADRON HAWKER TYPHOON IB. JULY 1942.

UNKNOWN SQUADRON PILOT AND ARTIST. ORB
DATED 25 OCTOBER 1943 GIVES DETAILS!.

Total pilot and known ground crew losses

Pilots.

Killed in Action.	24
Missing in Action.	23
Others. (Accidents etc.)	21
Total.	68

(Assuming 16 pilots in squadron this equates to the squadron being 'wiped out 4.25 times!)

Ground crew.

Killed on Active service.	4
Wounded on Active Service.	4

Total 8

Enemy aircraft claimed

Destroyed.

Me 109 x 4
Do 217 x 4
Me 110 x 1
He 111 x 6
Do 215 x 3
Ju 88   x 9
Me 210 x 1
Fw 190 x 12
Ju 52   x 2
Do 24   x 1
Ju 188 x 1
Bombers (Type Unspecified) x 5

Trainersx 3

Total 52

Damaged.
He 111 x 1
Do 215 x 5
Me 109 x 4
Ju 88 x 4
Fw 190 x 13
Trainer x 1
Other (Type Unspecified) x 10

Total. 41

Probables.
Bombers (Type Unspecified)   x 3

Grand total. 96 enemy aircraft

Roll of Honour 1939

Officers & NCOs recorded as having been with the Squadron during 1939.
Pilot Officer D. L.Armitage. RAFVR
Pilot Officer D. G. Ashton.
Missing in Action. 12 August 1940
Sergeant Pilot R. G. V. Barraclough
Pilot Officer E. G. Barwell
Pilot Officer N. G. Bowen.
Killed in Action. 16 August 1940.

Flying Officer N. W. Burnett
Pilot Officer C. A. G. Clarke

Pilot Officer S. W. Cobb. Squadron Adjutant. RAFVR
Flight Lieutenant J. B. Coward. Flight Commander
Sergeant Pilot A. W. Eade
Flight Lieutenant (Acting) I. R. Gleed. Flight Commander
Pilot Officer H. M. T. Heron
Squadron Leader J. W. A. Hunnard. Commanding Officer
Sergeant Pilot W. Jones
Pilot Officer P. H. G. Mitchell
Warrant Officer J. Pickard. Engineering Officer.
Pilot Officer R. J. B. Roach
Pilot Officer J. W. B. Stevenson.
Missing in Action. 2 June 1940
Pilot Officer R. M. Trousdale. (P7350 pilot)
Pilot Officer J. L. Wilkie
Pilot Officer W. S. Williams.
Killed in flying accident. 21 October 1940
Pilot Officer J. L. Willis

Known ground crew. 1939
530787 Leading Aircraftsman B. Walker.
Accidental injury. 13 November 1939 at RAF Sutton Bridge.

Roll of Honour 1940

Officers & NCOs recorded as having been with the Squadron during 1940.
Officers and NCOs from 1939 are not listed here.

Sergeant Pilot J. W. Allen

Sergeant Pilot L. O. Allton

Sergeant Pilot H. W. Ayres

Flight Lieutenant D. W. Balden. Flight Commander

Flight Lieutenant Bazley. Flight Commander

Killed in Action. 2 March 1941

Sergeant Pilot M. A. Beatty

Sergeant Pilot R. A.Boswell

Squadron Leader Bitmead

Sergeant Pilot R. A.Breeze

Pilot Officer F. W. Cale.

Killed in Action. 15 August 1940

Pilot Officer H. H. Chalder

Pilot Officer J. C. R. Clarke

Sergeant Pilot H. Cook. (P7350 pilot.)

Sergeant Pilot T. A. Cooper

Pilot Officer T. D. Davey DFC

Pilot Officer A. R. H. Downing. Intelligence Officer.

Sergeant Pilot J. T. Dumore

Sergeant Pilot W. Ellis

Pilot Officer F. P. Ferris

Missing in Action. Presumed drowned. 8 March 1941

Sergeant Pilot G. A.Ford

Sergeant Pilot S. A. Godwin

Flight Lieutenant Gleed

Sergeant Pilot S. A. Goodwin

Pilot Officer R. C. Gostling

Sub Lieutenant H. C. Greenshields. RNVR

Missing in Action 16 August 1940

Sergeant Pilot R. H. Gretton

Pilot Officer P. S. Gunning

Pilot Officer N. P. W. Hancock

Sergeant Pilot F. B. Hawley.

Missing in Action. 15 August 1940

Pilot Officer G. M. Hayton

Pilot Officer M. K. Hill
(Or M. R. Hill. KIA 12 March 1945)
Pilot Officer A. H. Humphrey
Squadron Leader P. G. Jameson.
Commanding Officer. 17 September 1940 (P7350 pilot)
Sergeant Pilot R. T. Kidman.
Missing in Action. 2 June 1940
Sergeant Pilot E. A. King
Sergeant Pilot D. E.Kingaby
Sergeant Pilot G. Land
Sergeant Pilot R. F. Lewis
Pilot Officer Logan. (P7350 pilot)
Sergeant Pilot MacGregor
Squadron Leader H. W. Mermagen AFC.
Temporary Commanding Officer 12 September 1940 (P7350 pilot.)
Pilot Officer W. A. Middleton
Sergeant Pilot F. W. Morse
Sergeant Pilot C. E. Ody
Pilot Officer J. G. Pattison
Sergeant Pilot K. C. Pattison
Pilot Officer H. E. Penketh
Killed in flying accident. 22 November 1940
Pilot Officer P. D. Pool
Pilot Officer H. A. R. Prowse
Sergeant Pilot W. Sadler
Sergeant Pilot J. E. van Schaich
Sergeant Pilot J. A. Scott
Sergeant Pilot J. Shircore
Pilot Officer S. A. C. Sibley
Sergeant Pilot Smith

Pilot Officer J. F. Soden

Squadron Leader D. G. H. Spencer
  (On attachment)

Flight Sergeant C. Sydney

Sergeant Pilot Terry

Pilot Officer R. H. Thomas

Flying Officer E. H. Thomas

Sergeant Pilot D. W. Thomas

Sergeant Pilot R. J. Thoburn
  Missing in Action. 3 July 1941.

Sergeant Pilot S. F. Tomalin

Pilot Officer B. E. Tucker

Pilot Officer T. A. Vigors

Sergeant Pilot Whewell

Pilot Officer E. P.Wells. (P7350 pilot)

Squadron Leader R. L. Wilkinson.

Commanding Officer. 6 July 1940
  Killed in Action. 16 August 1940.

Known ground crew. 1940

986486 Aircraftman Second Class. J. B. Brawley.
  Killed in action. 13 August 1940 at RAF Eastchurch.

973446 Aircraftman Second Class. E. Crossley.
  Wounded 13 August 1940 at RAF Eastchurch.

Roll of Honour 1941

Officers & NCOs recorded as having been with the Squadron during 1941.

Officers and NCOs from previous years are not listed here.

Pilot Officer N. N. Allen

Pilot Officer Allen-White
Missing in action. 11 January 1942.

Sergeant Pilot Barlow

Pilot Officer C. R. M. Bell
Drowned after ditching in his Typhoon. 3 February 1943.

Squadron Leader J. B. de la P. Beresford. Commanding Officer.

Sergeant Pilot Bowman

Sergeant Pilot Brandreth

Pilot Officer J. L. Browne. Intelligence Officer.

Sergeant Pilot Browne
Killed at Hawarden. 10 August 1941. No more details.

Pilot Officer Buchanan

Sergeant Pilot Carine
Killed in flying accident at Wittering. 31 August 1941.

Sergeant Pilot Chaplin

Squadron Leader Cheatle.
(Posted as supernumerary.)

Sergeant Pilot Cochran

Sergeant Pilot Cole

Pilot Officer E. O. Collcutt. Squadron Adjutant.

Pilot Officer Cook
Missing in Action. 27 June 1941

Wing Commander W. E. Coope
Missing in Action. 4 June 1941

Sergeant Pilot Copp

Pilot Officer Cunliffe

Pilot Officer Dawson
Killed in action. 19 August 1942.

Sergeant Pilot Deall

Sergeant Pilot Devenish

Sergeant Pilot Dick-Sherwood
(Some doubt as to this pilot's name.)

Sergeant Pilot D. A. Edwards

Sergeant Pilot G. Elcombe

Sergeant Pilot Gain
> *Killed in flying accident. 29 October 1941.*

Flight Sergeant A. D. Gillespie

Flying Officer Green

Flight Lieutenant C. L. Green

Sergeant Pilot Hagger

Sergeant Pilot Hardy

Pilot Officer Holland
> *Missing in Action. 27 June 1941.*

Sergeant Pilot F. S. Howard

Flying Officer J. S. Howitt. Medical Officer

Pilot Officer H. S. Jacques

Pilot Officer James

Pilot Officer Johnston.

Sergeant Pilot Lees

Sergeant Pilot Leggo

Sergeant Pilot Lucas

Sergeant Pilot MacNamara

Sergeant Pilot Main

Sergeant Pilot Matthews
> *Missing in Action. 3 July 1941.*

Flight Lieutenant McMullen

Pilot Officer Menelaws

Sergeant Pilot Miller

Sergeant Pilot Morris

Sergeant Pilot Munro
> *Commissioned, he held the rank of Flight Lieutenant when he was*
> *killed air testing a Typhoon at Exeter on 3 May 1943.*

Pilot Officer Parry.

Sergeant Pilot Plagis

Sergeant Pilot Reid

Flying Officer Scott. Medical Officer.

Sergeant Pilot Sergeant

Sergeant Pilot Sherwood

Pilot Officer J. Small

> *Killed in action. 21 January 1944. Buried near LeFtgoet.*

Sergeant Pilot Smith

Sergeant Pilot Smithyman

Sergeant Pilot Spence-Ross

Sergeant Pilot Thompson

Sergeant Pilot Welby

Sergeant Pilot Whiteford (Or Whitford)

Sergeant Pilot Wilson

Pilot Officer J. D. Wright

Known ground crew 1941

939607 Aircraftman First Class. P. P. Lowe.

> *Killed in action. 14 March 1941 at RAF Wittering*

972422 Aircraftman First Class. T. Gilmore.

> *Killed in action. 14 March 1941 at RAF Wittering.*

778141 Aircraftman Second Class. J. P. Kruger.

> *Wounded 14 March 1941 at RAF Wittering.*
> *Died from his wounds 18 March 1941 at the Stamford & Rutland*
> *General Infirmary.*

Roll of Honour 1942

Officers & NCOs recorded as having been with the Squadron during 1942.

Officers and NCOs from previous years are not listed here.

Sergeant Pilot D. D. Audley.

> *Killed in flying accident. 24 October 1942 at Warmwell.*

Sergeant Pilot C. Bailey.

Pilot Officer F. B. B. Biddulph.

Sergeant Pilot S. J. P. Blackwell.

Reported missing in action. 1 December 1943.

Held the rank of Flying Officer.

Sergeant Pilot Douglas C. Borland.

Sergeant Pilot N. V. Borland. (Brother of above.)

Killed in action on 23 April 1945. Held the rank of Flying Officer.

Flight Lieutenant Cook.

Medical Officer.

Sergeant Pilot Cooper.

Sergeant Pilot D. S. Eadie.

Promoted Flying Officer.

Shot down over Germany 25 December 1944.

Sergeant Pilot G. Eastwood.

Sergeant Pilot D. Erasmus.

Killed in action on 9 March 1945. Holding the rank Squadron Leader.

Aged 22.

Wing Commander Gillam.

Sergeant Pilot J. Hawarth. (Or Howarth)

Sergeant Pilot E. V. Horne.

Flight Sergeant J. Howarth.

Flying Officer Howarth.

(Possibly F/Sgt J. Howarth and/or J. Hawarth)

Wing Commander Kelly.

Flight Sergeant D. McGibbon.

Flight Lieutenant A. S. McIntyre

Pilot Officer J. D.Miller.

Sergeant Pilot M. B. Mollet.

Flight Sergeant W. V. Mollet.

Sergeant Pilot G. G. Osbourne.

Squadron Leader H. A. Pugh.

Sergeant Pilot J. L. Spence.

Sergeant Pilot R. K. Thompson.

Flight Lieutenant J. C. Thompson.
> *Prisoner of War. 11 January 1943.*

Pilot Officer Thompson.

Flight Lieutenant I. M. Umro.

Pilot Officer R. A. Wright.

Pilot Officer W. J. A. Wilson.
> *This pilot could be Sergeant Pilot N. J. A. Wilson previously listed in 1941. It is possible that he could have been commissioned and his initials mis-typed.*

Roll of Honour 1943

Officers & NCOs recorded as having been with the Squadron during 1943.

Officers and NCOs from previous years are not listed here.

Flight Sergeant C. W. Baillie.

Pilot Officer H. C. Ballance.

Flight Lieutenant T. A. Burke.

Flying Officer Cockburn. Engineering Officer.

Flying Officer H. A. Cooper.

Flying Officer J. H. Deall
> *This could also be Sergeant Pilot Deall previously listed in 1941 and Squadron Leader Deall in 1944.*

Sergeant Pilot D. Drummond.

Flight Sergeant Forrester. (Promoted Pilot Officer)
> *Killed in action. France 28 July 1944.*

Pilot Officer Furber.

Sergeant Pilot Henderson.
> *Badly injured during a forced landing at Exeter. 30 April 1943.*

Sergeant Pilot Horne.
> *Killed during a practice flight in cloud. 2 February 1943 at Exeter.*

Flight Sergeant A. O. Holland.
> *Killed when his Typhoon crashed into the sea. 19 May 1944.*

Sergeant Pilot I. O. Hulley.

Squadron Leader P. W. Le Fevre.

Flight Sergeant R. McElroy.
> *Shot down over France 19 July 1944.*

Flying Officer J. J. R. MacNamara.

Warrant Officer J. H. Meyer.
> *(Promoted to Pilot Officer)*
> *Shot down over France 19 July 1944.*

Flight Lieutenant A. S. MacIntire.
> *Rejoins the squadron from No. 245. 28 May 1943.*

Sergeant Pilot E. Palte.

Sergeant Pilot D. S. Peters.
> *Killed when his Typhoon crashed into the sea. 15 April 1943.*

Sergeant Pilot K. M. Rogers.

Flying Officer A. V. Sanders.

Known Ground crew 1943
Corporal Hosie
Leading Aircraftman MacMaster
Aircraftsman Cowan
Corporal Marshall

Roll of Honour 1944

Officers & NCOs recorded as having been with the Squadron during 1944.
Officers and NCOs from previous years are not listed here.

Flight Lieutenant Allen DFC
> *Shot down over France. 25 July 1944.*

Flight Sergeant I. E. T. Anton.

Wing Commander Baker DFC & bar.

Arrived 4th of January as Wing Commander Flying.

Killed in action 16 June 1944.

Flight Sergeant Bell.

Flight Sergeant Cambrook or Cambrooke.

Flight Sergeant R. A. Clack.

Captain Crabtree.

No further information as to his Service Branch. First noted in ORB *for 18 July 1944.*

Flight Sergeant P. Culligan.

Killed while taking off on the 26 March 1945. A burst tyre cartwheeled his Typhoon. Held the rank of Pilot Officer.

Flying Officer E. T. Cunnison.

Pilot Officer Dix. Intelligence Officer.

Flight Sergeant D. H. Dodd.

Released as a PoW and returned to squadron on the 15 May 1945. No information as to when he was captured.

Pilot Officer E. H. Donne.

Shot down by flak on the 1 April 1945 flying Typhoons.

Pilot Officer D. Donne.

Flight Sergeant W. H. Ewan

Sergeant Pilot R. Fishwick.

Flight Sergeant P. C. Green.

Shot down behind enemy lines in France 9 August 1944. Evaded capture.

Shot down over Germany 25 December 1944.

Flying Officer J. Harrison.

Flight Sergeant Harrold.

Shot down over France 19 July 1944.

Flying Officer Hayworth.

Flight Sergeant Haworth.

Flight Lieutenant Healey.

Missing in action 2 March 1944.

Flight Sergeant R. Hodnett.

Squadron Leader Holmes.

Commanding Officer. 9 February - 11 July.

Sergeant Pilot D. Hughes.

Sergeant Pilot A. Knoesen.

Flight Sergeant Laing.

Flight Sergeant R. Love.

Flight Sergeant Luhnenschloss.

Flying Officer R. McAdam.

Flight Lieutenant McGibbon.

> *Shot down and baled out over France 18 October 1944. Confirmed as Prisoner of War 31 December 1944. (Could possibly be Flight Sergeant D. McGibbon from 1942.)*

Sergeant Pilot McMurdon.

Flight Sergeant P. K. Mitchell.

Flying Officer L. L. Miller.

Flight Sergeant J. H. Moll.

Flight Sergeant D. Morgan.

Flight Lieutenant Nesbitt.

> *Killed in action. 12 June 1944.*

Flight Sergeant Paul.

> *Shot down over France. 6 October 1944. Held the rank of Warrant Officer.*

Warrant Officer D. Points.

Warrant Officer N. V. Phillips.

Flight Sergeant D. S. Shepherd.

> *Shot down by flak 28 February 1945. Prisoner of war. Held the rank of Pilot Officer. Returned to Squadron on the 15 May 1945.*

Flight Lieutenant Sheward.

Flying Officer Tidmarsh.

Flight Sergeant Wheeler.

> *Believed killed. Hit by flak over France. 15 August 1944*

Squadron Leader Wright. Commanding Officer. 11 July 1944.
Taken prisoner of war. 2 October 1944.

Known Ground crew 1944
Corporal Offley - Shore.
Injured in a V2 attack in France. 25/26 October 1944.
Leading Aircraftman Gold.
Injured in a V2 attack in France. 25/26 October 1944.

Roll of Honour 1945

Officers & NCOs recorded as having been with the Squadron during 1945.
Officers and NCOs from previous years are not listed here.

Warrant Officer Becks.
Flight Sergeant G. W. Godley.
Flight Sergeant J. O. Pascoe.
Flight Sergeant H. Wheeler.
Flying Officer D. Quick.

Commanding Officers 1939 - 1945
Squadron Leader J. W. A. Hunnard. 30 October 1939.
(Formation)
Squadron Leader R. L. Wilkinson. 6 July 1940
Squadron Leader D. G. H. Spencer. 17 August 1940
Squadron Leader H. W. Mermagen AFC. (Temp) 12 September 1940
Squadron Leader Patrick Geraint Jameson. September 1940
Squadron Leader T. B. de la P. Bereford. 9 June 1941.
Squadron Leader C. L. Green. October 1941.
Squadron Leader A. S. MaCintyre. 25 June 1943.

Squadron Leader P. W. Le Fevre. 18 August 1943.
Squadron Leader J. Holmes. 1944. England and France.
Squadron Leader Wright. 11 July 1944
Squadron Leader J. H. Deall. 7 October 1944. France.
Squadron Leader R. E. G. Sheward. January 1945.

Supermarine Spitfire P7350 and 266 Squadron.

The sole surviving airworthy Supermarine Spitfire IIa.
Based with the BBMF at RAF Coningsby.

Visitors to the Battle of Britain Memorial Flight (BBMF) at RAF
Coningsby in Lincolnshire can see the oldest airworthy Mk IIa
Supermarine Spitfire P7350 in the world today. (The author has
a 'direct link' with this particular aircraft in that while serving
in the RAF during the 1960s he served with No. 266 Squadron
when it was equipped with the Bristol Bloodhound Mk I at
RAF Rattlesden. The author is also a volunteer tour guide at
the BBMF so has the opportunity to inform visitors as to her
remarkable history.) She is the only Spitfire flying today that
fought in the Battle of Britain serving with No. 266 (Rhodesian)
(Fighter) Squadron.

Built at Castle Bromwich against Contract Number
981687/39 dated 12 April 1938 and having a fuselage number of
CBAF14, she is number 14 of some 11,989 built. She first flew
during August 1940 on an initial test flight and subsequently
taken on charge on the 13th of August, so entering RAF service
in August 1940. She was delivered from No. 6 MU at Brize
Norton to 266 Squadron at RAF Wittering on 6 September and
allocated the unit code letters 'UO-T'. The Squadron moved to
Hornchurch, but on 17 October P7350 was transferred to 603

City of Edinburgh Squadron of the AuxAF and the codes were changed to 'XT-D'.

Damaged in combat flying with 603 Squadron at RAF Hornchurch in October 1940, by a Me 109 over Hastings, crash landed, and was repaired at the No. 1 Civilian Repair Unit at Cowley. She was back in the air again on 15 November. (Repaired bullet holes are still visible in her port wing.)

On 18 March 1941 she was sent to 616 County of Yorkshire Squadron and the on 10 April transferred to 64 Squadron where it is claimed that when flying with this Squadron she shot down three enemy aircraft. The 5 August saw her delivered to Scottish Aviation Ltd at Prestwick for overhaul and repairs, when she was then sent on to No. 37 MU on 29 January 1942. Some time after April 1942 she was sent to the Central Gunnery School and 57 OTU, ending her operational career with No. 19 Maintenance Unit.

Her war service was not without incident however as she suffered no less than three separate flying accidents at RAF Tangmere, RAF Hornchurch and RAF Sutton Bridge.

She survived the war and was sold for scrap for the princely sum of £25 to Messrs.' John Dale Ltd in 1948. Luckily for us they recognised the historic significance of her and they promptly 'gave it back' to the RAF Museum at Colerne.

During 1967 she was removed from the museum and following a survey by John Simpson of Simpson Aeroservices Ltd, was delivered by road to RAF Henlow where an extensive overhaul programme commenced to return P7350 to flying condition. On 20 May 1968 she was flown to Duxford by Squadron Leader M. A. Vickers, the aircraft having been issued with a Restricted Category Certificate of Airworthiness where she took part in the film 'The Battle of Britain'. During September 1968 the Merlin XII engine, which had been installed in her since about 1944 (engine number 12312), was found to have metal contamination in the oil filters. This engine was removed and replaced with a Merlin 35. To complete her 'flying duties' in the film, she was flown to Bovingdon (Hertfordshire) for her last flying sequences.

It was during October 1968 that she was presented to the Battle of Britain Memorial Flight and flown to the then home of the BBMF at RAF Coltishall, by Squadron Leader Mills. She was flown to No. 5 Maintenance Unit at RAF Kemble on 28 April 1969 for an overhaul and respray in the colours and codes (ZH-T) of 266 (Rhodesia) (Fighter) Squadron, returning to the BBMF on 12 June.

P7350 is still with the BBMF at RAF Coningsby and can be seen flying during the Flight's programme of events, usual from April to October. A worthy and historically valuable example of a superb aircraft that by good luck and fortune survived the war to find its rightful place at the BBMF.

SUPERMARINE SPITFIRE P7350 IN HER BATTLE OF BRITAIN
266 SQUADRON MARKINGS. AUTHOR'S COLLECTION

The Pilots, and other Officers

The list that follows identifies many pilots and non-flying Officers that served with the Squadron from its formation in 1918. Obtaining information can be extremely difficult, as there may not be any recorded name or details about a specific pilot/ airman anywhere. Indeed, while conducting research I have discovered many family relatives who are searching for any information regarding their family members. Where I have been able to assist them I have done so. At the time of writing, this is all of 266 Squadron personnel I have been able to trace.

The reader should bear in mind that the official period for the Battle of Britain is July 10 to October 31 1940, and as such pilots that flew before or after this time frame with squadrons which were involved in the fighting - but not during it - are not noted as having fought in that battle.

Although personal details can be very sparse, I have included in some cases as much personal information as I am able to trace. In some instances I have included a brief description of actual combat reports for a particular pilot. Within the extracts of the ORBs included in this book, the pilot's names will be found, and I have included all those that are mentioned. The reader can therefore discover further details of a particular pilot by reading through the ORB extracts. Many of the reports include details of training flights and the weather. I have not included these in the majority of cases, unless a pilot is named.

The rank indicated in the biography is that which the pilot held at the time from the ORB records researched. This rank is not necessarily the highest achieved by that particular pilot and as such I have only used the pilot's name and not his rank in the photographs with the exception of one pilot whose initials are unknown. No disrespect intended.

Sergeant Pilot John Watson Allen.
Service number 89617. British.
Born in Cathcart, Scotland on 6 May 1918, he joined the RAFVR in 1938, qualifying as a pilot during 1940 and being promoted to Sergeant Pilot.

Flying initially with 266 Squadron from 7 October 1940, he was posted to 256 Squadron as a night fighter pilot. Posted to Malta in July 1943. Between the 12 July and 31 August he was credited with destroying 14 enemy aircraft.

Joining 151 Squadron in September 1943 undertaking night ranger operations over Northern Europe. (Large formations of aircraft on freelance intrusion operations over enemy territory with the aim of wearing down enemy forces). During December 1944 he took command of 29 Squadron, staying with them until after the end of the war.

Various postings followed, and in 1953 he led a flight of de Havilland Vampire night fighter jets (NF Mk Xs) for the Coronation Review Fly Past

Three appointments at the Air Ministry followed a period

with the Joint Warfare Establishment before he became
Commandant of the Officers and Aircrew Selection Centre at
RAF Biggin Hill, which was his final posting, reaching the rank
of Air Commodore. Retiring on 6 May 1973, he passed away on
9 July 1988. He fought in the Battle of Britain.

Flight Lieutenant R. N. Allen DFC
First noted in the ORB on 11 March 1944. Crashed in France 25
July 1944. Confirmed as Prisoner of War on 14 December 1944.

Pilot Officer N. N. Allen.
A Rhodesian pilot who was posted to the Squadron on 11
August 1941 for flying duties at Wittering. Sadly he was killed
while flying in a training interception practice on 24 April 1942
at Duxford.

Pilot Officer Allen -White.
A Rhodesian pilot posted to the Squadron at Wittering from 260
Squadron on 2 May 1941. On 18 October 1941 he was promoted
to Flight Lieutenant, taking up the role of a Flight Commander
on the squadron. While in combat with other squadron Spitfires
on 11 January 1942, all radio contact was lost with him. He did
not return to base and is listed as 'missing in action'.

Sergeant Pilot Leslie Charles Allton.
Service number 745436. British.
Joined 266 Squadron on 16 September 1940 at RAF Wittering,
posted from No. 7 Operational Training Unit. Killed in a
flying accident in Spitfire P3872 whilst with 92 Squadron near
Tuesnoad Farm, Smarden 19 October 1940. He fought in the
Battle of Britain.

Flight Sergeant I. E. T. Anton.
Arrived with the Squadron on 23 December 1944.

Pilot Officer Dennis Lockhart Armitage.
Service number 76573. British.
He learned to fly at the Lancashire Aero Club in 1934 and
joined the RAFVR during 1936 - one of the first to do so.
He completed his flying training on 1 September 1939 at No.
2 Flying Training School, Brize Norton. Commissioned 10
December 1939, he joined 266 Squadron on 16 December 1939
at RAF Sutton Bridge flying Fairy Battle light bombers. On
August 3 1940 he was appointed Flight Commander of 'A' flight
and destroyed a Ju 88 on 12 August.

He assumed temporary command the following day after
both the CO and 'B' Flight commander were shot down. By the
21 September there remained just five pilots in the Squadron.
These were posted to RAF Wittering to reform. During May
1941 He was posted from the Squadron and promoted to Acting
Squadron Leader. Awarded the DFC 18 July 1941.

He took command of 129 Squadron on 20 June 1941 that was
reforming with Spitfires at RAF Leconfield. Flying on a bomber
escort mission on 21 September 1941, he was shot down and
captured near Boulogne.

In late 1945 he left the RAF as a Squadron Leader. Sadly he
passed away on 5 March 2004. He flew from RAF Hornchurch
with 266 Squadron, and fought in the Battle of Britain.

Pilot Officer Dennis Garth Ashton.
Service number 76574. British.
Joining the RAFVR in June 1938 as an Airman (Under Training)
Pilot, he was called up on 1 September 1939 and commissioned
in December and was posted to 266 Squadron at RAF Sutton
Bridge as a Pilot Officer flying Fairy Battle light bombers.

At the commencement of the Battle of Britain Flying Officer Ashton was serving with 266 Squadron at RAF Wittering. On 18 July 1940 his Spitfire N3170 collided with a stationary tow tractor. For this incident he lost two months seniority.

He was reported as 'missing in action' whilst in combat over Portsmouth on 12 August 1940, when his Spitfire P9333 was shot down in flames, aged just 20. A Royal Navy minesweeper, HMS Cedar, found his body a month later, and he was buried at sea. He is commemorated on the Runnymeade Memorial, panel number 7. He flew from Hornchurch with 266 Squadron, and fought in the Battle of Britain.

Sergeant Pilot H. W. Ayre
Flew Spitfire Mk Is from RAF Wittering during 1940 before being posted (temporarily) to No. 1 Depot, RAF Uxbridge on 17 July 1940.

Sergeant Pilot D. D. Audley
He is recorded in the ORB for 24 October 1942 as being killed during a formation; tail chasing and aerobatics practice at Warmwell. His Typhoon was seen to break up at 18,000 feet. The wreckage was scattered over a five-mile radius. There was no known cause for the aircraft to break up, although a major structural failure is the most likely cause.

Sergeant Pilot C. Bailey
Serial number 778823.
Posted to the Squadron at Warmwell on 17 November 1942 flying Typhoons.

Flight Sergeant C. W Baillie
First noted in ORB on 2 September 1943. On 9 May 1944 is seen baling out of his Typhoon over France. He now has the rank

of Flying Officer.

Wing Commander E. R. Baker. DFC & Bar.

Flying Typhoons with the Harrowbeer Wing, 193 and 266 Squadrons, he led a flight of eight Typhoon Mk Ibs to an area east of Paris. He is credited with one Do 217 destroyed, also one Fw190. He was killed in action on 16 June 1944 his aircraft crashing near the small village of St. Mauvieu, which is approximately 3 miles west of Caen. Captain J. B. Lynd of HQ, 3rd Canadian Division, discovered it 10 days later. Wing Commander Baker was still in the cockpit of his aircraft.

He was buried with full military honours beside his aircraft within the battle area near to a British artillery gun position, on 26 June 1944.

Flight Lieutenant D. W. Balden

Joined the Squadron on 4 July 1940 from No. 5 SFTS for Flight Commander duties.

Pilot Office H. C. Ballance.

Service number 80450.
Rhodesian. Posted to the Squadron as a Pilot Officer on 26 November 1943.

Sergeant Pilot L. G. Barlow.

A Rhodesian pilot flying Spitfire Mk IIas from Wittering in August 1941. Commissioned at some time to Pilot Officer (no record in ORB), he was attached to Abbots Inch pending an overseas posting on 30 April 1942.

Sergeant Pilot Richard George Victor Barraclough.

Service number 66487. British.
Joined 266 Squadron at RAF Sutton Bridge on 16 December

1939 flying Fairy Battle aircraft. A pre-war pilot, he was with 266 Squadron throughout the Battle of Britain and flew from RAF Hornchurch with that Squadron. He claimed two Me 109s shot down, both 'unconfirmed', on the 23 May 1940, and shared in the destruction of a Ju 88 on 10 July, flying Spitfire P9374. After this, he damaged a Ju 88 on the 12 August, and then a He 111 damaged on the 11 September. On Boxing Day of 1940 he possibly destroyed a Do 17.

Shot down by German 'ace' Major Adolf Galland (Kommondore of Jagdgeschwader 26) during April 1941, he survived and eventually retired from the RAF with the rank of Squadron Leader.

Pilot Officer E. G. Barwell.
Joined 266 Squadron at RAF Sutton Bridge on 16 December 1939 flying Fairy Battle aircraft. He was posted to 12 Group Pool on 31 December 1939.

Flight Lieutenant S. H. Bazley.
Service number 90359. British.
Reported to the Squadron from 611 Squadron on 29 February 1940 as a Flight Commander. A former AuxAF pilot, he shot down a Bf 110 on 12 August 1940. Four days later he was shot down over Canterbury at 12.45 hours in flames by a Bf 109 and baled out of his Spitfire Mk I P9312, suffering burns and minor injuries. He was treated at Canterbury Hospital.

The first Squadron loss for 1941. On a dusk patrol, Flight Lieutenant S. H. Bazley was killed during a raid investigation. Flying Spitfire Mk I X4613, he crashed at Gedney Hill. He had been in command of 'B' flight since 5 March 1940. He was ordered to patrol Well-next-the-Sea at 10,000 feet. He was in radio contact with Wittering at 07.39 hours and this was the last

contact with him. His aircraft crashed in a field at Gedney Hill, Lincolnshire, and he was killed.
Warrant Officer Becks.
   First noted in ORB of 30 June 1945 flying the Squadron's Anson.

Sergeant Pilot M.A.Beatty.
Service number 69455. British.
Posted from the Squadron to 118 Squadron on 24 February 1941. He fought in the Battle of Britain.

Flight Sergeant Bell.
Posted to the Squadron on 2 June 1944 at Needs Oar Point.

Pilot Officer C. R. M. Bell.
Posted to the Squadron at Wittering from No. 58 OTU. Possibly a Rhodesian pilot, the ORB is not too clear on this point. Presumed drowned after ditching his Typhoon in the English Channel on 3 February 1943, flying out of Exeter.

Squadron Leader J. B. de la P. Beresford.
Arrived with the Squadron on 17 April 1941 as a supernumerary, from No. 58 OTU. Took command on 9 June 1941. Posted to RAF Station Wittering, the ORB does not state in which role, on 18 October 1941.

Pilot Officer F. B. Biddulph
Posted to the Squadron from 56 Squadron on 15 August 1942. This squadron was part of the Typhoon Wing at Duxford together with 266 and 609. Crashed into the English Channel in his Typhoon on 15 August 1943.

Squadron Leader E.R. Bitmead. DFC.

Service number 34139. British.

Based with 266 Squadron at RAF Wittering. He also flew with 310 (Czech) Squadron during the Battle of Britain. In January 1941 with 611 Squadron, (he was CO from 19 October 1940 to 18 May 1941) destroyed a Bf 109 and a Do 215. During May 1941 after an engagement over the English Channel, his aircraft was damaged and he made a forced landing in a field near East Grinstead. 14 September 1941 he was CO of 71 (Eagle) Squadron. (RAF North Weald). He died on active service in 1955.

Sergeant Pilot S. J. P. Blackwell

Serial number 777721.

Posted to the Squadron from 609 Squadron on 15 August 1942. This squadron was part of the Typhoon Wing at Duxford together with 266 and 56.

He was commissioned with effect from 12 October 1942 to the rank of Pilot Officer at Warmwell. Promoted to Flying Officer with effect from 4 April 1943 at Exeter. (ORB entry dated 24 June 1943.)

Sergeant Pilot Douglas C. Borland.

First noted in the ORB for 27 October 1942 as overshooting on landing at Warmwell, badly damaging his Typhoon. He was not injured. Promoted from Flight Sergeant to the commissioned rank of Pilot Officer with effect from 20 April 1943 at Exeter. (ORB entry of 24 April 1943.)

Flight Sergeant N. V. Borland.

Promoted from Flight Sergeant to the commissioned rank of Pilot Officer with effect from the 20 April 1943 at Exeter. (ORB entry of 24 June 1943.) Killed in action on 23 April 1945. Held the rank of Flying Officer. (Brother of above.)

Sergeant Pilot Reginald Arthur Boswell.
Service number 742295. British.
On 16 September 1940 he was posted to 266 Squadron at RAF Wittering, from No. 7 Operational Training Unit. Eventually posted on 28 September 1940 to 19 Squadron. He fought in the Battle of Britain.

Pilot Officer Nigel Greenstreet Bowen.
Service number 41984. British.
Eldest son of the Rector of St. Mary's Church in Wallingford, he was educated at Christ Church Cathedral in Oxford and then attended St. Edward's School. Joining the RAF in February 1939 on a Short Service Commission, he was posted to 266 Squadron at RAF Sutton Bridge at its re-formation in 1939.

He destroyed a Me109 over Dunkirk in June 1940, and a Ju 88 on 12 August 1940. He was shot down in flames in a Spitfire Mk I N3095, by Me 109s over Adisham and was killed, aged 20, on August 16 1940. He is buried in Wallingford Cemetery, Berkshire. He flew from Hornchurch with 266 Squadron.

Sergeant Pilot Bowman.
First reported in ORBs on 18 March 1941, flying Spitfire Mk I X4646 on patrol from Wittering. Possibly one of the Rhodesian pilots drafted in when the Squadron was named 'Rhodesia'.

Sergeant Pilot Brandreth
First mentioned in ORB for 21 February 1940 flying Spitfire Mk I X4997 on patrol. Possibly a Rhodesian pilot.

Sergeant Pilot Reginald Arthur Breeze.
Service number 54089.

Joined the RAF in September 1933 as an Aircraft Hand. He later remustered as an Airman (Under Training) Pilot. On 16 September 1940 he was posted to 266 Squadron at RAF Wittering from No. 7 Operational Training Unit. On 1 October 1940 he was posted to 222 Squadron. Flying a Spitfire N3164 on 8 November 1940, it was damaged in combat. He landed successfully at RAF Martlesham Heath, but as he was taking off the Spitfire caught fire, crashed, and was burnt out at nearby Oakley Poultry Farm at Mundersley Heath. He escaped uninjured from the crash.

Commissioned in September 1943, he was sadly killed on 28 January 1945 serving with No. 151 Repair Unit (Aircraft) at Wevelgem, Belgium and is buried in Calais Southern Cemetery, France.

He fought in the Battle of Britain.

Pilot Officer J. L. Browne
Posted to the Squadron at Wittering as an Intelligence Officer from No. 12 Group on 30 April 1941.

Sergeant Pilot Browne
A Rhodesian pilot who was posted to the Squadron on 5 August 1941 for flying duties at Wittering. Killed at Hawarden on 10 August 1941. No record of how he was killed is listed, but probably a flying accident.

Pilot Officer Buchanan
A Rhodesian pilot, he was posted to the Squadron on 12 May 1941 from 260 Squadron. Posted to 41 Squadron on 27 August 1941.

Flight Lieutenant T. A. Burke.
Posted to the Squadron at Exeter on 20 April 1943, flying

Typhoon Mk Ibs.

Flying Officer Norman Whitmore Burnett.
Service number 70101.
British. Commissioned on the Reserve Category of AA2 during August 1934, he transferred to the RAFVR in January of 1938, and was finally called up on the 1 September 1939. Posted to 266 Squadron at RAF Sutton Bridge on 16 December 1939. On 25 July 1940 has was posted to 46 Squadron at RAF Digby.

Following combat over Sheppey on the 8 September, he crashed at Hollingbourne and was admitted to hospital. The Hurricane V6631 he was flying was a write off. Out of hospital and returned to 46 Squadron he claimed a probable Italian CR42 in a raid in Italy on 11 of November 1940.

The squadron sailed for the Middle East on the aircraft carrier HMS Argus, transferring in Gibraltar to the carriers HMS Ark Royal and HMS Furious, flying off on the 6 June to Hal Far, Malta. Just five days later he was flying Hurricane Z2480 along side six others that had been scrambled to intercept a force of Italian fighters escorting a reconnaissance aircraft. He flew into the attack but was shot down by an Italian MC 200.

Although there was a search for him, no trace was found, and he was officially listed as 'missing in action' on 11 June 1941. He is commemorated on the Commonwealth Air Forces Memorial in Floriana. He fought in the Battle of Britain.

Pilot Officer F.W. Cale.
Service number 42104. Australian.
An Australian flying Spitfires with 266 Squadron, was shot down on 15 August 1940 whilst flying a Spitfire Mk I N3168 over Maidstone, Kent, at 18.50 hours and seen to successfully bale out by other pilots. However all that could be discovered on the ground was his parachute with the straps burnt. His body

was later recovered from the River Medway on 16 August. He was just 25. He flew from Hornchurch with 266 Squadron and fought in the Battle of Britain.

Flight Sergeant Cambrook or Cambrooke.
Appears in ORB Appendice of 16 October 1944. Shot down by flak over France flying Typhoons five days later on the 21st. Killed in action attempting to a force landing.

Sergeant Pilot V. L. Carine
Service number 778273.
A Rhodesian pilot. Posted to the Squadron on 1 August 1941 for flying duties at Wittering. On 31 August 1941 when taking off, his Spitfire struck a maintenance hanger with the port wing when airborne, crashing. Sergeant Carine was killed.

Pilot Officer H. H. Chalder.
Service number 43691. British.
Posted to 266 Squadron from 66 Squadron RAF Duxford on 15 April 1940. Injured in the foot during a German bombing raid on RAF Eastchurch on 13 August 1940. He was posted to 41 Squadron on 15 September 1940.

In action, he was shot down and baled out, seriously wounded, before his Spitfire Mk I X4409 exploded in mid-air. He was admitted to hospital, but he died of his wounds, aged 25, on 10 November 1940. Flew from Hornchurch with 266 Squadron and fought in the Battle of Britain.

Sergeant Pilot A. R. Chaplin
A Rhodesian pilot, posted from No. 58 OTU on 23 October 1941 to the Squadron at Wittering.

Squadron Leader Cheatle
Posted in a supernumerary post to the Squadron at Wittering on 26 August 1941. On 28 October 1941 was posted to 92 Squadron.

Flight Sergeant R. A. Clack.
Flew Typhoon Mk Ibs in Europe. Arrived with Squadron on the 23 December 1944.

Pilot Officer C. A. G. Clark.
Service number 42192.
Flew Fairy Battle light bombers from RAF Sutton Bridge when the Squadron re-formed in 1939.

Pilot Officer J. C. R. Clarke
Reported for flying duties on 27 August 1940 at RAF Wittering from No. 7 OTU.

Pilot Officer S. W. Cobb. (RAFVR)
The first Squadron Adjutant. He arrived on 20 November 1939 at RAF Sutton Bridge. On 14 April 1941 he was posted to Station Headquarters at Wittering.

Flying Officer Cockburn.
Posted to the Squadron at Exeter on 23 March 1943 as Engineering Officer.

Sergeant Pilot Cochrane
Posted to the Squadron at Wittering on 24 April 1941 from No. 57 OTU. On 3 May 1941 he was posted to 145 Squadron.

Sergeant Pilot Cole
Posted to the Squadron at Wittering on 24 April 1941 from No.

57 OTU. On 3 May 1941 he was posted to 145 Squadron.

Pilot Officer E. O. Collcutt
A Rhodesian Officer, he was appointed Squadron Adjutant at Wittering, on 14 April 1941, taking over from the Squadron's first Adjutant, Pilot Officer S. W. Cobb (RAFVR).

Now a Flight Lieutenant and the Squadron Adjutant since March 1941. Posted to 44 Squadron - the Rhodesian bomber squadron - on 11 November 1943.

Pilot Officer Cook.
Flew Spitfire Mk IIs from RAF West Malling during 1941. Is listed as 'missing' (from Combat Report) after combat with Me 109es on 27 June 1941 over St Omer, France.

Sergeant Pilot H. Cook.
Service number 126096. British.
Reported for flying duties on 26 August 1940 at RAF Wittering from No. 7 OTU. On the 11 September 1940 he was posted to 92 Squadron. He fought in the Battle of Britain.

Sergeant Pilot Cook
Appears in ORB (Appendix Eight) for 8 April 1941 as flying Spitfire Mk II P8188 from Wittering.

Flight Lieutenant Cook
With the Squadron since January 1942 as Squadron Medical Officer. Posted away on the 19 January 1944.

Wing Commander Coope
Written first in the ORB (Appendix Eight) for 7 April 1941. Flying Spitfire Mk I X4833 on patrol from Wittering. Was killed on 4 May 1941 when his Spitfire Mk IIa was observed to crash

into the sea.

Sergeant Pilot S. A. Cooper.
Posted from the Squadron on October 1940 to 92 Squadron at RAF Biggin Hill for flying duty.

Sergeant Pilot Cooper
Posted from the Squadron to 64 Squadron at RAF Hornchurch on 27 November 1940.

Sergeant Pilot Cooper
A Rhodesian pilot, he was posted to the Squadron at Duxford from No. 58 OTU, Grangemouth, on 22 April 1942. The author is assuming that these are all different pilots because of the posting dates.

Flying Officer H. A. Cooper.
Posted to the Squadron at Exeter flying Typhoon Mk Ibs on 23 March 1943. Posted to No. 5 PDC 8 November 1943.

Sergeant Pilot Copp
First noted in ORB (Appendix 14) on 14 April 1941, flying Spitfire Mk II P7611 out of Wittering on an interception that resulted in no enemy aircraft sighted. On 10 May 1941 he was posted to 46 Squadron.

Flight Lieutenant J. B. Coward
A Flight Commander from 11 November 1939 after the Squadron reformed on 30 October 1939.

Flight Sergeant Culligan
First noted in ORB for 3 August 1944 flying Typhoons. Killed while taking off on 26 March 1945. A burst tyre cartwheeled his

Typhoon. Held the rank of Pilot Officer.

Pilot Officer Cunliffe
Appears in the ORB (Appendix Seven) for 7 April 1941. Flying Spitfire Mk II P8014 on patrol from Wittering.

Flying Officer E. T. Cunnison
Appears in the ORB (Appendix 61) for 12 May 1944 flying Typhoon MN184 on patrol from Snaith. Operational flying in France/Belgium after the Normandy landings, was posted back to the UK sometime shortly after 24 November 1944. On 12 December 1944 he returned to Rhodesia.

Pilot Officer T. D. Davy.
Reported for flying duties on 28 August 1940 at RAF Wittering from 12 Squadron. From the Squadron he was posted to 72 Squadron on 28 September 1940. Killed in action on 13 September 1942.

Pilot Officer R. H. L. Dawson.
From a combat report of 26 February 1942. Pilot Officer Dawson Flying as 'White 1' attacked a Dornier bomber whist he was on convoy patrol duty with 266 Squadron. (Flying a Spitfire Mk Vb from RAF Coltishall). Firing two short bursts of 20mm cannon and machine gun fire from 250 yards astern, he observed hits. The bomber's rear gunner immediately returned fire.

Firing again at the bomber there was a large explosion from the bomber's port engine that began to burn fiercely. Pilot Officer Dawson used all of his remaining ammunition attacking the bomber. The flames spread rapidly inboard of the port engine and then along the fuselage. The Dornier dived in flames into the sea, leaving a wide area of burning petrol and wreckage.

He was killed in action on the 19 August 1942 flying

Typhoon R7815 near Dieppe. Tragically he was shot down by a Spitfire, crashing into the Channel. He held the rank of Flight Lieutenant.

Flying Officer J. Deall.
A Rhodesian Pilot, he was posted to the Squadron at Wittering on 2 September 1941 from 65 Squadron. As a Typhoon pilot, in early 1942 took part in a Ranger Operation from RAF Harrowbeer, with 193 Squadron, as part of the Harrowbeer Wing. In the action he is credited with one Ju 88 destroyed in air, one Ju 88 destroyed on the ground, and one Do 217 damaged on the ground. He was to became CO of 266 Squadron.

Sergeant Pilot Devenish.
Posted to the Squadron at Wittering on 26 May 1941 from 145 Squadron. A Rhodesian pilot.

Pilot Officer Dix.
First noted in ORB of the 22 / 23 October 1944. Squadron Intelligence Officer. Posted to 263 Squadron on these days.

Flight Sergeant D. H. Dodd.
A Typhoon pilot. On 18 April 1944 he shot down a Ju 188. Released as a PoW and returned to squadron on 15 May 1945. No information as to when he was captured.

Sergeant Pilot Edward Henry Donne
Born in Wimbledon, London, in August 1923, the family emigrated at some time to Rhodesia. Educated at Prince Edward School, Salisbury, Rhodesia, was attested as an Airman (Pilot Under Training), in the Royal Air Force in January 1942. He was trained in Rhodesia, and embarked for the U.K. in March 1943, joining 266 (Rhodesia) Squadron, flying Typhoons, as a Sergeant

Pilot on 13 January 1944 from OTU.

It was during January of 1944 that he was forced to bale out of his stricken aircraft five miles north west of Caen on D-Day, the 6 June 1944, reporting back to his unit 48 hours later. He was subsequently commissioned and remained actively employed on sorties with 266 Squadron until his death in action on 1 April 1945, when his Typhoon was downed by flak in the Lingen area during an armed reconnaissance mission.

The wreckage of his aircraft was later found at Lonneker, Holland and he was buried near the crash site, later his remains were exhumed and buried in the local cemetery. His mother was sent his campaign medals in August 1949 which consisted of the 1939-45 Star; Air Crew Europe Star, Clasp, France and Germany Star; Defence Medal and War Medal.

Pilot Officer A. R. H. Downing
Posted to the Squadron from the Air Ministry on 7 June 1940 as an Intelligence Officer.

Sergeant Pilot D. Drummond.
Posted to the Squadron at Exeter from No. 56 OTU on 16 August 1943. Shot down on fighter sweep 15 February 1944. Missing, believed killed.

Sergeant Pilot Jack Townley Dunmore.
Service number 741448. British.
From Egham, Surrey he joined the RAFVR on 15 April 1938 as an Airman (Under Training) Pilot. Called up for active service on 1 September 1939, he finished his flying training and was immediately converted to Spitfires at No.7 Operational Training Unit, Harwarden, joining 266 Squadron at RAF Wittering on 16 September 1940.

Posted to 222 Squadron at RAF Hornchurch two weeks later

FROM THE OPERATIONS RECORD BOOKS

on the 1 October. While there he shared in the shooting down of a Me109 on the 15th, but his aircraft suffered damage in the combat and he had to make a forced landing at RAF Hawkinge.

Promoted on 5 May 1941 to Flight Sergeant, he was instructing a pupil pilot (Pilot Officer V. C. Arnold. RCAF) flying a Master (T8780) from No. 58 Operational Training Unit at RAF Balado Bridge, Grangemouth, when the aircraft dived to the ground three miles north of Falkirk. Pilot Officer V. C. Arnold was killed. Dunmore was seriously injured and admitted to Larbert Military Hospital. He died from his injuries on 17 May 1941 and is buried in the churchyard of The Annunciation, Chislehurst, Kent. He fought in the Battle of Britain.

Sergeant Pilot A.W. Eade.
Service number 563253. British.
He flew Fairy Battle light bombers when the Squadron was re-formed in 1939, and he fought in the Battle of Britain. He was posted to 602 Squadron on the 13 September 1940.

Sergeant Pilot D. S. Eadie
Serial number 778745.
Posted to the Squadron at Warmwell on 17 November 1942 flying Typhoons. Received his commission. Was shot down over Germany on 25 December 1944, his rank Flying Officer. Released as a PoW at the end of the war and visited the Squadron on 4 July 1945.

Sergeant Pilot G. M. R. Eastwood
Serial number 778711.
Posted to the Squadron at Warmwell on the 17 November 1942 flying Typhoons.

Sergeant Pilot D. A. Edwards
Posted to 118 Squadron on the 24 February 1941.

Sergeant Pilot Elcombe
Posted to the Squadron for flying duties on 19 July 1941, but posted away to 19 Squadron on the 30 August 1941.

Pilot Officer G. Elcombe
Flew Typhoons from Duxford as part of the Duxford Wing during June 1942. Promoted to Flight Lieutenant at while at Warmwell, and posted to 66 Squadron on 26 December 1942.

Could this also be Sergeant Pilot Elcombe who could have been commissioned and posted back to the squadron? Without the pilot's initials it is difficult to confirm. The reader should be aware of this.

Sergeant Pilot W. T. Ellis.
Service number 110331.
Reported for flying duties on 26 August 1940 at RAF Wittering from No. 7 OTU. From 266 Squadron he was posted on 21 September 1940 to 92 Squadron for flying duties. Flying Spitfire Mk I X4552, he crash-landed on 10 October 1940 after attacking a Do 17 over Tangmere at 08.35, escaping any injury. He fought in the Battle of Britain.

Sergeant Pilot D. Erasmus
Service number 172607. British.
Posted to 266 Squadron at Warmwell on 17 November 1942. A Typhoon pilot who flew a Mk Ib EJ917 during 1944. He shot down a Fw190 that had just shot down the CO of 266 Squadron, Squadron Leader A. S. MacIntyre, during a dogfight over the Brest Peninsula, France.

Posted to 193 Squadron holding the rank of Flight Lieutenant during the 12 - 16 November 1944. Killed in action on 9 March 1945. Holding the rank of Squadron Leader. Aged 22.

Flight Sergeant W. H. Ewan
First noted in Appendice for 5 November 1944.

Pilot Officer Ferris
First noted in ORBs on 16 December 1940. Probably one of six un-named pilots posted to the squadron on 5 November 1940.

Sergeant Pilot R. Fishwick
Noted in ORB Appendice 66 of 19 May 1944 flying Typhoon MN243 from Snaith.

Sergeant Pilot G. A. Ford
Reported for flying duties from No. 7 OTU on 29 September 1940.

Pilot Officer I. H. Forrester
First appears in the ORB on 5 January 1944 flying Typhoons out of Harrowbeer.

Pilot Officer Furber
First appears in the ORB for 20 February 1943 flying Typhoon Mk Ibs from Exeter.

Sergeant Pilot Gain
A Rhodesian pilot. Reported for flying duties at Wittering on 1 September 1941 from No. 57 OTU. Was killed in a flying accident when returning to Wittering from Nottingham, crashing at Grantham during a snowstorm on 29 October 1941.

Wing Commander D. E. Gillam DSC. DFC & Bar. AFC.

Flew with 266 Squadron during 1942, as the Wing Commander for the Duxford Wing of Typhoons, with 56 Squadron.

Flight Sergeant A. D. Gillespie

First named in ORB for 20 March 1941 as being mentioned in dispatches. The London Gazette (No. 35107) dated 17 March 1941 refers.

Flight Lieutenant I. R. Gleed.

Born on 3 July 1916, Ian Richard Gleed had his first flight at Hatfield while still at school. He later became a member of the London Aeroplane Club. He gained his license on 12 July 1935 (No.12976) at Hatfield, although there are conflicting dates here, as one biographer states he qualified on 31 July 1936 (No. 8003) – after he joined the RAF in March 1936.

He was given the nickname 'Widge' – short for 'Wizard Midget', apparently due to his tendency to call things 'Wizard', and his short stature, he was just 5 feet 6 inches.

Already experienced in flying the Hawker Hurricane, Gleed first flew the Supermarine Spitfire while on the strength of 266 Squadron. Posted to 266 on 7 November 1939 as Flight Commander. However, testing one of their new Spitfires N3120 on 18 February 1940 nearly ended his career before it had really begun. A sudden, unexplained structural failure at 18,000ft found him falling through the air without an aeroplane (he had either been flung out or it had broken up around him.) Fortunately, he still had his parachute. Even so, his injuries meant a 3-week stay in hospital and a fight to regain his flying status.

On 17 May 1940 he arrived at 87 Squadron that operated Hurricanes and had first deployed to France on 9 September 1939. He possibly became the RAFs fastest ace: destroying two

Bf110cs on 18 May, and two Do17zs and a Bf109e the next day (he also shared in the destruction of a He111, and claimed another Me 109e as a probable).

He survived the Battle of France and the Battle of Britain. On Christmas Eve 1940 he became Squadron Leader and Commanding Officer of 87 Squadron. In November 1941 he was promoted to Wing Commander and took charge of the Ibsley Wing making fighter sweeps across the English Channel. The Ibsley Wing consisted of 118, 234 and 501 Squadrons. As a Wing Leader he was entitled to use personal markings instead of the usual squadron codes, he used his initials, 'IR-G', on his personal Spitfire.

Among the numerous missions he flew one was leading his wing as fighter escorts for bombers on Operation Veracity I and II, attacks on the German Navy in the port of Brest, during which a bomber scored a hit on the battleship Scharnhorst. This incident which triggered 'The Channel Dash' by three German capital ships, the Scharnhorst, Gneisenau, and Prinz Eugen. He also led his wing during Operation Fuller – the RAF's attempt to stop them.

Wing Commander Gleed was an exemplary commander and led his pilots into battle more times than his job required him to do. Also, later on, he had the option of flying the Spitfire IX but allowed less experienced pilots to do so. By 1943, his Spitfire Vb was outclassed by the German Fw190. Sadly, he pushed his luck too far and was killed in action on 16 April 1943, aged 26.

The exact circumstances of his death remain a mystery but he is thought to have fallen victim to one of the German aces of JG77. He was credited with 13 victories; 3 shared victories; 4 probables and 3 shared probables; and 4 damaged in air combat. He also destroyed and damaged a number of enemy aircraft in ground attacks.

Flight Sergeant G. W. Godley
First noted in the ORB Appendice for 20 January 1945 flying Typhoons.

Warrant Officer S. Godley
Flew Typhoons in Holland during 1945. Some confusion with the initials in the ORB. This pilot is possibly the Flight Sergeant listed above as he is on occasion listed as Warrant Officer G. Godley as well as 'S'.

Pilot Sergeant S. A Goodwin
Flying Spitfire Mk II P7296 with the Squadron on 4 October 1940 was forced to land at Little Bytham during bad weather. He was uninjured, but the aircraft was badly damaged. On 14 October 1940 he was posted to 66 Squadron at RAF Biggin Hill for flying duty. He fought in the Battle of Britain.

Pilot Officer R. C. Gosling. DFC & Bar
Service number 85245. British.
Posted from an unknown squadron and OTU on 29 September 1940. Flew with 266 & 229 Squadrons achieving nine victories. He fought in the Battle of Britain. Flew Spitfire Mk IIs from RAF West Malling during 1941.

Flight Sergeant P. C. Green.
While on an armed reconnaissance mission on 9 August 1944 flying a Typhoon over the Falaise area, he was shot down by flak, evading capture. Shot down over Germany on 25 December 1944. Flew as part of 146 Wing from Airfield B3 at St Croix.

Flying Officer Green.
Posted to Wittering on 13 May 1941. A Rhodesian pilot.

Flight Lieutenant C. L. Green

First noted in ORB dated 5 July 1941 as flying Spitfire Mk IIa P8608 from Wittering. Promoted to Squadron Leader on 18 October 1941. On 27 January 1943 he was awarded the DFC whilst CO of the squadron at Exeter. Posted to Hinkleigh on 25 June 1943 as Station Commander with the rank of Wing Commander.

Could this be Flying Officer Green? Without any initials in the ORB it is impossible to identify correctly between the two pilots.

Sub. Lieutenant Henry laFone Greenshields. (Fleet Air Arm). British.

Born in 1918 in Axminster, Devon. Medically turned down by the RAF with defective eyesight before the war, he joined the Royal Navy Volunteer Reserve (RNVR) and was among the group of Fleet Air Arm (FAA) pilots loaned to the RAF (who were seriously short of pilots) on 23 June 1940, joining 266 Squadron at RAF Wittering on 1 July 1940 after converting to Spitfires from No.7 Operational Training Unit, Hawarden. His fellow pilots quickly 'christened' him 'Sinbad'.

On 15 August he shot down a Me 109, and the following day he was involved in the pursuit of a number of Me 109s over the English Channel in Spitfire Mk I N3240, and was shot down and killed, aged 22, by (it is believed) Lieutenant Mueller-Duhe of JG 26. His aircraft crashed near Calais.

The Germans recovered his body but believed he was a French Canadian & buried him as a Frenchman. 36 years later - in 1976 - his true identity was revealed and he was reburied in the Military Section of Calais Southern Cemetery. He fought in the Battle of Britain.

Sergeant Pilot R.H.Gretton.
Service number 754187.

Joined 266 Squadron on 12 June 1940 from No. 5 OTU. He was
posted to 222 Squadron on 10 September 1940. It was while
on patrol with this squadron on the 27 September 1940 that he
was bounced by Bf 109s and was shot down, crashing his Spitfire
R6720 near Rainham, Essex, at 12:00hrs. Severely injured in the
subsequent parachute landing, he spent five months recovering
from a fractured pelvis and spine. He returned to operational
flying in November 1941 for three months before being posted
for a further two months treatment and rehabilitation in
February 1942, when he was also awarded the DFC. Although
not passed fit to fly, he returned to duty in April with the
Aircraft Delivery Flight, where he remained for the remainder of
the war. He fought in the Battle of Britain.

Pilot Officer P. S. Gunning.
Reported for duty with the Squadron on 22 April 1940 at RAF
Martlesham Heath.

Sergeant Pilot Hagger.
A Rhodesian pilot, he is first noted in ORB (Appendix Six) dated
6 July 1941, flying a Spitfire Mk IIa P8422 from Wittering. On
14 April 1942 he was attached from Duxford to Abbots Inch
pending overseas posting.

Pilot Officer N. P. W. Hancock.
Flew Spitfire Mk Is with the Squadron from RAF Martlesham
Heath during early 1940.

Sergeant Pilot Hardy
A Rhodesian pilot who was posted to the Squadron at Wittering
on 1 August 1941 for flying duties at Wittering. On 24
September 1941 he was posted to 129 Squadron.
Flying Officer J. Harrison.

First noted as flying Typhoons in France from the ORB Appendice of 6th of October 1944.

Flight Sergeant Harrold
First mention in the ORB for 9 April 1944.

Sergeant Pilot F.B.Hawley.
Service number 748286. British.
Joined 266 Squadron on 12 July 1940 from No. 5 OTU. Following the destruction of a He115 floatplane off Dunkirk, he is believed to have crashed into the sea and was reported 'missing in action' on 15 August, aged 23. He flew from RAF Hornchurch with the squadron and fought in the Battle of Britain.

Flying Officer Haworth.
A Typhoon pilot. In early 1942 took part in a Ranger Operation from RAF Harrowbeer with 193 Squadron as part of the Harrowbeer Wing. He is credited with one Me110 destroyed on the ground (shared with Warrant Officer Richardson), and one Harvard type damaged. (Unsure of the aircraft type, he described it as a Harvard.) First noted in ORB of 3 August 1944.

Pilot Officer G. M. Hayton
Reported for flying duties on 28 August 1940 at RAF Wittering from 12 Squadron. Posted to 66 Squadron on 26 October 1940.

Flight Sergeant Hayworth
Posted to 266 Squadron on 24 December 1944.
Flight Lieutenant Healey
First noted in ORB of 2 March 1944. Missing in action 2 March 1944.

Sergeant Pilot Henderson.

Known to have flown Typhoon Mk Ibs from Exeter. He was severely injured during a forced landing on 30 April 1943. Could also be Pilot Officer G. Henderson flying in Holland 1944/45.

Pilot Officer H.M.T. Heron.

Service number 41700. British.

Joined 266 Squadron at RAF Sutton Bridge on 16 December 1939 flying Fairy Battle aircraft. On 27 July 1940 attached to RAF St. Athen for 3 weeks Navigation Instructors Course. He was posted to 92 Squadron on 11 September 1940.

He was awarded the AFC on 7 September 1945. Flew from Hornchurch with 266 Squadron and fought in the Battle of Britain.

Pilot Officer M. K. Hill

Reported to Wittering on 28 September 1940 from No. 7 OTU.

Pilot Officer M.R. Hill.

Service number 72467. South African.

Killed in action 12 March 1945. He fought in the Battle of Britain.

Pilot Officer Hill.

A Rhodesian pilot. There is no further information for this pilot. There is a possibility that he is one of the pilots above. The reader should be aware of this.

Pilot Officer Holland.

Probably one of six un-named pilots posted on 5 November 1940. First reported in ORB dated 19 December 1940. Is listed as 'missing' (from Combat Report) after combat with Me 109s on 27 June 1941 over St Omer, France.

Flight Sergeant A. O. Holland.
Killed when his Typhoon crashed into the sea, 19 May 1944 following a No ball operation in the Cherbourg area.

Squadron Leader Joseph William Ernest Holmes.
Born in Yorkshire on 22 April 1916, he was educated at Normanton Grammar School, Trinity College, Carmathan and Carnegie Hall, Leeds. He entered the RAF in 1939, and was commissioned in 1941 joining 263 Squadron at RAF Charmy Down. During 1942 he was posted to 137 Squadron before returning to 263 Squadron in 1943 as a Flight Commander. Both of these squadrons were the only squadrons to fly the Westland Whirlwind fighter-bomber operationally during World War II.In 1944 he was made CO of 266 Squadron operating Typhoons, and it was while at this squadron that the strafing attack on German Field Marshall Rommel took place. Rommel was making an inspection tour of German frontline positions in Normandy.

Reports suggest that cannon fire from his Typhoon caused Rommel to be hit in the face by broken glass from the windscreen of the staff car he was travelling in, plus a severe blow to his left temple and cheekbone, fracturing Rommel's skull.

Research after the event indicated that it was indeed his attack that was responsible for the injuries. Now however, this action has been credited to a pilot of 193 Squadron, although the debate on which pilot actual did strafe and severely injure Rommel still continues to this day, with several other pilots making the claim at the time.During 1952 he was Chief Flying Instructor with No. 233 Operational Conversion Unit. In 1954 he was posted to the Far East involved in the air operations during the Malaysian Emergency.

It was during this period while flying in a Avro Lincoln bomber of 1 Squadron RAAF as second pilot that he had to take control of the aircraft after it struck high ground. Two of its engines caught fire, and he managed to ditch the crippled bomber in the sea. The crew evacuated the sinking aircraft and he pushed a dingy with injured crewmembers through shark-infested waters to the safety of the shore. Group Captain Holmes died, aged 77, at his home on Jersey during 1993.

Sergeant Pilot E. V. Horne
Serial number 778813.
Posted to Warmwell on 17 November 1942 flying Typhoons. He was sadly killed during a practice flight when flying in cloud at Exeter on 2 February 1943. His body and Typhoon aircraft were found near Hampton.

Sergeant Pilot Frank Stanley Howard.
Joined 266 Squadron on 15 September 1941 from No. 58 OTU. On 14 April 1942 he was attached from Duxford to Abbots Inch pending overseas posting. Went to Malta onboard the USS Wasp which was 'on loan' to the Royal Navy, delivering 64 Spitfires for the defence of the island from Italian and German air attacks. Died in Malta of wounds received in action some time prior to 24 December 1942. (Taken from Flight Magazine of 25 December 1942. Weekly RAF Casualty List.)

Flight Sergeant J. Howarth
Serial number 778630.
Flew with the Duxford Typhoon Wing in 1942. His name first appears in the ORB Appendix for 30 July 1942 flying Typhoon R7676. He was commissioned with effect from 12 October 1942 to the rank of Pilot Officer at Warmwell. Posted to an OTU on 5 March 1944.

Flying Officer J. S. Howitt

Is posted as Medical Officer on 1 January 1941. On 6 October 1941 is posted to RAF Station Wittering. (Flying Officer Scott arrived to take up the post of Medical Officer from the Princess Mary (RAF) Hospital at Halton Camp, Buckinghamshire on the 4 October 1941.)

Sergeant Pilot D. Hughes

First mentioned in the ORB Appendice for 23 April 1944.

Sergeant Pilot I. O. Hulley

Posted to Exeter on 18 August 1943 from No. 56 OTU, flying Typhoon Mk lbs. Promoted to Pilot Officer. After completing his first tour on operations in Europe was posted to a Tactical Evaluation Unit on 30 November 1944.

Pilot Officer A. H. Humphrey.

Service number 33543. British.

On 16 September 1940 he was posted to 266 Squadron at RAF Wittering aged 19, after a 21-hour conversion course undertaken in just 10 days at No. 7 Operational Training Unit. He flew with the massive 12 Group Wing lcd by Douglas Bader.

Had a very interesting career rising to Air Chief Marshall. His last post, in August 1976, was Chief of the Defence Staff. Admitted to Princess Mary RAF Hospital at RAF Halton near Aylesbury, Buckinghamshire, seriously ill, he died on 24 January 1977. He fought in the Battle of Britain.

Squadron Leader J. W. A. Hunnard.

First CO of 266 Squadron when it was re-formed on 30 October 1939 at RAF Sutton Bridge.

Sergeant Pilot H. S. Jacques
First mentioned in ORB for 6 March 1941 when he was posted to No. 58 OTU for instructor duties. Possibly a Rhodesian pilot.

Pilot Officer James
Posted to Wittering on 9 December 1941 from No. 57 OTU at Hawarden. He is a Rhodesian pilot.

Squadron Leader Patrick Geraint 'Jamie' Jameson. DFC & two Bars. DSO.
Service number 37813. New Zealand.
Born in Wellington, New Zealand on 10 November 1912. Educated in Lower Hutt, eventually employed as an assurance clerk. Learned to fly at the Wellington Aero Club in 1933. Left New Zealand in January 1936 to join the RAF. Completed flying training during January the following year, and was posted to 46 Squadron flying Hurricanes.

He flew in Norway in the campaign of 1940, destroying a Ju 88, plus he shared in the destruction of two Dornier Do 26 flying boats. 46 Squadron covered the withdrawal from Norway in June 1940. The squadron landed its Hurricanes on the flight deck of HMA Glorious. Sand bags were fitted under the tailplanes to shorten the landing run. Unfortunately the carrier was attacked and eventually sunk by the German battle cruisers Scharnhorst and Gneisenau with shellfire. Adrift with his CO and thirty others on a Carley float for three days, at the end of which just seven men survived the cold sea, the two RAF pilots being the sole survivors of the squadron. Awarded a DFC for his services in Norway in July.

When he was declared fit for active service he took command of 266 Squadron on 17 September 1940. On 9 June 1941 he was posted to RAF Station Wittering with the rank of Wing Commander, ending his command of the squadron. With nine victories, he survived the war, retiring with the rank of Air Commodore, returning to live in New Zealand. Listed wartime rank as Group Captain. He fought in the Battle of Britain.

Flight Lieutenant A. C. Johnston.

Flying as Blue Section with Sergeant Pilot Osbourne from RAF Duxford, and with Green Section (Pilot Officers Miller and Wilson), took off at 18.55 hours on 13 August 1942 to carry out a Sea Patrol flying Typhoon Mk Ibs.

Off the coast of Lowestoft they encountered a Ju 88. Flight Lieutenant Johnston as leading Blue 1 attacked the Ju 88 and observed strikes on the aircraft's starboard engine. Closing to 400 yards he fired a series of short bursts and saw the port engine smoking and the starboard engine and fuselage in flames. He observed the hood eject and one crewmember baled out. At this point Flight Lieutenant Johnstone was so close to the tail of the Ju 88 that he had to violently pull up to avoid a collision. The crewmember who baled out was seen to land in the sea.

Flight Lieutenant Johnston was credited with one Ju 88 destroyed. The other pilots in the patrol also attacked the aircraft. On 20 November 1942 he was promoted to Squadron Leader and posted to 56 Squadron.

Pilot Officer Johnston.

A Rhodesian pilot flying Spitfire Mk IIas. First noted in ORB dated 11 July 1941 flying P8422 from West Malling on an Offensive Fighter Sweep to Northern France.

Pilot Officer W. R. Jones.
Service number 44635.

British. Shared in shooting down a He115 off Dunkirk on 15 August 1940. In 1944 and 1945 he carried out many 'special flights' to southern France, Belgium, Holland and Germany carrying 'important passengers', possibly from RAF Tempsford flying Lysanders. Awarded the AFC 1 January 1946. Flew from Hornchurch with 266 Squadron and fought in the Battle of Britain.

Sergeant Pilot W. Jones.

He flew Fairy Battle light bombers from RAF Sutton Bridge when the squadron was re-formed in 1939. Commissioned August/September 1940 to Pilot Officer was posted to 612 Squadron on 13 September 1940.

Sergeant Pilot Ronald T. Kidman.

Service number 741442.

Joined the RAFVR. Shot down whilst on patrol flying a Spitfire Mk I over Dunkirk on 2 June 1940. Buried in the Dunkirk Town Cemetery, aged 26. (See also Pilot Officer James W. B. Stevenson also shot down on same patrol.)

Sergeant Pilot E. A. King

Reported for flying duty on 7 October 1940. Was posted to 602 Squadron on the 27 November 1940.

Sergeant Pilot Donald Ernest Kingaby.

Service number 112406. British.

The son of a clergyman, he was born in London on 7 January 1920. Enrolling in the RAFVR in April 1939 aged 19. Called up for active service in September 1939, eventually being posted as a Sergeant Pilot to 266 Squadron on 23 June 1940, but was not credited with any combat successes with them.

Posted to 92 Squadron on 25 September where he had better fortune destroying four enemy aircraft before the end of the Battle of Britain. Between the end of the Battle and 2 July 1942, he destroyed twelve Me109s and was described in the press as 'the 109 specialist'. Awarded the DFM on 6 December 1940. The citation read -

> 'This airman has displayed great courage and tenacity in his attacks against the enemy.
>
> He has destroyed at least nine hostile aircraft, four of which he shot down in one day.'

A Bar was awarded on 29 July 1941. The citation read -

> 'This airman pilot has continued to prove himself a very able section leader who fights with coolness and courage. He has now destroyed at least 14 enemy aircraft and damaged others.'

Shooting down three more Me 109s up to 3 October for which he was then awarded a second Bar on 11 November 1941, the only pilot to receive two Bars to the DFM during the war, the citation reading -

> This airman leads his section, and occasionally the Flight, with great skill and courage. He has participated in 36 operational sorties during which he has destroyed 17, probably destroyed six, and damaged a further seven enemy aircraft. F/Sgt Kingaby has at all times displayed the greatest determination and sound judgement, combined with a high standard of operational efficiency.

In October 1941 he was commissioned and taken off operations so that his experience could be put at the service of a training unit. But by March 1942 he was back in the conflict with 111 Squadron. Later in the war he was posted to 122 Squadron initially as a Flight Commander and then Squadron Commander. In March 1943 he was promoted to lead the Hornchurch Wing.

After a further period at Fighter Command HQ he was again back as a Wing Leader in the summer of 1944. In the air battles that raged during the D-Day landings at Normandy his last victory was a share in a Me109 on June 30. This was his last combat victory, bringing his total to 23 confirmed. He also claimed eight probables.

After the war he was given a permanent commission and

in the 1950s took naturally to jet aircraft. He was awarded the DSO on 9 March 1943, CdeG (Belgium) in October 1944, the DFC (USA) on 15 May 1945, and the AFC on 5 June 1952. He attained the rank of Group Captain. Retiring from the RAF in 1958, he moved with his wife and two daughters to live in the United States of America. He flew from Hornchurch with 266 Squadron and fought in the Battle of Britain.

Sergeant Pilot A. Knoesen

First noted in ORB Appendice 79 of 28 May 1944 flying Typhoon MN297 from Snaith.

Flight Sergeant Laing

First noted in ORB of 9 September 1944 flying Typhoons in France. Shot down on 19 November 1944. Was 'picked up' by the French Resistance and returned to the Squadron later in December un-harmed.

Sergeant Pilot G. Land

Flew Fairy Battle light bombers with 266 Squadron during December 1939 and early January 1940 before being posted to No. 12 Group Pool at RAF Aston Down on 17 January 1940.

Sergeant Pilot Lees

First noted in ORB of 17 July 1941, flying a raid investigation in Spitfire Mk IIa P8608 from Wittering.

Pilot Officer Lees

A Rhodesian pilot, he was sadly killed flying a Typhoon aircraft from Duxford on 8 March 1942. He was seen to go into a spin from 5,000 feet with the aircraft engine stopped, crashing about a quarter of a mile from Duxford village.

The author is uncertain as to whether Pilot Officer Lees is

the same pilot as Sergeant Lees above. It is possible that Sergeant Lees was commissioned, but without further details of each pilot it is not possible to correctly identify each.

Squadron Leader P. W. Le Fevre. DFC

Commanding Officer of the Squadron after the death of Squadron Leader MacIntyre on 15 August 1943. Flying with the Harrowbeer Wing (France) in Typhoon Mk Ibs along with pilots from 193 Squadron, the Wing took off towards St Brieuc Bay, crossing the French coast north of St Alban to meet up with six aircraft of 183 Squadron.

As the formation passed west of Lannion, two Me 109s were spotted. Squadron Leader Lefevre flying as 'Brandy Port 1' attacked an Me 109, destroying it, firing a short burst from 175 yards range. This action took place on 21 January 1944.

Sergeant Pilot Leggo.

A Rhodesian pilot flying Spitfire Mk IIas. From a Combat Report of 23 July 1941, he was on patrol over the French Coast, and attacked several Me 109s with no apparent damage to the enemy aircraft. Following instructions to remain with the squadron he did not pursue the enemy aircraft. On 25 November 1941 he was commissioned.

Sergeant Pilot R. F. Lewis.

Posted to No. 57 OTU for further training on 21 November 1940. Is mentioned in ORB for 8 March 1941 as being on the Squadron strength flying Spitfire Mk I N3100 on patrol.

Pilot Officer Colin Logan.

Service number 44178. British.
He joined the RAF as an apprentice in September 1928, passing out in August 1931. Remustering as an Airman (Under Training)

Pilot, he was commissioned on 20 July 1940 serving with 12 (Bomber) Squadron. It is not certain when he moved to Fighter Command, possibly volunteering, but he was posted to No. 7 Operational Training Unit, Hawarden on 8 March 1940.

He was posted to 266 Squadron at RAF Hornchurch on 20 August 1940 from 12 Squadron, RAF Eastchurch. Posted to 222 Squadron on 4 November 1940 where he sadly lost his life. On 27 March 1941 he was killed in action aged 29, and is buried in Brookwood Military Cemetery, Woking. He fought in the Battle of Britain.

Flight Sergeant R. Love.
Posted for flying duties on 15 June 1944. Missing in action over France flying Typhoons on 17 August 1944.

Sergeant Pilot N. J. Lucas
A Rhodesian pilot who was posted to the Squadron at Wittering (WB2) from 19 Squadron on 4 November 1941 flying Spitfire Mk Vbs.

Flying Officer N. J. Lucas
A Typhoon pilot who flew Mk Ibs. Operating near Lorient, France, he shot down a Ju 52 minesweeping aircraft of the Minensuchgruppe. This action was shared with fellow 266 Squadron pilot, Flying Officer W. V. Mollet. Posted to No. 59 OTU on 16 February 1944.

The reader should be aware that this pilot could be Sergeant Pilot N. J. Lucas above. Possibly commissioned at some time.

Pilot Officer Lunnenschloss.
Four Typhoon Mk Ib aircraft from 266 Squadron took off on an armed reconnaissance mission on 11 April 1945, flying close to a German held airfield at Varrelbusch where they spotted three

parked enemy aircraft (a Ju 88, Me 109 and a Fw 190). All four Typhoons strafed the German aircraft and destroyed all on the ground. Pilot Officer Lunnenschloss was given 'a share' along with Squadron Leader Sheward (the Flight leader), and Flight Sergeants' Clack and Wheeler.

Sergeant Pilot A. N. MacGregor.
Service number 109895. British.
Joined 266 Squadron at RAF Wittering on 16 September 1940 when posted from No. 7 Operational Training Unit. On 28 September 1940 he was posted to No. 19 Squadron. He fought in the Battle of Britain.

Sergeant Pilot MacNamara.
A Rhodesian, he was posted to the Squadron on 15 September 1941 from No. 58 OTU.

Pilot Officer J. J. R. MacNamara
Flew Typhoons from Duxford during 1942 when the squadron was re-equipped. On 13 January 1943 while at Exeter, he had to leave the Squadron because of illness.

This could be the same pilot as Sergeant Pilot MacNamara above, but without more details of when he was commissioned or any initials it cannot be confirmed. The reader should be aware of this.

Flying Officer McAdam
First noted in ORB of 2 September 1944 flying Typhoons in France.

Pilot Sergeant Main
First mentioned in ORB (Appendix Five) on 5 April 1941, flying Spitfire Mk II P8167 on patrol from Wittering.

Sergeant Pilot Matthews.

A Rhodesian pilot flying Spitfire Mk IIs from Wittering, he was posted to the Squadron on 7 May 1941 from 145 Squadron.

Flight Sergeant D. McGibbon

Serial number 778635.

Noted in the ORB (Appendix) for 19 July 1942, flying Typhoons out of Duxford. He was commissioned with effect from 12 October 1942 to the rank of Pilot Officer at Warmwell.

In early 1942 took part in a 'Ranger Operation' from RAF Harrowbeer with 193 Squadron as part of the Harrowbeer Wing. He was credited with one He111 destroyed on the ground, and three Harvard type aircraft destroyed in the air. (Unsure what types these three were, he describes them as Harvard's.)

Promoted to Flying Officer with effect from 4 April 1943 at Exeter. (ORB entry dated 24 June 1943). Posted to an OTU on 5 March 1944. A Flight Lieutenant McGibbon is listed as being shot down, but baling out successfully, over France flying Typhoons with 266 Squadron on 18 October 1944. Confirmed as a Prisoner of War on 31 December 1944.

Flight Lieutenant A. S. MacIntyre.

Posted to the Squadron at Warmwell on 30 September 1942 from Annan. Posted to 245 Squadron, date not known. Re-joined 266 Squadron at Exeter on 28 May 1943 flying Typhoon Mk Ibs. On 25 June 1943 he was appointed CO of the Squadron. Killed in action on 15 August 1943 flying Typhoons over France.

Flight Lieutenant D. A. P. McMullen. DFC and Bar.

Noted in ORB (Appendix 26) dated 30 July 1941 as flying a Spitfire Mk IIa P7850. The 3 November 1941 ORB entry lists him as having a DFC and Bar and has now been posted to 257 Squadron.

Sergeant Pilot R. McElroy.
Arrived at Exeter from No. 56 OTU on 26 August 1943, flying Typhoon Mk lbs.

Sergeant Pilot McMurdon
Arrived from OTU on 10 January 1944. Shot down over France on 9 May 1944 flying a Typhoon.

Pilot Officer J. R. D. Menelaws
A Rhodesian pilot, he was posted to Wittering from 19 Squadron on 4 November 1941.

Squadron Leader Herbert Waldemar Mermagen.
Service number 29097. British.
Born in Swansea on 1 February 1912, he first became interested in flight as a child when he first saw a Sopwith Camel land near the family home. Educated at Brighton College, he was granted a short service commission, and in June of 1931 was posted to 43 Squadron flying Hawker Fury bi-planes. As an aerobatic pilot in the squadron he was selected to fly in the RAF aerobatic team at the 1933 Brussels Air Show.

Qualifying as an instructor at the Central Flying School (CFS), he moved on to the Oxford University Air Squadron. In 1936 he was posted back to the CFS where he gave a brilliant solo aerobatic display in front of George VI. He was later promoted to Squadron Leader at the very young age (then) of 26.

During October of 1939 he formed 222 Squadron at RAF Duxford, flying Bristol Blenheim bombers. March 1940 and he was instructed to convert the squadron to Spitfires, for which he was awarded the AFC. On 12 September of 1940 he was appointed temporary CO of 266 Squadron at RAF Wittering, flying Spitfires. His Spitfire, P7350, is still flying with the Battle of Britain Memorial Flight at RAF Coningsby. (See informative item in this book).

Promoted to Wing Commander in the summer of 1941 he was posted to the Middle East where he served for over two years before taking up a staff appointment in 1944 at Supreme Headquarters Allied Expeditionary Force. At the end of the European War he commanded the British Air Command in the British Sector of a divided Berlin.

He remained in the RAF after the war and qualified as a Gloster Meteor pilot while commanding RAF Leconfield, before retiring in 1960. He was appointed OBE in 1942, CBE in 1945 and CB in 1960. Marshal Zhukov personally invested him with the Soviet Distinguished Services Medal in 1946, and he also held the United States of America Legion of Merit and French Legion d'Honneur. He died in 1997 aged 85, and fought in the Battle of Britain.

Warrant Officer J. H. Meyer.
A Rhodesian with 266 Squadron, flying Typhoon Mk Ibs from the Harrowbeer Wing in France.

Pilot Officer W.A. Middleton.
Service number 39928. British.
Reported for flying duties on 26 August 1940 at RAF Wittering from No. 7 OTU. Was posted from the squadron to 485 Squadron for flying duties. Declared as 'missing in action' on 27 August 1941. A pilot who fought in the Battle of Britain.

Sergeant Pilot Miller
Joined the 266 Squadron at Wittering on 15 September 1941 from No. 58 OTU.

Pilot Officer J. D. Miller
Flew Typhoons from Duxford during 1942. Promoted to Flying Officer on 1 December 1942. (ORB entry dated 24 June 1943). Shot down on a fighter sweep 15 February 1944. Missing, believed killed.

The author is uncertain as to whether this pilot is the same pilot as Sergeant Miller above. It is possible that Sergeant Miller was commissioned, but without further details of each pilot it is not possible to correctly identify each. The reader should be aware of this.

Flying Officer Miller.
Noted in the ORB Appendice dated 10 September 1944.

Pilot Officer P. H. G. Mitchell.
Service number 42252. British.
He flew Fairy Battle light bombers from RAF Sutton Bridge when the Squadron was re-formed in 1939 and was with the squadron throughout the Battle of Britain. Posted to No. 57 OTU on 9 June 1941.

Sergeant Pilot Mitchell
Arrived from OTU on 10 January 1944.

Flight Sergeant Moll.
Arrived at 266 Squadron on 23 December 1944.

Sergeant Pilot M. B. Mollet
First noted on the ORB (Appendix) for 30 July 1942 flying Typhoons from Duxford and West Malling. This pilot could also be Flight Sergeant W. V. Mollet below with incorrect initials. The reader should be aware of this.

Flight Sergeant W. V. Mollet
Serial number 778597.
A Typhoon pilot who flew a Mk Ib. Operating near Lorient, France, he shot down a Ju 52 minesweeping aircraft of the Minensuchgruppe. This action was shared with fellow 266 Squadron pilot, Flying Officer N. J. Lucas. He was commissioned with effect from 12 October 1942 to the rank of Pilot Officer at Warmwell. Promoted to Flying Officer with effect from 4 April 1943 at Exeter. (ORB entry dated 24 June 1943.)

Flight Sergeant Morgan
Posted to 266 Squadron on 2 June 1944 at Needs Oar Point.

Sergeant Pilot Morris
First noted in ORB (Appendix Eight) during April 1941 as flying Spitfire Mk II P7611, on patrol from Wittering. On 3 May 1941 he was posted to 260 Squadron.

Lieutenant Morrison.
With the Squadron at its formation in 1919.

Sergeant Pilot F. W. Morse
Posted to the Squadron (latter part of 1940) from 56 Squadron for flying duties.

Sergeant Pilot Ian M. Munro.
A Rhodesian pilot flying Spitfire Mk IIas. Posted in for flying duties on 19 July 1941. On 25 November 1941 he was commissioned with the rank of Pilot Officer. On 9 August 1942, flying a Typhoon Mk Ib from RAF Matlask on Sea Patrol with Pilot Officer Lucas (Typhoon Mk Ia) as Red Section, 266 Squadron, they encountered a Ju 88 which they both immediately chased.

The Ju 88 opened fire, and the pilot took evasive action, weaving from side to side. Pilot Office Munro opened fire with 20mm cannon observing strikes on the water. Both pilots attacked the Ju 88, and set both engines on fire. The Ju 88 pilot attempted to ditch on the water, but 'bounced', dropping a wing and dived in nose first. There were no survivors.

Sadly on 3 May 1943 he was killed when air testing a Typhoon at Exeter. He held the rank of Flight Lieutenant. He is buried at Exeter Cemetery.

Flight Lieutenant Nesbit
Arrived on 6 May 1944 from 237 Squadron at Salisbury. Killed in action on 12 June 1944 flying Typhoons.

Sergeant Pilot C. E. Ody
Reported for flying duty on 14 October 1940 from No 7 OTU. Noted in ORB for 21 December 1940. Posted on 26 March 1941 to No. 58 OTU for instructors duties

Sergeant Pilot G. G. Osbourne.
Serial number 777692.
A Rhodesian, flew Typhoon Mk Ibs from Duxford and Warmwell during 1942. He was commissioned with effect from 12 October 1942 to the rank of Pilot Officer at Warmwell. Killed while flying a Typhoon on a formation practice flight on 28 November 1942 after flying into cloud.

Sergeant Pilot E. Palte.
Posted to the Squadron on 12 November 1943. Promoted at some time to Pilot Officer. After completing his first tour on operations in Europe was posted to a Tactical Evaluation Unit on 30 November 1944.

Pilot Officer Hugh L. Parry.
A Rhodesian pilot. He was posted to Wittering from 260 Squadron on 2 May 1941. Flying on patrol over the Calais area on 3 July 1941, he was attacked by an Me 109. Cannon fire scored hits on his port wing. The enemy aircraft broke off the attack,

Returning to base (West Malling possibly) crossing over the Channel, he observed an Me 109 climbing and fired a three second burst at it - only his starboard machine guns were firing - but did not observe any strikes. On 3 November 1941 he was promoted to Flight Lieutenant and given command of 'B' Flight.

Flight Sergeant J. O. Pascoe.
First noted in ORB on 6 February 1945.

Sergeant Pilot K. C. Pattison.
Service number 742457. British.
Posted to RAF Wittering on 23 September 1940 from an OTU. From 266 Squadron he was posted to 611 Squadron on 25 September 1940 for flying duties. He died from injuries on 13 October 1940. He fought in the Battle of Britain.

Pilot Officer J. G. Pattison.
Service number 39931. New Zealand.
Reported for flying duties on 26 August 1940 at RAF Wittering from No. 7 OTU. Posted to 92 Squadron on 11 September 1940. He fought in the Battle of Britain.

Flight Sergeant A. W. Paul
Arrived from OTU on 10 January 1944. Shot down over France on 6 October 1944 flying Typhoons. Held the rank of Warrant Officer at the time.

Pilot Officer H. E. Penketh

Posted to the Squadron on 8 November 1940 from 611 Squadron for flying duties. Killed in action flying Spitfire Mk I X4593 on 22 November 1940 when his aircraft was seen to dive into the ground at full throttle at Holme, near Upwood aerodrome. His body was recovered on 30 November from the crater made by the crashing aircraft.

Sergeant Pilot D. S. Peters.

He appears in the ORB for 15 April 1943. He was killed on that day when his Typhoon Mk Ib flew into the sea. He was with the Squadron at Exeter.

Warrant Officer J. Pickard

First named in ORB for 20 March 1941 as being mentioned in dispatches. The London Gazette (No. 35107) dated 17 March 1941 refers.

On 1 November 1941 was commissioned to Pilot Officer for engineer duties. Promoted as some unknown date to Flying Officer, he was posted to No. 59 OTU as a Flight Lieutenant from Exeter on 11 March 1943. He was one of the original members of the squadron when it re-formed, having been with it since 1 November 1939.

Warrant Officer N. V. Phillips

Arrived to the Squadron on 23 December 1944.

Sergeant Pilot Johnny Plagis. (Ioannis Agorastos "John" Plagis.)

A Rhodesian pilot born of Greek parents in 1919. Joined 266 flying Spitfire Mk IIs. Posted for flying duties on 19 July 1941. (The ORB doesn't state where to.) While serving in Malta he shot down four German aircraft in one day. He had 16 confirmed victories in total.

After a spell as an instructor in the UK during 1942, he returned to action in September 1943 as commander of 64 Squadron, flying Spitfire Mk Vcs over northern France. He took command of 126 (Persian Gulf) Squadron in June 1944, and led many attacks on German positions during the invasion of France. He was shot down over Arnhem during Operation Market Garden, but only lightly wounded. After converting to Mustang IIIs, he commanded a Wing based at RAF Bentwaters that supported bombing missions. He finished the war with the rank of Squadron Leader and remained with the RAF afterwards, operating Gloster Meteors at the head of 266 Squadron.

He was the top-scoring Rhodesian of the war, and the highest-scoring ace of Greek origin, with 16 confirmed aerial victories, including 11 over Malta. Awarded the Distinguished Service Order and other medals.

The Southern Rhodesian capital, Salisbury, honoured his wartime contributions by naming a street in its northern Alexandra Park neighbourhood after him. He returned home in 1945 still serving in the RAF until 1948. Retiring with the rank of Wing Commander, he set up home at 1 John Plagis Avenue. He married and had four children. Sadly during in 1974 he committed suicide.

Warrant Officer Points
First noted in ORB Appendice of 25 November 1944 flying Typhoons.

Pilot Officer Pool.
Reported for flying duties on 26 August 1940 at RAF Wittering from No. 7 OTU. On 3 October 1940 was posted to RAF Biggin Hill for flying duties. Missing in action on 19 August 1942. He fought in the Battle of Britain.

Lieutenant H. G. Pratt.
With the Squadron at its formation in 1919.

Pilot Officer H.A.R. Prowse.
Service number 42358. British.
Posted to 266 Squadron at RAF Wittering on 16 September 1940 from No. 7 Operational Training Unit. On 20 October 1940 he was posted to 603 squadron. He fought in the Battle of Britain.

Squadron Leader H. A. Pugh
Is first recorded in the ORB (Appendix 5) as flying Typhoons from Duxford and Thorney Island on 6 September 1942.

Flying Officer D. Quick
Posted to the Squadron on 17 March 1945 from Bulawao.

Sergeant Pilot Reid
Posted to Wittering on 15 December 1941 from 275 Air/Sea Rescue Squadron. A Rhodesian pilot.

Flight Lieutenant Roach.
Flew Spitfire Mk IIs from RAF West Malling during 1941. As there are no initials or service number for this pilot the reader should be aware that he could be the same pilot below.

Pilot Officer R. J. B. Roach.
Service number 42263. British.
Flew from RAF Sutton Bridge in Fairy Battle light bombers during 1939, and from RAF Wittering with 266 Squadron.
   Shared in downing a He115 off Dunkirk on 15 August 1940. (Also see Pilot Officer J.F. Soden below). He shot down a Do117 on 7 September and was shot down by defensive fire from a

He111 on 11 of September 1940, successfully baling out of his Spitfire P7313 at 16.20 hours over Billericay, uninjured. On 25 September 1940 he was sent to Hendon for flying demonstration in a Supermarine Spitfire Mk II for factory workers. The Squadron had just been re-equipped with the Mk II Spitfire

Sergeant Pilot K.M. Rogers.
Posted to Exeter from No. 59 OTU on 29 August 1943. Could also be Flying Officer Rogers flying Typhoons in France/Belgium.

Sergeant Pilot Ross
A Rhodesian pilot, who was posted to the Squadron on 1 August 1941 for flying duties at Wittering.

Sergeant Pilot W. Sadler.
Joined the Squadron on 23 September 1940 from 92 Squadron. From the 266 Squadron he was posted to 611 Squadron on 26 September 1940 for flying duties.

Flying Officer A. V. Sanders.
Posted from MSFU on 19 May 1943. Flew Typhoon Mk Ibs from Exeter. His first flight is recorded as taking place on 25 May 1943. He takes over the role of Squadron Adjutant while remaining as a pilot on 16 November 1943. On 18 April 1944 shot down a Ju 188 prior to the D-Day invasion.

Sergeant Pilot John Alan Scott.
Service number 745385. British.
Born in 1918 at Greenford, West London, he joined the RAFVR during March of 1939 as an Airman (Under Training) Pilot. With the outbreak of war he was called up in September 1939 and after initial training was sent to No. 7 Operational Training Unit at Hawarden in September 1940. Converting to Spitfires he

joined 266 Squadron at RAF Wittering on 23 September 1940 from No. 7 OTU.

From this Squadron he was posted to 611 Squadron at RAF Tern Hill on 26 September 1940 for flying duties, and then to 74 Squadron at RAF Biggin Hill on 23 October.

He was shot down by a Me 109 over Maidstone on 27 October 1940, and crashed in flames in his Spitfire P7526 near to Dundas Farm, Elmstead, not far from Ashford. On the side his Spitfire's cowling, just forward of the cockpit are the words 'The Flying Scott'. Just 22 years of age, he is buried in the Alperton Burial Ground at Wembley. He fought in the Battle of Britain.

Sergeant Pilot Sergeant
First appears in the ORB (Appendix 14) for 14 May 1941, flying a Spitfire Mk IIa P8092, from Wittering. Posted to 129 Squadron on 1 July 1941.

Flying Officer Scott
Flying Officer Scott arrived to take up the post of Medical Officer from the Princess Mary (RAF) Hospital at Halton Camp, Buckinghamshire on 4 October 1941, taking over from Flying Officer Howitt.

Sergeant Pilot Shepherd
Arrived from OTU on 10 January 1944. Forced landing in France on 9 April that year with engine trouble.

Squadron Leader R. R. G. Sherwood.
Flew Typhoon Mk Ibs in Europe.

Sergeant Pilot E. S. Sherwood.
A Rhodesian pilot flying Spitfire Mk IIas from Wittering. First noted in ORB for 12 June 1941, flying P8167 on a raid

investigation. On 25 November 1941 he was commissioned to Pilot Officer, and on 30 April 1942 was attached to Abbots Inch pending overseas posting.

Flight Lieutenant Sheward.
Posted to 266 Squadron on a temporary posting on 1 November 1944 before being posted to 263 Squadron on 25 November 1944. Appears to be CO of the Squadron from January 1945. Signs off the ORB for that month as 'Commanding 266 Squadron'.

Sergeant Pilot J. Shircore
Probably one of six un-named pilots posted on 5 November 1940. First noted in ORB entry 19 December 1940.

Pilot Officer S. A. C. Sibley.
Flew from RAF Sutton Bridge during December 1939 and early January 1940 before being posted to No. 12 Group Pool on 17 January 1940.

Pilot Officer J. Small
A Rhodesian pilot, posted to the Squadron at Wittering on 7 October 1941 from No. 58 OTU. Shot down while flying Typhoons from Exeter on 15 August 1943. Was seen to bale out of his aircraft. No further information available.

Sergeant Pilot Smith
He is first mentioned as flying Spitfire Mk I X4021 in Appendix 20 of the ORB entry dated 28 November 1940. Probably one of six un-named pilots posted to the Squadron on 5 November 1940. On 31 May 1941 he is posted from Wittering to 145 Squadron.

Sergeant Pilot W. R. Smithyman

A Rhodesian pilot who was posted to the Squadron on 1 August
1941 for flying duties at Wittering. He was commissioned at
Duxford with the rank of Pilot Officer, on 21 April 1941, still
flying for the Squadron. Reported as missing in action on 19
August 1942 while attacking Do 217 bombers near Dieppe.

Pilot Officer John Flewelling Soden.

Service number 42903. British.
Joined the RAF on a short service commission during August
1939 undergoing training at No. 9 Flying Training School, he
arrived at No. 5 Operational Training Unit, Aston Down, on 10
June 1940.

Converting to Spitfires he was posted to 266 Squadron at
RAF Wittering on June 26. It was on 15 August 1940 that he
shared with another pilot in destroying a He 115 floatplane off of
Dunkirk covering the evacuation of the BEF and French forces.
(See also P/O R.J.B. Roach above).

The next day flying a Spitfire Mk I K9864, he was shot down
over Canterbury by Me 109s, he successfully force landed near
Oare, Faversham, suffering wounds in both legs. Posted to 603
Squadron at RAF Hornchurch on 14 September 1940 he shot
down two Bf109s and was himself shot down again on 25th
October in Spitfire Mk I P7635, baling out near Canterbury,
injuring his right leg on landing and was admitted to East Sussex
Hospital, Hastings. His Spitfire crashed at Stonelink Fann, Brede.

He also flew Tomahawks in the Western Desert. Returning
to the UK, he was lost on the troopship SS Laconia when it was
sunk on 12 September 1942 by a German U-boat, the U-156.
(The U-boat's Captain, Werner Hartenstein, actually stopped
to pick up survivors. Towing lifeboats and carrying survivors on
his U-boat until they could be transferred to other U-boats and
Italian ships. As well as civilian passengers on the SS Laconia, it

also carried Italian prisoners of war.) He is remembered on the Alamein Memorial, and he fought in the Battle of Britain.

Sergeant Pilot Spence Ross
A Rhodesian pilot who was posted to the Squadron on 1 August 1941 for flying duties at Wittering. Posted to 129 Squadron on 27 August 1941.

Sergeant Pilot J. L. Spence
Serial number 778522.
Posted to the Squadron from 66 Squadron on 22 June 1942. He is recorded in the ORB Appendix for 29 August 1942 as flying Typhoons out of Duxford as part of the Duxford Typhoon Wing.

Was reported as missing in action on 15 September 1942. His Typhoon was seen to be smoking after an engagement, and he was heard to say over the R/T that he was baling out over the Channel, which he was seen to do. He was about 25 miles from Cherbourgh and was seen sitting in his dinghy. Six squadron aircraft orbited him for 30 minutes to get a fix on his position, but had to leave because of low fuel. Air-Sea rescue tried to find him but with no luck. The wind was very strong, and the sea was roughish. He was not seen again.

Squadron Leader. D.G.H. Spenser.
Service number 34114. British.
An experienced pilot who had spent most of his pre-war service in India, he was attached to 266 Squadron on 25 July 1940, taking command on 18 August 1940 until posted away on 10 September 1940. Flew from Hornchurch with the Squadron, and he fought in the Battle of Britain.

Lieutenant Spike.
With the Squadron at its formation in 1919.

Pilot Officer J. B. Stevenson

Joined 266 Squadron at RAF Sutton Bridge during October or November 1939 flying Fairy Battle aircraft. This pilot could also be the pilot listed below. The reader should be aware of this.

Pilot Officer James W. B. Stevenson.

Lost on 2 June 1940 flying Spitfire Mk I on patrol over Dunkirk aged 24. Listed as 'missing in action'. See also Sergeant Pilot Ronald T. Kidman also shot down on same patrol.

Flight Sergeant C. Sydney.

Service number 564940.

Reported for flying duties on 24 August1940 at RAF Wittering from 19 Squadron.

Sergeant Pilot Terry

Posted from the Squadron on 3 October 1940 to RAF Biggin Hill for flying duties.

Sergeant Pilot R. J. Thoburn

Reported to the Squadron for flying duty on 14 October 1940 from No. 7 OTU.

Sergeant Pilot Thorburn.

Listed as missing after combat over Calais on 3 July 1941 flying a Spitfire Mk IIa. This pilot could also be the pilot listed above. The reader should be aware of this.

Sergeant Pilot E. H. Thomas.

Service number 83282. British.

No further information available at the time of writing.

Sergeant Pilot D. W. Thomas
Reported for flying duty on 14 October 1940 from No. 7 OTU.

Flying Officer E. H. Thomas
Service number 39138.
Reported for flying duties on 24 August 1940 at RAF Wittering
from No. 19 Squadron. Posted to No. 222 Squadron on 19
September 1940.

Pilot Officer R. H. Thomas
Posted to 266 Squadron on 26 August 1940, then two days later
was posted to 66 Squadron.

Pilot Officer Thomas
From 266 Squadron was posted to 129 Squadron as a Flight
Commander. As no initials are given in the ORB, it has to be
assumed that this pilot is not Pilot Officer R. H. Thomas, as that
pilot was posted away during August 1940.

Sergeant Pilot R. K. Thompson.
Service Number 160052.
Posted to the Squadron at Warmwell on 30 September
1942 from Llandow. Promoted from Flight Sergeant to the
commissioned rank of Pilot Officer with effect from 20 April
1943 at Exeter. (ORB entry dated 24 June 1943). Killed in action
3 August 1943. Buried at Gouesnou Church, northwest France.

Pilot Officer J. C. Thompson
First recorded in the ORB for 4 January 1942 as flying from
Wittering and Duxford. He flew Spitfire Mk Vbs and Typhoon
Mk Ias and Mk Ibs. At Warmwell he was promoted to 'B' Flight
commander with the rank of Flight Lieutenant on 22 November
1942. After a forced landing in occupied France on 11 January

1943, he was captured and reported as a Prisoner of War.

Flying Officer Tidmarsh
First noted in ORB on 15 March 1944 as Intelligence Officer. Returned to the Squadron on the 22/23 October 1944.

Sergeant Pilot S. F. Tomalin
Posted to the Squadron on 7 October 1940. Was posted to 602 Squadron on 27 November 1940.

Pilot Officer Richard. M. Trousdale.
Service number 42163 New Zealand.
Born in New Zealand in the Old Mission House, Waimate North on 23 January 1921. Having applied to be a heavy bomber pilot and undergoing initial bombing instruction, he was posted to 266 Squadron on 6 November 1939 when it was still intended for the squadron to fly Fairy Battle bombers.

He covered the Dunkirk evacuation of the BEF on 2 June 1940, and he claimed a probable Me 109 destroyed, and scored five victories by the end of the Battle of Britain

He was posted to 255 Squadron as a Flight Commander on 23 November 1940. After the Battle of Britain he became a night fighter pilot, flying Defiants, destroying a He111 on 10 February 1941, and two He111s on the 9th May. He never flew heavy bombers operationally.

Awarded the DFC on 4 March 1941 and a Bar on 8 May 1942. Sadly he was killed in a flying accident on 16 May 1947. Flew from RAF Hornchurch with 266 Squadron.

Pilot Officer B. E.Tucker.
Service number 86349. British.
Posted to the Squadron at RAF Wittering on 7 October 1940. On 25 October 1940 he was posted to 66 Squadron. He fought

in the Battle of Britain.

Sergeant Pilot John van Schaich.
Probably one of six un-named pilots posted to the Squadron on 5 November 1940. Flew Spitfire Mk IIs from RAF West Malling during 1941. Attacked three Me 109s on 3 July 1941 over the Calais area, one of which was seen to be 'going down smoking'. Claimed as destroyed.

Pilot Officer T. A. Vigors.
Flew from RAF Sutton Bridge during December 1939 and early January 1940 before being posted to No. 12 Group Pool on 17 January 1940.

Sergeant Pilot Welby
A Rhodesian pilot who was posted to the Squadron at Wittering on 8 September 1941 from RAF Leconfield. He was killed flying a Typhoon Mk Ia from Duxford when taking part in a training exercise flying in cloud, on 13 June 1942. He crashed into the ground near March.

Pilot Officer E.P. Wells.
Service number 58786. New Zealand.
Reported for flying duties on the 26 August 1940 at RAF Wittering from No. 7 OTU. Flew in the Battle of Britain with 266 Squadron before transferring to RAF Hornchurch and No. 41 Squadron on 2 October 1940.

Known as 'Hawkeye' Wells. His first victory was on 17 October 1940, destroying a Me 109 off of the French coast. On 29 October he possibly destroyed a second, and on 2 November he destroyed a third.

'Hawkeye' Wells had a number of victories credited to him during World War 2. He finally retired from the R.A.F. with the rank of Group Captain in June 1960. He sadly died on 4 November 2005.

Flight Sergeant Wheeler.
Posted to Squadron on 15 June 1944. Believed killed when his Typhoon was hit by flak over France on 15 August 1944.

Flight Sergeant H. Wheeler.
He is possibly the above pilot. There are no initials in the ORB for him and there is no discovered record of Flight Sergeant Wheeler's fate after he was shot down.

Sergeant Pilot H. Whewell
Probably one of six un-named pilots posted to the Squadron on 5 November 1940. First reported in ORB dated 17 December 1940.

Sergeant Pilot Whiteford.
The first Rhodesian pilot to join the Squadron at Wittering on 14 April 1941 from No 58 OTU. On 3 July 1941 while on patrol, he damaged one Me 109, and claimed as a probable another. This took place over the Calais area. He was posted to 41 Squadron on 27 August 1941.

Pilot Officer J. L. Wilkie
Flew Fairy Battle light bombers when Squadron re-formed at RAF Sutton Bridge.

Squadron Leader Rodney Levett Wilkinson.
Service number 26192. British.
Born in Rotherfield, Sussex, he was educated at Wellington College and entered RAF Cranwell during January 1929 as a Flight Cadet, graduating in December 1930. He was posted to 3

Squadron at RAF Upavon and from there onto the staff at HQ Transjordan and Palestine where he was the personal assistant to the Air Officer Commanding, Sir Wilfred Freeman.

Returning to the UK in 1934 he joined the Station Flight at RAF Duxford on 22 October. Various other posts followed this until in June 1940 he was sent on a refresher course at No. 5 Operational Training Unit at RAF Ashton Down where he converted to Spitfires.

He took command of 266 Squadron on 6 July 1940 at RAF Wittering. He destroyed a Do117 on 12 August and a Ju 88 on the 15th. He claimed a Do17 destroyed on 12 August and a Ju 88 on the 15th. The following day in combat over Deal it is believed that he collided with a Me109, possibly that flown by Uffz. Bruder of 4/JG51 who baled out. (It should be noted that various other reports say that he was actually shot down.)

He didn't survive this combat and was killed when his Spitfire, R6768, crashed and burned out at Eastry Court. He was 30 years of age, and is buried in Margate Cemetery, Kent. He fought in the Battle of Britain.

Pilot Officer W. S. Williams.

Service number 42173. New Zealand.

Joined the newly formed 266 Squadron at RAF Wittering during November 1939. On 12 August 1940 he shot down a Ju 88, but his Spitfire Mk I N3175 was damaged in the combat and he was forced to belly-land his damaged aircraft. He barely got clear of the blazing Spitfire when it exploded. He shot down two more aircraft during the Battle of Britain.

On 21 October 1940 he took part in an interception near Cambridge and after the action landed at RAF Stradishall airfield to re-fuel. As he took off he flew low across the airfield and the Spitfire Mk I X4625 appeared to stall. The engine stopped and he was unable to pull out of the ensuing dive. He crashed and was killed, aged 21. Mentioned in dispatches. The London Gazette (No. 35107) dated 17 March 1941 refers.

Sergeant Pilot N. J. A. Wilson
A Rhodesian pilot who was posted to the Squadron at Wittering, from No. 58 OTU on 7 October 1941.

Pilot Officer W. J. A Wilson
Flew Typhoon Mk Ias and Mk Ibs as part of the Duxford Typhoon Wing in 1942. Could this be Sergeant Pilot N. J. A. Wilson? It is possible that he was commissioned and that the initials have been mis-typed in the ORB. The reader should be aware of this.

Squadron Leader Wright
Commanding Officer from 11 July 1944. Shot down over France flying Typhoons and taken prisoner of war on 2 October 1944.

Pilot Officer J. D. Wright
A Rhodesian pilot who was posted to the Squadron on 11 August 1941 for flying duties at Wittering. He was posted to an unknown squadron as a Flight Lieutenant on 27 December 1942 when he was at Warmwell.

Pilot Officer R. A. Wright
Posted to the Squadron at Duxford from 72 Squadron (Ayr) on 16 September 1942 flying Typhoons.

JOHN WATSON ALLEN

LESLIE CHARLES ALLTON

DENNIS LOCKHART ARMITAGE

DENNIS GARTH ASHTON

S. H. BAZLEY

M. A. BEATTY

E. R. BITMEAD

REGINALD ARTHUR BREEZE

A. W. EADE   D. E. GILLAM

I. R. GLEED

HENRY LAFONE GREENSHIELDS.
(FLEET AIR ARM)

J. HOLMES

PATRICK GERAINT JAMESON

D. E. KINGABY

W. A. MIDDLETON

J. G. PATTISON

K. C. PATTISON

PILOT OFFICER POOL

JOHNNY PLAGIS

H. A. R. PROWSE

JOHN ALAN SCOTT. ON THE SIDE COWLING, JUST FORWARD
OF THE COCKPIT, ARE THE WORDS 'THE FLYING SCOTT'.

JOHN FLEWELLING SODEN

RODNEY LEVETT WILKINSON

Not forgetting the ground crews

'They also serve who only stand and wait'

When I consider how my light is spent
Ere half my days in this dark world and wide,
And that one Talent which is death to hide
Lodged with me useless, though my soul more bent
To serve therewith my Maker, and present
My true account, lest He returning chide,
"Doth God exact day-labour, light denied?"
I fondly ask. But Patience, to prevent
That murmur, soon replies, "God doth not need
Either man's work or his own gifts. Who best
Bear his mild yoke, they serve him best. His state
Is kingly: thousands at his bidding speed,
And post o'er land and ocean without rest;
They also serve who only stand and wait.

On His Blindness
John Milton 1608 - 1674

Little if any information exists regarding specific members of the squadron's ground crews, which is particularly sad. Without these 'unsung heroes' no aircraft of any squadron would have taken to the air. Their role in keeping the fighting arm of the RAF is one which, to my mind, cannot be praised enough.

So, in general terms, I have put together the following as a tribute to these men and women who, sometimes under the most primitive of conditions, kept the RAF in the air.

The lower ranks were usually referred to as 'erks', these highly trained people worked as a team, keeping aircraft in the air, and of course keeping the ground equipment on 'top line'. Without them the RAF simply could not have operated.

Armourers would attend to the Browning .303 machine guns, Hispano 20mm and 30mm cannons, rocket projectiles and bombs. Airframe mechanics and fitters would be responsible for the fuselage, wings and all things 'structural'. The aircraft instruments had to be maintained, repaired and replaced as required. Electricians looked after the electrical circuits and switches etc. Engine fitters and mechanics - to service the aircraft power plant - its beating heart. Hydraulic systems, tyres, linkages, the coolant system and umpteen other items that go to keeping an aircraft in the air - all have to be checked, serviced, repaired and maintained to the highest order possible.

Often working through the night in conditions that would not be tolerated in these modern days, they toiled relentlessly to ensure that their pilots would be flying the following day to take the battle to the enemy.

Aircraft returning from combat - the ground crews would have to examine and repair any combat damage the aircraft had sustained. The decision had to be taken in some cases as to whether the damage could be repaired at the base or was it perhaps, beyond the tools and scope that was available to the squadron.

Particularly during the Battle of Britain, the stress on ground crews was at times unbearable. Often snatching a quick bite to eat and a mug of tea when they could, but more often than not, eating and drinking while working. Many were unable, because of the work demanded of them, to even change their clothes, working and sleeping in the same dirty uniforms for days on end.

The fighting status and combat record of any squadron was so reliant on the efficiency and dedication of their ground crews, just as it was with the flying and fighting skills of its pilots.

But lets not forget those other 'erks'. The petrol bowser driver, the parachute packer, the lasses that served the ground crews with hot mugs of tea - these were normally civilians representing the 'Sally Ann' better known as the Salvation Army, and of course the NAAFI (Navy, Army, Air Force Institute) - so in essence everybody was involved in keeping the RAF's aircraft in the air. The list of people involved is endless.

The author is slightly biased on this topic as, serving as a ground crew member with 266 Squadron at RAF Rattlesden, he too, had to work outside in all weathers and conditions to keep, not aircraft, but surface to air Bloodhound missiles fully operational.

The list that follows is of all ground crew members that I have been able to trace from ORBs. The date (where indicated) is of the date recorded in the ORB.

1939 - 1945 known ground crew members.
530787 LAC. B. Walker. Injured. 13 November 1939. Sutton Bridge.
986486 AC2. J. B. Brawley. Killed. 13 August 1940. Eastchurch.
973446 AC2. E. Crossley. Wounded. 13 August 1940. Eastchurch.
939607 AC1 P. P. Lowe. Killed. 14 March 1941. Wittering
972422 AC1 T. Gilmore. Killed 14 March 1941. Wittering.
778141 AC2 J. P. Kruger. Wounded 14 March 1941. Wittering. Died 18 March 1941 at Stamford & Rutland General Infirmary.
Corporal Hosie. ORB entry for 28 December 1943 refers.
Leading Aircraftsman MacMaster. ORB entry for 28 1943 December refers.
Aircraftsman Cowan. ORB dated 21 July 1943 refers.
Corporal Offley - Shore. Injured in a V2 attack in France. 25 / 26 October 1944.
Leading Aircraftman Gold. Injured same V2 attack in France. 25 / 26 October 1944.

Corporal Marshall. ORB dated 22 July1943 refers.

Post 1945 known ground crew members.
2581086 Michael Hull. RAF Wunstorf. September 1953 -
January 1955.
4264801 SAC. F. B. Woodhouse. 1961. RAF Rattlesden. FUSF.
Corporal Neil Kirkham. Station Headquarters. RAF Rattlesden.
Corporal Dave Hilton. 1960 - 1962. RAF Rattlesden. RAF
Police.
Junior Technician Dennis Gilliland. RAF Rattlesden. Engine
Fitter. April 1962 - October 1962.

Aircraft type, squadron service dates, squadron codes to 1962.

The intention of this book is not to give detailed information
about the types of aircraft flown by this squadron. I have
included some very basic information only. There are ample
excellent technical books available to pursue any additional
information that the reader may wish to investigate.

The reader should be aware that throughout the various
Marks of Supermarine Spitfire and other listed aircraft, that
there are many variations within each Mark, that is - Mk II, Mk
IIa, Mk IIb etc. Where these variations to the same Mark are
shown below I have not given a description to that variant, that is
beyond the scope of this book.

Short Admiral Type 184.

Reconnaissance/torpedo bomber floatplane. Manufactured by
Short Brothers, and designed by Horace Short, it first flew in
1915 and was introduced into service shortly after. In squadron
service until 1933, its main users were the Royal Naval Air

Service (RNAS) and the Royal Flying Corp (RFC). Some 936 were built.

266 Squadron service September 1918 - March 1919. Squadron code - not known.

Short Admiral Type 320.

Reconnaissance/torpedo bomber floatplane built by Short Brothers and the Sunbeam Motor Car Company. Its first flight was during 1916, introduced into service during 1917. Main users RNAS and the Royal Air Force. (The RFC became the RAF on 1st of April 1918). Numbers built 127.

266 Squadron service September 1918 - March 1919. Squadron code - not known.

Felixstowe F3.

Military flying boat manufactured by Short Brothers, Dick, Kerr and Company, Phoenix Dynamo Manufacturing Company. It first flew in February 1917 and went into service the same year. Flown by the RNAS, RAF and US Navy, some 182 were built. It was developed from the Felixstowe F2, other variants being the F5 and F5L.

266 Squadron service September 1918 - March 1919. Squadron code - not known.

Magister.

Three are recorded in the ORB. Possibly used for training/transport purposes. As such no technical details are listed here.

Fairy Battle.

A light bomber used by 266 Squadron as a training aircraft. Designed by Marcel Lobelle of the Fairy Aviation Company, its first flight was on 10 March 1936. Went into RAF service in June 1937 and was withdrawn from service in 1949. In service with the RAF, Belgian Air Force, RAAF, RCAF and the Free Polish Air Force.

266 Squadron service December 1939 - May 1940. Squadron code - UO

Supermarine Spitfire Mk I.

Designed by Reginald J. Mitchell to specification F.5/34, the prototype first flew on 5 March 1938. The last operational Spitfire was retired from the RAF in 1955. Production deliveries to the RAF began in July 1938, with No. 19 squadron at RAF Duxford being the first unit to re-equip with Mk Is. The Supermarine Spitfire was the only Allied aircraft of World War II to take part in the conflict from the declaration of War (September 1939) through to the end in August 1945, proving what an adaptable fighter aircraft it was. Altogether there were 19 Marks of Spitfire with 52 sub-variants and 5 different wing designs. Following the death of Reginald J. Mitchell in June 1937, all further variants of his iconic and brilliant design were designed by Joseph Smith and a dedicated team of engineers and draftsmen.

Built at Castle Bromwich and Woolston, some 2,160 were ordered - 1,000 from Morris Motors at Castle Bromwich, 200 from Woolston followed by another 450 a few months later.

Armed with 8 x .303 machine guns (4 in each wing), each gun having approximately 400 rounds. Mk Is were able to reach a maximum speed of 362 mph (583 km/h) at 18,500 ft. (5,600 m), with a maximum rate of climb of 2,490 ft/min at 10,000 ft. (3,000 m). The service ceiling was 31,900 ft. (9,700 m)

266 Squadron service January 1940 - September 1940. October 1940 - April 1941. Squadron code - UO

Supermarine Spitfire IIa.

A new Merlin power plant, the XII, was fitted to an early Mk I

Spitfire and this type was designated the Mark II. Various other improvements were incorporated including a Coffman engine starter, a larger diameter propeller and 2 x 20mm cannons replacing some of the .303 machine guns.

Some Mk IIs were also converted to Long Range Spitfires by the addition of a 40-gallon (182 litres) wing tank fitted under the port wing. Some 50 were also converted for air - sea rescue work. A total of 921 were built, all from Castle Bromwich.
266 Squadron service September 1940 - October 1040. March 1941 - September 1941. Squadron code - UO

Supermarine Spitfire IIb
266 Squadron service September 1941 - September 1941. Squadron code - UO

Supermarine Spitfire Vb
This Mark became the main production variant of the Mk V. Fitted with a new Merlin, the 45 series with 4 propeller blades, and a 'B' wing. The exhaust stubs were modified from the normal round section to 'fishtails' that marginally increased the exhaust thrust. A bigger oil cooler was also fitted under the port wing. Armament consisted of 4 x .303 machine guns and 2 x 20mm cannons.
266 Squadron service September 1941 - June 1942 Squadron code - UO

Hawker Hurricane
A solitary Hurricane was with the squadron during 1942. It is reported in just two entries in the ORB during August 1942. No reason is given as to why the squadron had this Hurricane, or to its Mark number or aircraft number. As the purpose of this aircraft is unclear (part of the Station Flight?) no technical details are shown here.

Hawker Typhoon Ia

Manufactured by the Hawker Aircraft Company and designed by Sydney Camm, the Typhoon prototype first flew on 24 February 1940, flown by Hawkers Chief Test Pilot Philip Lucas from Langley. It was brought into squadron service as a fighter-bomber in 1941. Production ceased in 1945 when some 3,317 of various Marks entered not only RAF service but also RCAF service. It was given the nickname 'Tiffy' by RAF pilots.

It was an extremely versatile aircraft used as a long-range fighter, as a fighter-bomber and also as a ground-attack aircraft armed with cannons as well as un-guided rocket projectiles. It could also carry two 1,000lb (454kg) bombs.

It had a maximum speed of some 412 mph (with the Sabre IIb engine and a 4 bladed propeller), a range of 510 miles (821 km), the service ceiling being 35,200 ft. (10,729 m). Armaments consisted of four x 20mm Hispano Mk II cannons, 8 x 3 RP-3 unguided air to ground rocket projectiles and/or 2 x 500lb (227kg) or 2 x 1,000lb (454kg) bombs.

At the time of writing only one example of this aircraft still exists. Hawker Typhoon MN235 can be seen on display at the RAF Museum in Hendon.
266 Squadron service January 1942 - September 1942. Squadron code - UO and ZH (From July 1942 - July 1945)

Hawker Typhoon Ib

266 Squadron service March 1942 - July 1945. Squadron code - UO and ZH.

Gloster Meteor F Mk III

Manufactured by the Gloster Aircraft Company, its first flight was on 5 March 1943. Powered by twin turbojets developed by Sir Frank Whittle. It went into squadron service on 27 July 1944 and was retired from RAF service during the 1980s. Number produced in all types and Mark was 3,947, flying not only with the RAF but also the RAAF, Belgian Air Force and Israeli Air Force. 616 Squadron was the first to be equipped with Meteor F1s ('F' denotes 'fighter') during July 1944. Its primary role then was as a counter measure for the German V 1 flying bomb threat.

The Meteor Mk III first flew on 11 September 1944 and some 210 of this type were built. A maximum speed of 600 mph (965km/h), approaching Mach 0.82 at 10,000ft (3,050m), service ceiling of 43,000ft (13,100m), and a range of 600 miles (965km). Armament consisted of 4 x 20mm British Hispano cannon, with provision for up to 16 x 60lb (3 inch) rockets or 8 x 5 inch HVAR rockets. 2 x 1,000lb (454kg) bombs could also be carried. (These are for later Marks of Meteor).
266 Squadron service. September 1946 - April 1948. Squadron code - FX

Gloster Meteor F Mk IV
266 Squadron service February 1948 - February 1949. Squadron code - FX

de Havilland Vampire FB Mk V
266 Squadron service August 1952 - May 1953. March 1954 - July 1954. Squadron code - L (July 1952 – 1953.) Squadron code - A (1953 – 1955.)

de Havilland Venom FB Mk I
Manufactured by the de Havilland Aircraft Company, it first flew on 2 September 1949. Introduced as a fighter-bomber to replace the de Havilland Vampire. Entering squadron service in 1952, it was retired from RAF service in 1962, but variants were still flying with the Swiss Air Force in 1983. It is possibly thanks to this long Swiss Air Force service that there are many examples

not only as static displays in museums, but also still flying in private ownership today.

The FB Mk I Venoms was a single seat fighter-bomber, of which 375 were built. Some 1,431 of all types were built, seeing service world wide with the RAF, from the United Kingdom to the Near and Far East.

Its specification are a crew of 1, maximum speed 640 mph (1,030 km/h), range 1,080 miles (1,730 km) and a service ceiling of 39,400 ft. (12,000 m). Armaments consisted of 4 x 20mm Hispano Mk V cannon (just 150 rounds per gun), 8 x 3 inch (60 lb.) rocket projectiles or 2 x 1,000 lb. bombs.
266 Squadron service April 1953 - September 1955. Squadron code - L and A (See above.)

de Havilland Venom FB Mk IV
266 Squadron service July 1955 - November 1957. Squadron code - A

Bristol Bloodhound Mk I
Developed during the 1950s as the United Kingdom's main air defense weapon. This was at a time when RAF thinking was towards a missile system as opposed to a piloted jet aircraft.

Classed as a SAM - Surface to Air Missile, the Mk I entered RAF service in 1958, followed in 1964 by the Mk II. Manufactured by the Bristol Aeroplane Company some 783 of both Marks were produced. A proximity fuse, intending not to score a direct on its target, but to explode in front, would detonate the warhead; the target would then fly through the debris and shrapnel. An operational range of just over 10 miles (85 km) and reaching Mach 2.2. It was fired from a fixed launching pad, reaching 720 mph (the speed of sound) just 25 feet away from its launching ramp. Three seconds after launching it had already attained Mach 2.2 - more than twice the speed of sound.

Intended to protect the RAF's 'V' Bomber bases from attack by aircraft of Warsaw Pact countries, the missile squadrons comprised of eight missile sites - RAF Dunholme Lodge, RAF Watton, RAF Marham, RAF Rattlesden (266 Squadron), RAF Woolfox Lodge, RAF Carnaby, RAF Warboys, RAF Breighton and RAF Mission, these sites being chosen specifically to protect the 'V' Bomber bases.

The role of nuclear deterrent was transferred to the Royal Navy in 1970 and all Bloodhound systems based in the UK were closed.

266 Squadron service December 1959 - June 1964. Squadron code - none denoted.

Aircraft type and missile operational dates.

August 1918 - September 1919	Admiral Short Type 184
August 1918 - September 1919	Admiral Short Type 320
August 1918 - September 1919	Felixstowe F.3
Dates are un-clear. 1941-42	Magister. (Three aircraft)
December 1939 - April 1940	Fairey Battle Mk.I
January 1940 - September 1940	Supermarine Spitfire Mk.I
September 1940 - October 1940	Supermarine Spitfire Mk.IIa
October 1940 - April 1941	Supermarine Spitfire Mk.I
May 1941 - September 1941	Supermarine Spitfire Mk.IIa
September 19th 1941.	Supermarine Spitfire Mk IIb
September 1941 - May 1942	Supermarine Spitfire Mk.Vb
January 1942 - July 1945	Hawker Typhoon Ia, Ib
September 1946 - April 1948	Gloster Meteor F.3
February 1948 - February 1949	Gloster Meteor F.4
July 1952 - June 1954	de Havilland Vampire FB.5, FB.9
April 1953 - September 1955	de Havilland Venom FB.3

July 1955 - November 1957   de Havilland Venom FB.4

December 1959 - June 1964   Bristol Bloodhound Mk I

Squadron Formation & Disbandment dates.

27 September 1918 -   1 September 1919

30 October 1939   -   31 July 1945

1 September 1946 -   11 February 1949

14 July 1952   -   16 November 1957

1 December 1959 -   30 June 1964.

Squadron Codes

UO   January 1940 - July 1942

ZH   July 1942 - July 1945

FX   September 1946 - February 1949

L   July 1952 - 1953

A   1953 - 1955

Squadron Stations

Mundos (Greece) Formed.	27 September 1918
The Caucasus	February 1919
Skyros (Detachment)	March 1919
Petrovsk	May 1919
Chechen (Detachment)	May 1919
Disbanded	1 September 1919
Reformed	30 October 1939
Sutton Bridge	30 October 1939
Martlesham Heath	1 March 1940
Wittering	14 May 1940
Collyweston	May1940 (Detachment)
Tangmere	9 August 1940 (Detachment)
Eastchurch	12 - 14 August1940
Hornchurch	14 August 1940
Manston (Advanced base)	August 1940

Wittering (Wittering Wing)	21 August 1940
Duxford (Duxford Wing)	September 1940 (Detachment)
Martlesham Heath	(Detachment)
Martlesham Heath	28 September 1941
Collyweston	3 October 1941
Kingscliffe	24 October 1941
Docking	(Fighter Sweeps)
	November 1941
West Malling	1941
Duxford	29 January 1942
Coltishall	February 1942 (Detachment)
Digby	6/7 July 1942 (Sector cover)
Matlask	3 - 11 August 1942
Duxford	11 August 1942
Warmwell	21 September 1942
Predannack	November 1942 (Detachment)
Exeter	8 January 1943
Warmwell	(Detachment)
Gravesend	7 September 1943
Exeter	10 September 1943
Harrowbeer	21 September 1943
Bolthead	7 March 1944
Harrowbeer	12 March 1944
Acklington	15 March 1944
Tangmere	23 March 1944
Oar Point. (Lymington)	10th April
Snaith. Yorkshire. (Temporary)	27 April - 6 May 1944
Oar Point (Lymington)	6 May 1944
Eastchurch	29 June 1944
Hurn	13 July 1944
Ste-Croix-sur-Mer (Airfield B3)	20 July 1944
Sommervieu (Airfield B8)	25 July 1944
Morainville (Airfield B23)	6 September 1944

Manston	8 September 1944
Tangmere	9 September 1944
Manston	10 September 1944
Lille/Vendeville (Airfield B51)	11 September 1944
Deurne (Airfield B70)	2 October 1944
Mill (Airfield B89)	14 February 1945
Drope (Airfield B109)	16 April 1945
Fairwood Common	25 April 1945
Ahlhorn (Airfield B111)	4 June 1945
Hildesheim (Disbanded)	8 June 1945
Boxted	(Reformed) 1 September 1946
Acklington	24 September 1946
Boxted	31 October 1946
Wattisham	4 November 1946
Boxted	5 December 1946
Wattisham	4 January 1946
Tangmere	16 April 1947
Lubeck	28 April 1947
Tangmere	26 June 1947
Acklington	5 July 1948
Tangmere	24 August 1948
Renumbered as No. 43 Squadron	
Disbanded.	11 February 1949
Reformed as No. 266 Squadron	14 July 1952
Wunstorf (Germany)	14 July 1952
Fassberg (Germany)	16 October 1955
Wunstorf (Germany)	15 October 1956
Disbanded	16 November 1957
Reformed	1 December 1959
Rattlesden	1 December 1959
Disbanded	30 June 1964

Abbreviations used

AA	Anti Aircraft.
AC	Aircraftman.
AOC	Air Officer Commanding.
AFC	Air Force Cross.
AFV	Armoured Fighting Vehicle.
AMC	Armoured Military Convoy possibly.
AOP	Army Observation Post.
ASI	Air Speed Indicator.
ATA	Air Transport Auxiliary.
Bogey	Suspected enemy aircraft.
Beehive	A term for a number of aircraft, usually bombers, taking up a defensive formation.
CO	Commanding Officer.
CTU	Central Training Unit.
DH	Direct Hits.
DR	Dispatch Rider possibly.
DFC	Distinguished Flying Cross.
de Wilde	Incendiary bullets.
ETA	Estimated Time of Arrival.
FTS	Flying (or Flight) Training School
HDT	High Definition Targets.
HSL	High Speed Launches.
HQ	Head Quarters.
IO	Intelligence Officer.
Intruder	Offensive patrols intended to destroy enemy aircraft over their own territory, patrols were usually carried out at night.
Jim Crow	Coastal patrols to intercept enemy aircraft crossing the British coastline.
KIA	Killed in Action.
LAC	Leading Aircraftman
MRCP	Mobile Radar Control Post.

MET	Possibly Motorised Enemy Transport.
MDV	Possibly Men Deployed with Vehicles.
MU	Maintenance Unit.
MG	Machine Gun.
MIA	Missing in Action.
MT	Motor Transport.
MTB	Motor Torpedo Boat.
NDEA	Possibly Not Damaged by Enemy Action.
NCO	Non Commissioned Officer
Noball	V-weapon launch sites and related targets. (Also NOball and no - ball.)
ORB	Operation Record Book.
Ops	Operation or Operations.
PTC	Possibly Pilot Training Command or Centre.
Queen Mary	Possibly a squadron term for a V2 carrying trailer.
Ramrod	Short-range bomber attacks to destroy ground targets, similar to Circus attacks.
Ranger	Freelance flights over enemy territory by units of any size, the intention was to occupy and tire enemy fighter pilots.
Rhubarb	Operations when sections of fighters or fighter-bombers, taking full advantage of low cloud and poor visibility, would cross the English Channel and then drop below cloud level to search for opportunity targets such as railway locomotives and rolling stock, aircraft on the ground, enemy troops and vehicles on roads.
Roadstead	Dive bombing and low level attacks on enemy ships at sea or in harbour.
Rodeo	Fighter sweeps over enemy territory.
RAFVR	Royal Air Force Voluntary Reserve
RNVR	Royal Navy Volunteer Reserve.

RSU	Repair and Servicing Unit or Repair and Salvage Unit. (Probably the latter.)
R & I Section	Radio and Instrument Section.
RT	Radio Transmitter.
RP	Rocket Projectiles.
Rover	Armed reconnaissance flights with attacks on opportunity targets.
Scramble	Fast takeoff and climb to intercept enemy aircraft.
SSQ	Station Sick Quarters.
SFTS	Services Flying (or Flight) Training School.
SP	Self propelled gun.
Tally-ho	Radiotelephony code phrase for 'enemy in sight'.
TIT	No obvious meaning. Lost in history unfortunately.
TEU	Technical (or Tactical) Evaluation Unit.
TAF	Tactical Air Force.
VCP	Vehicle Command Post.
V1, V2, V3	German 'Vengeance' weapons.
X Raid	Suspect enemy raids.

Acknowledgements

The National Archives. Kew.
Michael Biggs. England.
Alan Harris. South Africa.
Dennis Boswell. USA.

Sources

266 Squadron Operations Record Books
AIR 27/1558 30 October 1939 – 31 December 1940
AIR 27/1558 1 January 1941 – 31 December 1941
AIR 27/1558 1 January 1942 - 31 December 1942
AIR 27/1559 1 January 1943 - 31 December 1943
AIR 27/1559 1 January 1944 - 31 December 1944
AIR 27/1559 1 January 1945 - 31 July 1945

Lightning Source UK Ltd.
Milton Keynes UK
UKOW06f0102141117
312689UK00003B/286/P

9 781912 183210